安廸師：

此文自始至終承蒙詳加批改指正、

謹獻上衷心之謝忱。

學生

孫康宜敬上

THE EVOLUTION OF *TZ'U* FROM LATE T'ANG TO NORTHERN SUNG:

A GENRE STUDY

Kang-i Sun Chang

A DISSERTATION

PRESENTED TO THE

FACULTY OF PRINCETON UNIVERSITY

IN CANDIDACY FOR THE DEGREE

OF DOCTOR OF PHILOSOPHY

RECOMMENDED FOR ACCEPTANCE BY THE

DEPARTMENT OF

EAST ASIAN STUDIES

May, 1978

To

CHEZY CHANG

and to

YU-KUANG SUN

CONTENTS

Preface

The subtitle of this dissertation, "A Genre Study," underscores the fact that the conceptual framework of my study rests on the notion of generic development in literature. Every important age in literary history has its own special forms and styles, reflecting closely its particular taste. As will be demonstrated, the rise of a new genre corresponds to the need of an age for a new set of aesthetic and cultural values. It follows that studying the development of an emergent genre or genres is indispensable to our understanding of a literary period. Yet a genre does not remain static; it emerges, is developed, is employed widely, then falls from favor. Its essential qualities depend on the conventions followed by individual poets, critics, and readers over the centuries. When we contemplate the slow formation and gradual changes of a genre--with all its formalistic and thematic variations--we can see that it is through such developments that the correlation between genres and literary history can be properly perceived. Thus, this generic study is based on two assumptions: (1) that a genre evolves in response to the new demands of an age, (2) that its ultimate significance rests on its dynamic evolution.

The genre of Chinese poetry known as *tz'u* first emerged in the High T'ang and became a prominent literary form during the Sung (960-1279). On the one hand, *tz'u* was basically a song form, taking shape at a time when Chinese music was undergoing radical changes. And yet

as a literary genre, its evolution represents a departure from and a continuation of certain principles characteristic of established genres. Within its tradition we find gradual developments of sub-genres (i.e., the earlier hsiao-ling and the later man-tz'u) and widely different stylistic possibilities (which in turn condition the nature of the genre as a whole). The present study attempts to bring to light the unique structural principles of tz'u poetry by focusing on a few representative poets during the 250-year history of the early tz'u (from approximately A.D. 850 to A.D. 1100).

All literary civilizations share a common concern with genres in literature, but it is important to note that each culture has its particular approach to perceiving the value of genre study. The Chinese tradition offers one kind of literary judgment, and the Western tradition provides another. As in the West, the Chinese generic kinds were chiefly distinguished by form and purpose. Yet what was unique about traditional Chinese criticism was the unusual attention it gave to the classification of "styles" and the mutual dependence of genres and styles. For example, Liu Hsieh (465-522) perceived eight different styles in shih poetry. Chung Hung (fl. 502-519) distinguished poets whose style followed the Ch'u-tz'u tradition from those who followed the Kuo-feng tradition. Ssu-k'ung T'u (837-908) described twenty-four styles in shih poetry. The tz'u criticism (tz'u-hua) also classified poets according to two basic styles: "delicate restraint" (wan-yüeh) and "heroic abandon" (hao-fang).

This Chinese notion of style was grounded in a particular traditional perspective in Chinese thought. To the Chinese critic,

style was the manifestation of a person's inner self and thus was a measure of his life's achievement. Therefore, a distinction of style was not simply a literary accomplishment, but rather a direct expression of one's level of self-cultivation. The classification of styles was not considered to be arbitrary, as it came from a firm conviction that a qualitative assessment of individuals had an ultimate value, a belief rooted in Chinese literary tradition and made explicit as early as the Eastern Han (A.D. 25-A.D. 220).

This concern with detailed classification of styles was so important to the traditional critics that it sometimes caused them to confuse the notion of genre with that of style, as can be seen from the fact that they often used the term t'i to refer to both genres and styles. For example, in Yen Yü's (fl. 1200) Ts'ang-lang shih-hua the 110 t'i include such genres as ku-shih (Ancient Style poetry), chin-t'i (Recent Style poetry), etc., and such styles as Tung-p'o t'i (Su Shih's style) and Wang Ching-kung t'i (Wang An-shih's style). To the modern student of literature this confusion between generic and stylistic conceptions on the part of traditional critics can be very perplexing. However, this problem also provides us with a key to understanding the nature of Chinese genre criticism and reveals what a major role stylistic distinction has played in that tradition. This suggests that without considering the particular styles within the framework of genres we can never do full justice to the significance of generic development in China.

One of the difficulties confronting us today is that traditional Chinese critics, especially those after the T'ang, tended to be

impressionistic rather than analytical in their approach. The metaphorical expressions they use in their critical comments sometimes seem vague and arbitrary. It is true that they often called attention to generic distinctions and stylistic differences, but they rarely specified what factors underlie the differences. The fact is that the critics generally attempted to suggest rather than to argue. Like the lyric poet, they valued the concentrated but profound moments of self-expression. As a result, critical comments generally take the form of fairly short remarks, approximating the expression of a momentary feeling. In other words, the critical statements are expressed in such a way that they resemble the lyrical situation and effect.

The fact that the Chinese critical approach is sharply determined by its cultural context assists, rather than hinders, our study of its literature. Our task today is to work out a method by which to simultaneously draw inspiration from the traditional Chinese criticism and to take advantage of the analytical approach available to modern students of literature. In studying *tz'u* poetry I have attempted to undertake two basic procedures: first to look into the verbal meaning of the text through using some technique of philological analysis, and then to proceed to judge its importance with respect to the generic development as a whole. The first stage concerns the elucidation of textual meaning, and the second touches upon the function of interpretation. It is in the second stage of interpreting the significance of the text that traditional *tz'u* criticism will come to the aid of our analytical approach. In so doing I hope to clarify some of the aesthetic values cherished by the Chinese poets and critics.

Thus, what may seem impressionistic or elusive in the traditional commentaries may be crystallized into clear analytical language.

Certainly there is no problem in using modern critical terms to interpret traditional Chinese poetry. Terms do not have absolute values; they are significant only when they are useful for explaining the ideas behind them. For example, readers will find that the concept of "rhetoric" plays an important part in the methodology of the present study. In this context, "rhetoric" is taken to mean a poet's "manner of expression," through which he establishes a proper relationship between himself and an imagined audience, even when he himself is the "audience." It is employed here as a convenient means of locating the important devices by which the poet expresses his inner world, but it does not imply that devices are the very stuff of poetry itself. It is assumed that there is something about the power of creative energy which cannot always be analyzed, for great poetry is an organic unification of individual genius and technical devices.

The backbone of the present study will be an analysis of _tz'u_ on two levels. First, _tz'u_ poetry as a whole must be defined in terms of its unique form (i.e., meter, stanzaic division), structure (i.e., methods of organization), and function (i.e., subject and audience). Second, the diachronic dimension of the generic development must be traced and analyzed--in other words, we must attempt to find the links which connect significant poets in chronological order. In each individual case stylistic analysis will form the basis of inquiry: i.e., the style of each poet will be examined according to both formal and non-formal considerations. Beginning with the linguistic and the

structural dimensions of poems, we shall move on to study the scope of the poet's poetic vision which is embodied in his expression of feelings. This last point corresponds to our earlier statement on the basic approach to studying poetry: the formal considerations including an inquiry into the textual meaning, and the non-formal study of individual poetic vision requiring an act of interpretation.

Of particular significance is the fact that the emergence of *tz'u* was closely related to the impact of popular literature. The genre was first recognized and appreciated by the common audience in the form of popular songs or songs of entertainment long before literati poets started to compose their own *tz'u* poetry. In the course of its development, one witnesses the poets' continual attempt to absorb popular songs into literati poetry, and the introductory chapter of the present study deals mainly with this topic.

The five *tz'u* poets to be studied in the present work, Wen T'ing-yün (ca. 812-ca. 870), Wei Chuang (ca. 836-910), Li Yü (937-978), Liu Yung (987-1053), and Su Shih (1036-1101) represent milestones in the early development of *tz'u*. Like most Chinese literary genres, *tz'u* poetry evolved from a simpler to a more complex form. The shorter form *hsiao-ling*, which came to define the scope of late T'ang and Five Dynasties *tz'u* poetry, will be covered in Chapters II and III. The importance of Wen T'ing-yün and Wei Chuang lies mainly in their establishing two distinct stylistic modes, which were to become the two important schools of *tz'u* writing. Li Yü then synthesized these modes and exploited new poetic devices, marking the turning point of

the development of hsiao-ling.

In Chapter IV Liu Yung's achievement will be evaluated with respect to his innovations in the longer form called man-tz'u. Both his new conception of lyrical exploration and his extended experiment with sequential structure are crucial to the development of Sung tz'u. In this chapter we will see most clearly the way in which a creative poet can change the direction of a literary genre by boldly seeking inspiration from popular literature.

Chapter V examines how in the hands of Su Shih the tz'u genre finally entered the inner circle of Sung poetics. Su Shih's enlargement of poetic vision was directly responsible for this significant achievement. This chapter is the culmination of the present study, because in the view of the traditional Chinese a new genre was considered mature only after it became a literary form through which a poet could express the full range of his ideas and feelings. At the same time we shall find that the transformation of a lesser genre into a major genre often occurs when a literary genius extends the potentialities of his medium by combining in a new way old accepted devices from other genres.

In preparing this dissertation I have received help from many individuals. I am most indebted to Professor Yu-kung Kao who, with his tremendous scope of knowledge and highly theoretical mind, provided me with an inexhaustible source from which I constantly draw new inspirations. I am immensely grateful to Professor Andrew H. Plaks, who patiently read through all my earlier drafts, suggested changes, and encouraged me to consider the impact of popular songs. Special

thanks also go to Professor Frederick W. Mote, who corrected many errors in my work, and whose breadth of learning in history and literature has led me to view poetic developments in a much larger perspective than I formerly would have envisioned. I am grateful to Professor Earl Miner who enriched my understanding of poetics in general and gave valuable comments on the dissertation. I should also like to thank some other teachers whose assistance has been invaluable to me: Professor H. T. Tang for his help in Chinese linguistics, Professor Ralph Freedman for providing me through the past several years with a background in comparative literature and literary theory, Professor Seiichi Nakada for elucidating problems in Japanese sources, and Professor James T. C. Liu for discussing issues in Sung history. Thanks are also due to friends who offered help in various ways: Frances LaFleur, Dore Levy, and Lucy Loh. I owe a great debt to the library staff of Gest Oriental Library, especially to the past and present curators James S. K. Tung and David Tsai for their encouragement. I wish also to thank Maureen Donovan who as a librarian helped me with reference sources, and as a friend made useful suggestions after having read portions of an earlier draft. In addition, I wish to express my thanks to Professor Denis Twitchett of Cambridge University who directed me to important materials on the T'ang, to Professor Shuen-fu Lin of the University of Michigan who kindly lent me his manuscript on the _tz'u_ poetry of the Southern Sung, to Professor Kun Chang of the University of California at Berkeley who gave valuable comments on a section of the present work, and to Professors James J. Y. Liu of Stanford University, Chia-ying Yeh Chao of the University of British Columbia, and J. Thomas

Rimer of Washington University, who all encouraged me at an early stage of my research. I am grateful to the members of the Chinese Poetry Group of the East Coast, and particularly to Professors Hans H. Frankel, Nathan Sivin, Marsha L. Wagner, Stephen Owen, Adele Rickett, C. T. Hsia, and Jonathan Chaves for their faith and interest in my work. Thanks also go to Ernest Tsai, Librarian of East Asian Library at Washington University in St. Louis, who generously gave me access to books there. I wish to acknowledge the help of Jeannette Mirsky, the biographer of Sir Aurel Stein, whose interest in the art of writing has been a great inspiration to me. The names of many authors--too numerous to mention--to whom I owe an intellectual debt will appear in the bibliography and footnotes. I would like to express my thanks to the Whiting Foundation for the award of a Whiting Fellowship in the Humanities, through which the completion of this work was made possible. Finally I must thank Professor James R. Hightower of Harvard University who kindly agreed to read this dissertation and be one of my examiners.

I. Introduction

Some modern readers of Western lyric may forget that lyric as a genre originally referred to poems to be sung to the lyre. Likewise, today's readers of Chinese *tz'u* often overlook the primary importance of the musical element in early *tz'u* poetry. At first the genre was known as *ch'ü-tzu-tz'u*, meaning simply "song words" or "words accompanying tunes." "*Tz'u*" as a literary term did not come into use until late in the Sung.

As music changed and as the old *yüeh-fu* ballads during the Sui and T'ang times ceased to be sung, *tz'u* gradually appeared as a new song form.[1] In terms of musical function, *tz'u* was often viewed as a continuation of the *yüeh-fu* songs, and thus many critics and poets throughout the Sung continued to place *tz'u* under the category of *yüeh-fu*.[2] Although the music of *yüeh-fu* and *tz'u* has long been lost, it is worth noting that these two poetic forms share a common affinity with musical presentation.[3]

Tz'u, however, did not emerge merely as an extended form of *yüeh-fu* songs. It initiated a special tradition of composition. Whereas the *yüeh-fu* titles do not point to fixed metric patterns, the *tz'u* titles specify the particular tune patterns (*tz'u-p'ai*) to which the poems are composed.[4] During the T'ang and Five Dynasties period, the subject of a *tz'u* poem often corresponded to the meaning of its

tune title.[5] After the Sung the subject of the poem gradually lost its thematic connection with the tune pattern. "Filling in words" (*t'ien-tz'u*) was the term used to describe this unique practice of *tz'u* writing. These tune patterns were of great variety: according to the prosodic manual *Tz'u-lü* and its supplement there were 825 tunes in total (i.e., more than 1670 forms when the variants of each pattern were taken into consideration).[6] It was the use of these tune patterns which first marked *tz'u* as a new song form, distinct from the earlier poetic forms which were generally included in the larger category *shih*.

It is often noted that *tz'u* is distinguished by its use of lines of unequal length, and that it was this particular feature which led the traditional scholars to give *tz'u* an alternative name: the "long-and-short" line verse (*ch'ang-tuan-chü*). Upon closer scrutiny, however, one realizes that such is by no means the most crucial structural principle in *tz'u*. The practice of using lines of unequal length is as old as the *Book of Songs* (800 B.C.-600 B.C.). Besides, a few *tz'u* tunes requiring regular lines, such as *Yü-lou ch'un* (i.e., *Mu-lan hua*) and *Huan hsi sha* remained current through Sung times, and in fact *Yü-lou ch'un* bears a particularly striking resemblance to the 7-character line *lü-shih*.[7] Thus, it is quite clear that the length of poetic lines should not be viewed as the only criterion upon which to distinguish between the *tz'u* form and other poetic forms.

Yet it is undeniable that, viewed historically, no poetic forms previous to *tz'u* ever employed lines of unequal length on such a large scale. This very fact is of great importance to our understanding of the *tz'u* aesthetics. But the question remains: how can this seemingly

minor point be important in Chinese poetics?

Before this question is answered, we should briefly review the development of the various forms in shih poetry which preceded the tz'u tradition. Two of the most notable phenomena in the development of shih poetry during the Han (206 B.C.-A.D. 219) were its preference for lines of equal length and its tendency to employ lines composed of an odd number of characters. This started with the emergence and the increasing popularity of the 5-character lines (wu-yen shih), followed by the poems of 7-character lines in a later period. Although admixtures of irregular lines were by no means absent during Han times, the 5-character-line poems stood out as the most popular poetic form. What was most striking was that when admixtures of irregular lines were found in a poem, the combinations were in most cases made up of odd-numbered lines (i.e., 5-7 character lines, 3-7 character lines, or 3-5-7 character lines).[8] In contrast with the poetic sensibility of the Book of Songs where a standard 4-character line form was employed, the practice of using odd-numbered lines created a new kind of poetic rhythm.

The gradual rise of 8-line lü-shih (Regulated Verse) at the end of the Six Dynasties period, and its consequent popularity throughout the T'ang dynasty (618-906), brought to the Chinese tradition a whole new spectrum of poetic experience. Its insistence on a rigid tonal system and structure of parallelism was believed to represent the perfect form of poetry. In this period the long established chüeh-chü quatrain in lines of equal length, which has been found to constitute a major portion of the popular songs during the Six Dynasties period,

also began to be written in a similar manner. Thus, "Recent Style poetry" (*chin-t'i shih*) became a term to refer to this "new" poetry, as opposed to the "Ancient Style poetry" (*ku-shih*) which was meant to include both old poems produced before that age and new poems written in the old style.

The aesthetics of Recent Style poetry stressed the notion of regularity, which included a system of tonal variations.[9] When the development of the 5-character-line and the 7-character-line *lü-shih* poetry reached its most mature stage, poets began to follow consciously or unconsciously a tonal system which was based on the systematic alternation of oblique and level tones (e.g., in the conventional method of noting tonal patterns, — — | | — / | | — — |). The rhymes normally fall on the level-tone syllables, though in extremely exceptional cases oblique-tone rhymes also were used. The two middle couplets (i.e., the second and third couplets of a poem) are often characterized by semantic parallelism. The scheme of parallelism is complex and manifold, but the basic rule is that the two parallel elements should usually belong to the same semantic category (e.g., in the strict sense, number parallels number, color parallels color, location parallels location, proper name parallels proper name; and in a loose sense, adjectival form parallels adjectival form, adverbial form parallels adverbial form, and verbal form parallels verbal form). Of course, the structure of parallel lines had been a major concern of Chinese poets since the time of the *Book of Songs*, but it did not mature into a definitive structural principle until the age of Recent Style poetry.

After the rise of Recent Style poetry, the continuing tendency to employ lines of equal length and odd numbers of characters persisted, and in fact was reinforced. There was in this new tradition no further admixture of irregular lines, and only 5-character or 7-character lines were permitted.

At this juncture *tz'u* poetry suddenly emerged, and began to mix odd-numbered character lines with even-numbered character lines. Thus, *tz'u* became what Claudio Guillén might call a "countergenre,"[10] a reaction against the previous firmly-entrenched regulated verse tradition. Yet the use of lines of unequal length represents only one aspect of *tz'u* which distinguishes it from the 8-line *lü-shih*. There is another important technical feature of *tz'u* that deserves our attention--i.e., the increasing use of oblique tone rhymes, and the mixture of level and oblique tone rhymes in a single poem (e.g., a a b b / a a b b). According to the traditional patterns in practice the rhymes of *lü-shih* are normally confined to level tones (oblique tone rhymes appear very rarely); and only the ends of even-numbered lines (except for the opening line) are expected to rhyme with one another (i.e., x a x a x a x a).[11] Thus, the rhyming pattern in most *tz'u* poems would have been considered to be in most serious violation of the conventional *lü-shih* requirements.

Such a simple distinction of formal structure merely serves as our point of departure for examining the evolution of the *tz'u* form in a broader perspective. Our next important question is: what gave rise to the emergence of this "countergenre"?

1. The Cultural Milieu of *Tz'u* Poets

The Tun-huang Cave findings which have provided so many significant clues to T'ang and Five Dynasties cultural conditions are indispensable to our study of *tz'u* poetry.[12] Among the Tun-huang discoveries one finds a considerable number of popular *tz'u* songs sung during the T'ang and Five Dynasties period which may be dated back to the Early T'ang (ca. A.D. 650) and possibly to A.D. 600.[13] The form of these songs varies from that of "separate songs" (*tsa-ch'ü-tzu*) to that of "song cycles" (*ting-ko lien-chang*).[14] These range from very short songs consisting of less than 25 characters to relatively long songs of more than 100 characters. These songs are generally composed of irregular lines, though a small portion of them are poems carrying lines of regular length.[15]

The discovery of the Tun-huang songs immediately proved that the earlier theory held by the scholars of *tz'u* was incorrect. They had claimed that *tz'u* poetry in the form of "long-and-short" lines did not come into being until Middle T'ang and that the T'ang poets Po Chü-i (772-846) and Liu Yü-hsi (772-842) were responsible for the beginning of *tz'u* writing.[16] This mistaken assumption has caused scholars since the Ming critic Hu Ying-lin (1551-1618) to claim that the *P'u-sa man* songs attributed to Li Po (760-762) were forgeries.[17] For in their view, the "long-and-short" line *tz'u* could not have been produced as early as the High T'ang.

It was true, however, that *tz'u* poetry as a clearly defined literary form was not sufficiently realized until the Late T'ang poet

Wen T'ing-yün put great effort into producing individual collections of *tz'u* poetry.[18] It was in his hands that *tz'u* was gradually transformed from mere songs of entertainment to lyric verse of high literary quality. But this should not make us forget that the occasional *tz'u* poems produced by earlier poets--however few there were--remain important as milestones in the history of the development of *tz'u*. In order to locate those structural principles which later became important in the *tz'u* tradition as a whole, we have to study the general trend of *tz'u* poetry before Late T'ang.

It is uncertain whether Li Po wrote the *P'u-sa man* songs or not. Yet this problem of authorship, which has become the main controversy in *tz'u* scholarship, should not be our main concern. Rather, the important question for us to ask is: Could any poet in Li Po's time possibly have written these *tz'u* songs in "long-and-short" line form?

As was mentioned, a large number of Tun-huang songs consisting of lines of unequal length can be traced back to Li Po's time (i.e., High T'ang). Moreover, 65% of the titles of the Tun-huang songs appear in the *Chiao-fang chi*, a book on the activities of musicians and singers during the period 713-740, and *P'u-sa man* is one of them.[19] This shows that this, along with many other *tz'u* tunes, was already popular among musicians in the first half of the eighth century. It was quite possible that a creative poet such as Li Po would attempt to employ a new "popular" form. In fact it has been proved that one of the *P'u-sa man* songs in question was written on the wall of Lung-hsing Temple in 742, at least twenty years before Li Po's death.[20] If Li Po did not compose the poem, some other poet of his time must have done so.

The basic question arises: why did popular *tz'u* tunes begin to flourish at this particular time? The two most crucial periods in *tz'u* history, during which time new song forms developed, were the early part of the eighth century and again that of the eleventh century. The former period witnessed the initial appearance of the *hsiao-ling* form and the latter the gradual adoption of the *man-tz'u* form. In both cases changes in poetic structure were stimulated by the invention of new musical tunes. And in each case the reigning emperor played an active role in the promotion of new music--in the early eighth century the T'ang emperor Hsüan-tsung (reigned 713-755), and in the early eleventh century the Sung emperors T'ai-tsung (reigned 976-997) and Jen-tsung (reigned 1023-1063) all knew and loved music.[21]

What T'ang Hsüan-tsung did to change the direction of Chinese musical performance was to establish the *chiao-fang* (Palace Music School) in the capital district where hundreds of musicians and singers were trained to perform new music.[22] Even more significant was the fact that he admitted both "popular" and foreign musical tunes (*hu-yüeh*) into the court, and thus destroyed the earlier rigid dichotomy between "elegant music" (*ya-yüeh*) and "popular music" (*su-yüeh*).[23] This unconventional act on the part of Hsüan-tsung no doubt promoted the growth of *tz'u* songs, in that musicians and courtesans in the *chiao-fang* and literati poets began to write song-words for the new tunes.[24] Some of the Tun-huang songs were probably produced in response to this cultural milieu. Hsüan-tsung himself also engaged actively in the invention of tunes and *tz'u* composition. For example, his *tz'u* song to *Hao shih-kuang* (6-3-3-7-5/5-3-3-5-5) is listed as the first poem in the T'ang and Five Dynasties *tz'u* anthology *Tsun-ch'ien*

chi.[25]

Ironically Emperor Hsüan-tsung's greatest impact on the development of the new music and *tz'u* poetry was to be realized only after his downfall and death. As an immediate consequence after the outbreak of the An Lu-shan Rebellion in 755 which shook the foundations of the T'ang dynasty, courtesans and musicians of the *chiao-fang* were scattered, and began to seek new locations for their musical performances.[26] This consequently led to the sudden booming of entertainment halls (*chi-kuan*) in the cities where the new *ch'ü-tzu-tz'u* were sung, produced, and popularized. It was from these places that poets after the Middle T'ang drew most of their inspiration in writing *tz'u* poems. From the beginning of the Sung, entertainment halls were so expanded that some contained more than a hundred rooms.[27]

This is not to say that entertainment quarters began to emerge only after the downfall of Hsüan-tsung, but simply to say that the dispersion of the trained members of the *chiao-fang* after the rebellion had a direct impact on the gradual popularity of *tz'u* songs after the Middle T'ang. These musicians and courtesans coming from the capital district knew the art of the new music, and by joining the existing professional singers of *tz'u* in the cities they naturally made *ch'ü-tzu-tz'u* a fashionable art form. To accompany this new music they sometimes wrote their own song words and sometimes asked famous poets to provide *tz'u* poems for them.

Another important subject which comes in at this time concerns a parallel literary development. The High T'ang is also known as the zenith of the Recent Style *chüeh-chü* quatrain. The *chüeh-chü* poems by

such poets as Wang Ch'ang-ling (689-ca. 756), Wang Chih-huan, Ts'en Shen (714-770) and Kao Shih (702-765) were often sung by singers, and were simply called *yüeh-fu*.[28] The practice of setting quatrains to music can be traced back to the Six Dynasties period. In the Southern Dynasties the two major groups of *yüeh-fu* songs, *wu-ko* and *hsi-ch'ü*, were made up of Ancient Style *chüeh-chü*, and these quatrain-ballads were found to be particularly popular in urban centers.[29] Thus, the practice of singing *chüeh-chü* during the first half of the T'ang was merely a continuation of this old tradition.

It was also during this time that the new music for *tz'u* emerged. On the one hand, the "long-and-short" line *tz'u* began to be produced for the purpose of accompanying the new melodies. On the other hand, Regulated *chüeh-chü* poems were written to this music, sometimes with interpolated words (*ho-sheng*) conforming to the length of the melody. Since these quatrains were sung to various melodies, they bear the name of *tz'u* tunes as titles. In terms of literary form, these were merely *chüeh-chü* poems. But as song words they were regarded as *tz'u*.[30]

Although courtesans and musicians had been singing and composing such *tz'u* songs for a long time, *tz'u* poetry did not become a noticeable genre for literati poets until entertainment quarters in major cities were in full bloom. One fact which supports this is that the life of Wen T'ing-yün, the first prolific *tz'u* writer, falls in the period during which the T'ang entertainment quarters reached their peak of prosperity. The work entitled *Pei-li chih* by the Late T'ang literatus Sun Ch'i describes in great detail the courtesans' singing abilities and literary accomplishments, and the educated

elite associated with them, during the mid-ninth century, the heyday of such quarters in the city of Ch'ang-an. According to Sun almost all the regular visitors to these quarters were scholar-officials and literati poets (which included himself, a _Han-lin_ academician).[31]

The term _Pei-li_ (literally "Northern Ward"), which later became a popular name for all entertainment quarters after the appearance of Sun Ch'i's work, originally referred to the particular quarter north of P'ing-k'ang _fang_ in Ch'ang-an, existing since the time of Emperor Hsüan-tsung.[32] This entertainment quarter was perhaps the earliest one of its kind, and in Sun Ch'i's view the singing girls there were unsurpassed in musical skill, so much so that they outshone the famous courtesan Hsüeh T'ao in Szechwan.[33] Many courtesans in _Pei-li_ were well versed in poetry aside from their musical talents. Poems by singers such as those referred to by Sun Ch'i as Ch'u-erh, Yen Ling-pin, Lai-erh and Fu-niang were all well written and admired by their literati friends.[34] A few decades before Sun Ch'i's time the T'ang writer Po Hsing-chien (the brother of Po Chü-i) had already written about the lives of courtesans in the _Pei-li_ quarter in his famous tale "Li Wa chuan", although at that time the entertainment quarters had not yet blossomed into a center of city life.

Ch'ang-an was the earliest city to have developed such entertainment quarters, but later many other cities also came to be known for courtesans. In the Lower Yangtze region, the cities of Yangchow, Soochow, and Hangchow were all famous for such quarters.[35] Wen T'ing-yün traveled through Yangchow during his younger days, and Wei Chuang wandered around the cities in the South after the Huang

Ch'ao Rebellion (874-884). And prior to that, Po Chü-i wrote his famous tz'u poems to the tune I chiang-nan, in which he expressed his love for the South after visiting the Hangchow and Soochow areas. During the same period Liu Yü-hsi stayed in Soochow for a few years, and composed his tz'u poetry to match Po Chü-i's I chiang-nan songs.[36] All of these poets knew musical technique, loved popular tunes, and enjoyed the company of courtesans. They experimented with the "long-and-short" line tz'u mainly as a response to the popularity of new tunes. Sometimes in their tz'u poems they indicated that the song-words were set to new music:

> Ancient songs, old music--don't listen to those,
> Listen to the newly revised Yang-liu chih tune.
>
> (Po Chü-i, CTWT, I, 33)

古歌舊曲君休聽
聽取新翻楊柳枝

> Please do not play the music of the former reigns,
> Listen and sing to the newly revised Yang-liu chih tune.
>
> (Liu Yü-hsi, CTWT, I, 23)

請君莫奏前朝曲
聽唱新翻楊柳枝

This connection with new music, singing girls and entertainment quarters was vital to the development of tz'u poetry. During the Northern Sung this convention not only continued but increased its

overall impact. As entertainment quarters became more and more prosperous in the cities, the chiao-fang gradually reduced in influence.[37] Consequently not only did scholar-officials frequent these quarters but the emperors themselves had liaisons with professional singers. In the tz'u poetry of the T'ang and Five Dynasties period, names of two famous courtesans of former times "Hsieh-niang" and "Hsiao-niang" were often used as general names to refer to singing girls. But during the Sung the real names of singers began to appear in tz'u poems.[38] This no doubt reveals a change in attitude on the part of Sung poets.

A case in point was the poet Liu Yung who spent most of his youth in the entertainment quarters. When musicians invented new tunes, he was always ready to write song words for them. And in fact he himself was a competent musician who knew how to compose tunes for his own tz'u poetry. Thus, he was immensely popular among singing girls. A legend has it that after his death there emerged a general custom for courtesans to visit his tomb annually.[39] Another Sung poet Chang Hsien (990-1078) even kept singing girls at home, and continued to enjoy the company of these girls even in his 80's.[40] And Su Shih did not start to write tz'u poetry until he went to Hangchow as a local official, at which time he began to appreciate the courtesans' musical art.

This shows how various cultural phenomena combined to promote the popularity of tz'u poetry. But this discussion is still peripheral to our study of tz'u poetics. The following sections of this chapter will therefore turn to the "literary" aspects of the

early *tz'u*, with the hope of demonstrating to the readers how *tz'u* slowly grew into a recognizable literary genre.

2. A Stylistic Comparison of Literati *Tz'u* and Popular Songs

The concept of *tz'u* poetry as a genre was not officially or fully realized until the appearance of *Hua-chien chi* (940), an anthology of 500 *tz'u* poems by eighteen authors from 850 to 940. Its famous preface by Ou-yang Chiung (896-971) reveals a conscious wish on the part of literati poets to establish a separate literary tradition from the popular *tz'u* songs. This preface, written in the respectable *p'ien-wen* form, describes the 500 *tz'u* poems not simply as *ch'ü-tzu-tz'u* but as *shih-k'o ch'ü-tzu-tz'u* (the song words of poets). The tradition linked *tz'u* poets from Li Po to Wen T'ing-yün and then to later authors. In Ou-yang Chiung's view the popular *tz'u* songs were "not only vulgar in style" but also "empty in substance, though beautiful in appearance."[41] Thus to him the purpose of *Hua-chien chi* was to provide the "Southern singing girls" (*nan-kuo ch'an-chüan*) with *tz'u* songs possessing high literary value.

Prior to the compilation of *Hua-chien chi*, a collection of popular *tz'u* songs entitled *Yün-yao chi* had already appeared (i.e., before 922).[42] This *Yün-yao chi*, which has become the oldest group of songs in the Tun-huang *tz'u* collection, was already well-known even before it was put into its written form. Sometimes the term *yün-yao* was used loosely to refer to casual *tz'u* songs, as can be seen from

the following quotations from the poetry of the time:

> Secretly the fairy messenger shows off his writing;
>
> He composes *yün-yao* songs in private and gives them
> to friends.
>
> (CTS, X, 7348)
>
> 玉童私地誇書札
> 偷寫雲謠暗贈人

> Suddenly a torchlight announces the arrival of an
> imperial edict--
>
> The emperor expresses his appreciation for my *pai yün-yao*
> songs .
>
> (CTS, XI, 8603)
>
> 蠟炬乍傳丹鳳詔
> 御題初認白雲謠

> We feast on the *yün-yao* melodies,
>
> As she sings, flashing her white teeth.
>
> Let us make merry!
>
> (CTWT, I, 96)
>
> 讌雲謠
> 歌皓齒
> 且行樂

In contrast to *Hua-chien chi*, in which all the poets were given

their official titles in addition to their names, the *tz'u* songs included in *Yün-yao chi* were all anonymous. Clearly the significance of *Hua-chien chi* does not lie in the mere fact of being an anthology, but rather in its distinction from the other current mode, that of the *yün-yao* songs. What is more significant is that the concept of a distinct literary genre was set forth in its preface, a discussion which serves as the first piece of critical literature on the *tz'u* form. It is in this sense that we can claim that the establishment of a particular poetic tradition often coincides with the presence of an important preface to a representative anthology. This indeed echoes what Earl Miner has said about the emergence of poetic systems in general in his discussion of the preface to the first Japanese imperial collection, the *Kokinshū*: "A systematic poetics emerges in the encounter of a great critical mind or minds with the dominant genre of the time."[43]

Can we then make the assumption that there is an absolute distinction between the literati *tz'u* poetry and popular *tz'u* songs since their purposes were so different? The problem is that the total extant corpus of Tun-huang *tz'u* songs includes not only the popular songs of the streets but also a few works by literary poets which appealed to popular taste.[44] Moreover, the known Tun-huang songs may be only a small portion of the songs existing in the T'ang and Five Dynasties which were of that kind. Obviously it is dangerous to base our argument on purely statistical comparisons. What we should be most concerned with here is not the notion of absolute generic boundaries, but rather the common stylistic features

characterizing a particular group of tz'u poems existing in a given range of time. Therefore, the question is not whether the literati tz'u were "popular" or not; by definition, of course, tz'u emerged as a popular form. In other words, the pertinent question here is: what is the stylistic common denominator of early literati tz'u that distinguishes it from other contemporary popular songs, and vice versa?

The "Hua-chien" tz'u poems, which represent the early efforts of the literary tz'u poets, were found to be almost exclusively characterized by love themes. This seems to be a logical outcome of the actual interrelations between poets and singing girls. Yet the issue has a deeper meaning than may appear at first sight. I believe that by focusing on the love themes, the poets were attempting to follow the conventions established by the Palace Style poetry (kung-t'i shih), a poetic style developed during the Six Dynasties period. The Palace Style poetry was promoted by an anthology compiled under the auspices of Emperor Chien-wen of the Liang dynasty, namely Yü-t'ai hsin-yung. The anthology was partly a collection of love poems; it represented the flowering of a sensuous poetic taste nourished by a group of poets during the time.[45] It was probably due to the importance of the love themes in tz'u poetry that Ou-yang Chiung traced the origin of tz'u back to the Palace Style poetry in his preface to Hua-chien chi.

The Tun-huang songs, on the other hand, represent something quite different in terms of subject matter. That collection includes numerous kinds of subjects, chief among them songs on religious ceremonies, and on social injustice. The love theme, which

characterizes much of the literati *tz'u*, constitutes only a portion of the Tun-huang songs. In fact these popular songs can be viewed as realistic descriptions of contemporary events. Songs on war, conscription, and the hardships experienced on the frontiers stand out in the majority of the poems. In the Tun-huang songs one reads about the true story of Emperor Chao-tsung (i.e., Li Chieh) who escaped to Hua-chou when Li Mao-chen invaded the capital in 897 (THC, #046-051), as well as the disaster caused by the Huang Ch'ao Rebellion in 880 (THC, #070-072). Even weapons used on actual battlefields were often described in great detail (e.g., THC, #078-080).

This obvious difference of subject matter between the literati *tz'u* and popular *tz'u* songs points to a more basic difference regarding modes of poetic expression. Whereas the former is characterized almost exclusively by the lyrical mode, the latter contains a variety of modes--narrative, dramatic, and lyrical. In fact a major portion of the Tun-huang songs is narrative or dramatic, rather than lyrical, in nature. By "lyrical poem" I mean a sustained expression of inner feelings felt in the present, such that external realities are shaped and molded to form part of the artistic world of the self and the present. The dramatic or the narrative modes, on the other hand, focus on the presentation of a concrete human encounter or the development of an event. In the Tun-huang songs one witnesses not only a strong preoccupation with external realities but also a well-developed system of dramatic and narrative devices conforming to them. The song cycle (*lien-chang*) is a basic formal device which carries out this purpose. In a song cycle each individual song serves

as part of an integral story, as in the case of *Tao-lien tzu* which tells the story of Meng-chiang-nü in temporal sequence (THC, #127-130). When such individual songs serve as dialogues the dramatic function becomes primary, and the device is called *yen ku-shih*, which in Jen Erh-pei's view means "to perform the story." One out of six songs in the Tun-huang *tz'u* collection belongs to the *yen ku-shih* song cycles.[46] This seems to suggest the early dramatic and dance performances in the popular *tz'u* tradition which anticipated the later Chin and Yuan dramatic literature.[47] The use of narrative-descriptive *tz'u* in the *chia-men* section of the Ming *ch'uan-ch'i* plays may also be traced back to this combined effect of the narrative and the dramatic as found in the early popular *tz'u* tradition.[48]

The device of song cycles, however, is not the only possible means by which the Tun-huang songs manifest narrative or dramatic dimensions. Many separate songs are structured so that the actual occurrence of events forms the main issue of the poems, and often dialogues are used to heighten the effect of dramatic action. The following song to *Ch'üeh t'a chih* exemplifies this very common technique employed by popular *tz'u* songs:

> "Darn it! The magpie often lies.
> When he brings good tidings, does he ever provide
>   any evidence?
> How many times has he flown here to be captured alive?
> I have locked him in a golden cage, forbidding him to talk." [4]
>
> "I just wanted to bring her good tidings with good will,

Who would expect that she would lock me in this
golden cage?
I hope her husband will soon return from the war,
Then she will set me free to soar into the blue sky." 8

(THC, #115)

叵耐靈鵲多瞞語
送喜何曾有憑據
幾度飛來活捉取
鎖上金籠休共語

比擬好心來送喜
誰知鎖我在金籠裏
願他征夫早歸來
騰身却放我向青雲裏

Unlike a lyric poem in which everything is seen through the eye of the persona, this song presents two distinct points of view by the use of a dialogue between a woman and a magpie. The poet seems to retreat to the background, as if he were letting the two characters

converse with each other.

If we look into those popular songs which are more lyrical in nature, we can also find significant poetic devices that distinguish them from most of the literary *tz'u*. One of the common devices found in the Tun-huang lyrics is the use of short, straightforward statements of feelings or interrogatives in the opening lines of the poem before an introduction to the situation is given. These opening lines often appear to be abrupt, carrying the tone of unusual extremity:

(1) I *regret* having married this charming husband,
He is charming, but cannot be relied upon.

(THC, #119)

悔嫁風流壻
風流無準憑

(2) How can I not think of you?
Afraid that your heart may have changed.

(THC, #124)

爭不教人憶
怕郎心自偏

(3) *Darn it!* I don't know where to go.
At this moment the flowers bloom, but who is the master?

(THC, #007)

叵耐不知何處去
正值花開誰是主

What these examples above have in common is the expression of mental attitudes in a head position where one would not normally find these in contemporary literati Recent Style poetry, accomplished through the use of "verbs of thought" (e.g., "regret," "afraid"),[49] modal words (e.g., "darn it"), and interrogatives (e.g., Examples 2 and 3). There seems to be an unwritten aesthetic principle in Recent Style poetry to reserve comparable devices such as hypothetical, negative, and interrogative statements for the concluding lines of the poem, so that we do not usually expect them in the opening lines.[50]

The tendency to state feelings in a straightforward manner is characteristic of the T'ang popular *tz'u* songs, in keeping with the tone of simplicity and directness in all such literature. The persona in a popular song often starts by expressing a particular feeling explicitly and then dwells on it throughout the poem. When we compare a Tun-huang song to the tune *Wang chiang-nan* and Po Chü-i's *tz'u* poem to the same tune,[51] we can see the basic differences of the two types of *tz'u* songs:

Tun-huang song:

Don't pluck me,
Plucking me will stir your heart.
I'm a willow by the pond near the Ch'ü River;
This man plucked me (*che le*), and that man plucked me,-- 4
Each loved me for a moment.

(THC, #086)

莫攀我
攀我太心偏
我是曲江臨池柳
者人折了那人攀
恩愛一時間

Po Chü-i:

The South of Yangtze, how great!

Its scenery I once knew by heart.

At sunrise the river blossoms, more red than flames,

In spring the river waters, as blue as indigo. 4

How can I not think of the South of Yangtze?

(CTWT, I, 31)

江南好
風景舊曾諳
日出江花紅勝火
春來江水綠如藍
能不憶江南

The Tun-huang song starts with a modal word *mo* ("don't") which leads up to a command in a clear and explicit manner: "Don't pluck me!" It is this particular feeling of the persona (in this case, a woman) that is repeatedly emphasized. The poem is almost wholly structured by the verb "pluck" and its object "me" (line 1, line 2, line 4). In other words, all the parts of the poem are connected by a single concern of the persona; it does not permit us to leap beyond the confinement of this world even for a minute.

In sharp contrast to this, Po's poem displays a careful distribution of feeling and scene (what the traditional critics call *ch'ing-ching chiao-jung*) to make natural images the artistic elements of a complex whole. Line 1 is a formulaic expression, but nonetheless expresses the persona's feeling and judgment. Yet the lines immediately following it do not elaborate on the intensity of this feeling. Instead they move on to depict a natural scene (lines 3-4), thus providing us with the picture of a world outside. Here the illusion of an objective world and a vision of a perceptual space are seemingly dissociated from the actual "self." Then suddenly this impression of reverie leads us back to the actual situation: "How can I not think of the South of Yangtze?" (line 5) The entity of the poem is not maintained by continuous, successive statements of a particular feeling, but by an artistic structure in which perception as well as conception, natural scenes as well as inner feelings, form a world of correspondence and mutual relatedness.

This comparison shows how much the style of literati *tz'u* may differ from that of popular songs even when both kinds of *tz'u*

developed from the same, or at least a similar, milieu. The contrast can also be seen from another angle: i.e., the diction of popular songs is generally closer to the spoken, colloquial usage. For example, in the Tun-huang song cited above we find the use of a colloquial function word *le* (line 4) indicating the completion of the action "pluck" (*che le*), an expression so colloquial that most of the literati poets of the T'ang and the Five Dynasties would regard it as unpoetic.

Chinese grammarians often classified Chinese locutions into two large categories: *shih-tzu* (literally "full word") and *hsü-tzu* ("empty word" or function word). The criteria for such a classification may often seem arbitrary, but at least we may say that the former generally refers to words which have substantive lexical meanings (e.g., nouns and predicates) and the latter to particles, prepositions, interjections, etc.[52] Although "full words" contribute the basic meaning to a sentence, it is often the "empty words" that underline the syntactic structure and reflect the attitude of the speaker or the writer. When most of the "empty words" employed in a poem are those which actually appear in daily, colloquial speech, the poem will immediately be recognized as possessing a "popular" style.

The Tun-huang songs employ a wide range of colloquial "empty words." The following *le*, *mo*, and *che*(-ing) are the most noticeable ones:

No more problems (*le*).

(THC, #014)

無事了。

Assume that we are loosening our friendship, O.K. (mo)?

(THC, #026)

淡薄知聞解好麼

My heart is broken, do you know (mo)?

(THC, #003)

腸斷知麼

Carefully thinking (che) it over.

(THC, #026)

子細思量着

The effect of colloquialism is further reinforced by the use of colloquial idioms composed of "full words":

Don't hand over (kuo-yü) your true heart to him.

(THC, #026)

莫把真心過與他

Her singing voice is bell-like (chien-hsin).

(THC, #023)

歌令尖新

To pester (yu-ni) me.

(THC, #010)

把人尤泥

Don't disappoint heaven (ku-t'ien fu-ti)!

(THC, #113)

你莫辜天負地

Such expressions appeared to be common in the daily speech of the time, but were not yet accepted as poetic language by the contemporary _tz'u_ poets. Colloquialism used by the T'ang and Five Dynasties poets were still limited to pronouns such as _nung_ ("I") and _lang_ ("you"). It was not until the Sung that colloquial "empty words" gradually appeared in the literary _tz'u_ poetry. But since this particular point will come up again in Chapter IV we shall wait until then for a more thorough investigation.

3. The Concept of a New Genre

The literati tradition formed its separate conventions in other significant aspects. While the Tun-huang songs employed many widely different poetic forms "simultaneously" and without discrimination, the literary _tz'u_ poetry was at first based on the poetics of the _chüeh-chü_ quatrain. Here I believe lies the crucial conceptual framework by which the development of early _tz'u_ should be traced and analyzed.

If we choose Wen T'ing-yün as a historical point of reference in the development of early _tz'u_, we will see that before Wen the favorite _tz'u_ tunes among the literati poets were those whose song words were written in exactly the same pattern as the 7-character _chüeh-chü_ quatrain (e.g., _Yang-liu chih_, _Chu-chih_, _Lang t'ao sha_, _Ch'ing-p'ing tiao_, _Ts'ai-lien ch'ü_).[53] After Wen these tunes gradually disappeared from _tz'u_ writing; or else they changed into different metrical patterns (as in the case of _Lang t'ao sha_). From this we

can draw one conclusion: the literati *tz'u* poetry before 850 was greatly conditioned by the poetics of the *chüeh-chü* quatrain, and after 850 the *tz'u* genre slowly acquired its independent structural principles, departing from the *chüeh-chü* conventions.

(1) *Hsiao-ling* before circa 850

Earlier I mentioned that when the popular *tz'u* songs in the "long-and-short" line form began to emerge in the High T'ang the *chüeh-chü* quatrain was also reaching its culmination. Thus, it was only natural that most early *tz'u* poets preferred to write *tz'u* poems in the form of *chüeh-chü*. What generally distinguishes the popular song tradition from the literati tradition is that the former tends to adopt new forms immediately in response to new musical requirements; whereas the latter, staying within the conceptual framework of past rigid poetic conventions, progresses slowly and in an orderly fashion until a new set of systems is properly established for an emerging genre. The notion of a tradition is paramount in the development of a literary form.

The conventions of the *chüeh-chü* quatrain played so important a role in the formation of early *hsiao-ling* that even those *tz'u* songs which did not take the exact form of *chüeh-chü* conformed to it in terms of length. Since a *chüeh-chü* poem consists of four lines, with a combined length of either 20 or 28 characters (depending upon whether it is a 5-character line or 7-character line *chüeh-chü*), most of the early literati *tz'u* poems do not exceed 30 characters and contain four distinct line-units, as is shown in the most widely used

tunes before the time of Wen T'ing-yün:

San-t'ai	6/6/6/6	(24 characters)
Yü-fu	7/7/3-3/7	(27 characters)
Ho-na ch'ü	5/5/5/5	(20 characters)
I chiang-nan	3-5/7/7/5	(27 characters)
Yang-liu chih	7/7/7/7	(28 characters)
Chu-chih	7/7/7/7	(28 characters)
Lang t'ao sha	7/7/7/7	(28 characters)
Hsiao-hsiang shen	3-3/7/7/7	(27 characters)

Traditional critics called these short hsiao-ling poems tan-tiao, meaning a single stanza, as distinguished from the other form shuang-tiao, meaning double stanza. The latter became popular later.

This insistence upon chüeh-chü or quasi-chüeh-chü structure on the part of early hsiao-ling poets was special to the literati tradition. By this I am not saying that the chüeh-chü form and single-stanza tz'u were absent from the popular songs. Quite the contrary, many of the Tun-huang songs were composed of less than 30 characters and some of them took the exact chüeh-chü form. What is worth noting, however, is that the Tun-huang songs did not rigidly adhere to the formal rule of chüeh-chü quatrain as those of the contemporary literati poets did. This statement can be amply demonstrated by the fact that while some Tun-huang tunes (e.g., Wang chiang-nan and T'ien-hsien tzu) could have either single-stanza or two-stanza poems as song words, the literati poets in the same period used only the single-stanza form for these tunes. Of particular significance is

the fact that the two most favorite tunes for chüeh-chü tz'u among the poets, namely, Yang-liu chih and Chu-chih, were in the Tun-huang collection found to possess only two-stanza song words, with metrical patterns radically different from the chüeh-chü form:

Yang-liu chih	7/4/7/5	7/4/7/5	(46 characters)
Chu-chih	7/5/7/7/7	7/5/6/7/7	(65 characters)

Of course, Tun-huang songs represent only a small portion of the T'ang and Five Dynasties popular songs; it would be wrong not to assume that many of the popular Yang-liu chih and Chu-chih songs by unknown writers did employ the chüeh-chü form. The fact remains, however, that while the contemporary literati tz'u poets clung to the formal principles of a previously established genre, the various different tz'u forms became popular among musicians, courtesans, and other unknown writers.

Later, even when the literati hsiao-ling poetry developed a poetic structure quite different from that of chüeh-chü, the two genres continued to share some similar aesthetic principles. For example, according to traditional critics and poets, the most vital part of a chüeh-chü poem is its ending couplet.[54] It is believed that the power of a chüeh-chü lies both in its concentrated poetic world and the overtones suggested by it. "Simple words with profound meanings" is an expression used frequently to describe the aesthetic value of chüeh-chü.[55] The critics of tz'u also affirm a similar poetics in terms of poetic closure. Starting with the Southern Sung poet and critic Chang Yen, scholars have been extremely, perhaps

overly, concerned with the aesthetic value of the ending lines in *tz'u*, thus reflecting their awareness of a close relationship between *hsiao-ling* and *chüeh-chü*. Chang Yen suggested that the ending couplet of Wang Wei's famous *chüeh-chü* poem *Wei-ch'eng ch'ü* is a particularly good model for *tz'u* poets to emulate.[56] He claimed that the *hsiao-ling* verse may be compared to *chüeh-chü* poetry because of its similar emphasis on the aesthetic value of the final lines:

> The difficulty of writing *tz'u* is realized in the *hsiao-ling* form, as the difficulty of writing *shih* is realized in the *chüeh-chü*. Since a *hsiao-ling* is composed of only ten-odd sentences, not a single line or word can be neglected. The concluding sentence demands the most careful attention; only when it has lingering overtones is it considered good.[57]

This theory, which sharply pointed out the essence of *hsiao-ling* poetics, eventually became the conventional view in *tz'u* criticism. Most critics from Shen I-fu in the Sung to Li Yü in the Ch'ing emphasized the importance of creating overtones in *hsiao-ling* poetry, a critical view we find continuing early in this century as well.[58] This long-standing critical attention to the aesthetics of poetic closure in *tz'u* reflects the manner in which the *tz'u* poets from the beginning paid special attention to the metrical tonalities of the ending portion of a *tz'u* poem.[59]

The perceived connection between the forms of *tz'u* and *chüeh-chü* in the traditional study of *tz'u* was useful--but very misleading. It

is useful because it reveals how traditional critics were sensitive to the various interrelations between old and new genres. It is misleading, however, because scholars so exaggerated the connection between the two forms that they often overlooked the possibility of further generic development in _tz'u_ , or the coexistence of "long-and-short" line _tz'u_ and _chüeh-chü_ _tz'u_ in the popular milieu from the High T'ang on. For instance, almost all the T'ang and Five Dynasties _tz'u_ poems included in the famous poetry anthology _Yüeh-fu shih-chi_ (by the Sung scholar Kuo Mao-ch'ien) were in the form of _chüeh-chü_.[60] The "long-and-short" _tz'u_ poems, so popular after the middle of the ninth century, were excluded as though they had never existed. Unfortunately later scholars of _tz'u_ often respected this anthology as representing the total picture of poetic development. This consequently led to many incorrect theories.

(2) _Hsiao-ling_ after circa 850

In the light of the generic development of _tz'u_, we can see that by circa 850 the structure of _tz'u_ poetry moved in a new direction which contrasts sharply with the earlier _tz'u_. At this point the standard _tz'u_ poem no longer resembles a _chüeh-chü_ in structure or length, but rather is recognized as containing two equal structural units termed _p'ien_, with a combined length not exceeding 58 characters.[61] In other words, the two-stanza verse has gradually replaced the single-stanza poem. Among the 20 _tz'u_ tunes used by Wen T'ing-yün, 11 had two-stanza song words; in Wei Chuang

17 out of 22 tunes employed the two-stanza verse. It is obvious that by the time of Wen and Wei the two-stanza structure was on the verge of becoming a convention in *tz'u* poetry. Indeed later in the Northern Sung almost all the single-stanza *tz'u* tunes disappeared. Yen Shu used only one single-stanza tune (i.e., *Ju-meng ling*) among his 137 *tz'u* poems in the *Chu-yü tz'u* collection; Yen Chi-tao did not use any single-stanza tune at all in his *Hsiao-shan tz'u* (a collection of 258 *tz'u* poems). All of Ou-yang Hsiu's 171 extant *tz'u* poems (collected in *Liu-i tz'u*) had the two-stanza structure. As for Li Ch'ing-chao, her three *tz'u* poems to the tune *Ju-meng ling* were the only single-stanza poems among a total of 79.

One might argue that the two-stanza structure might have developed from the simple practice of repeating the same tune. As a poetic form, however, its impact upon the later development of *tz'u* aesthetics was a crucial one. What was most important to this new development in *tz'u* was the rule governing stanzaic transition (the so-called *huan-t'ou*, literally "changing heads"). This poetic principle could have no application in either the *chüeh-chü* or the *lü-shih* form.[62]

The structural significance of the stanzaic transition in *tz'u* poetry gave rise to a new convention of poetry reading, different from the reading convention in other previous genres. Although structurally a *hsiao-ling* poem may look like something developed from a combination of two *chüeh-chü* poems, they were not so read by traditional readers, for whom the ending lines of the first stanza in a *hsiao-ling* did not aim at producing overtones as a regular *chüeh-chü* would, but projected ahead to the second stanza of the poem.

The convention of reading hsiao-ling in such a manner was supported by the traditional critical views. Many tz'u critics have suggested that the transition from the first stanza to the second should be carefully handled; it should serve both as a conclusion to the first stanza and as an introduction to the second:

> Generally in a tz'u poem the most critical parts are the conclusions to the first and final stanzas. The first conclusion is like a running horse being reined up; it should come to a halt, but there still is room for further progression, conveying a force of stopping and yet not stopping. . . .[63]

This remained an essential issue in tz'u poetics for many centuries. Nowhere is the significance of the relation between poetic structure and the notion of conventions more evident than here. It implies that the traditional reader's sense of anticipation in reading a tz'u poem arose largely from his expectation of a second stanza, for he had come to learn that tz'u poetry had a particular structure, different from other poetic forms. And the function of stanzaic transition was strengthened by the poets' continual efforts to make it a structural principle. Generally, the way a poet connects the two stanzas in tz'u reflects not only his stylistic predilections but also, as the following chapters will attempt to show, his personal relation to the world in general.

The period around 850 was crucial to the development of tz'u, because it was then that the aesthetic principle of the two-stanza

hsiao-ling began to take shape. It was a watershed. Before that the *tz'u* poetry was not yet an independent literary genre; after that it assumed a new phase, slowly growing into a distinct system. It is in this sense that Wen T'ing-yün and Wei Chuang can be regarded as the pioneer poets in the *tz'u* tradition.

II. Wen T'ing-yün and Wei Chuang:

Toward a Formation of Conventions

Although Wen T'ing-yün was Wei Chuang's senior by only about 20 years, the two poets lived under very different political circumstances. And the crucial difference was that Wen did not live to see the Huang Ch'ao Rebellion (880) which virtually brought about the end of the T'ang dynasty by causing China to be divided into several independent states. A series of wars followed the Huang Ch'ao Rebellion, and a great many people lost their homes or merely disappeared. Living in such times of turbulence, Wei Chuang did not have a peaceful life as Wen T'ing-yün did. At the age of 45 Wei Chuang encountered the dangerous Huang Ch'ao uprising in Ch'ang-an, and for about 20 years he led a wanderer's life in the lower region of the Yangtze until he finally settled down in Szechwan (901) by serving the Shu ruler Wang Chien. Many of his lü-shih poems describe his nostalgia for the past and his sorrow over the dismal situation caused by the Rebellion:

(1) Crossing Yangchow

In those years people did not know about the affairs
of the sword and spear;
Everywhere there were brothels, night after night
songs were sung.

Blossoms from the caves, spring days everlasting.

Bright moonlight on my garments; pleasant breezes frequent. 4

Since the Lord of Huai departed, there are no more chickens and dogs;[1]

When Emperor Yang returned, he was strangled with a silk scarf.[2]

The Twenty-four Bridges, deserted and lonely;

Along the old imperial canal, green willows are broken. 8

(CTS, X, 8021)

過揚州

當年人未識兵戈
處處青樓夜夜歌
花發洞中春日永
月明衣上好風多
淮王去後無雞犬
煬帝歸來葬綺羅
二十四橋空寂寂
綠楊摧折舊官河

(2) Recalling the Past

In bygone years I used to make merry in Wu-ling,[3]

At midnight songs were lovely and the moon filled the tower.

Silvery candles hung in front of the tree; it always seemed like daylight.

Amid the peach blossoms growing by the well, 4

I forgot the coming of autumn.

The prince of the Western Garden was named Wu Chi,

And the maiden of the Southern Country was called

Mo Ch'ou.[4]

Today I suffer war and separation; it is all a dream.

Beyond the sunset I see only rivers flowing east. 8

(CTS, X, 8007)

憶昔

昔年曾向五陵遊
子夜歌清月滿樓
銀燭樹前長似晝
露桃華裏不知秋
西園公子名無忌
南國佳人號莫愁
今日亂離俱是夢
夕陽唯見水東流

It was "in those years" when "people did not know about military affairs" (Poem 1, line 1) that the Late T'ang poet Wen Ting-yün spent his life. Wei Chuang could not help but reveal his nostalgia for the wonderful past which he knew so well in his youth. In poetry, as well as in life, Wen and Wei exhibited two widely different styles. It is the purpose of this chapter to discuss the

differences between these two pioneer poets, so that we will see how later generic conventions in *tz'u* were influenced by the poets' individual stylistic features.

1. The Rhetoric of *Tz'u*: Implicit Meaning versus Explicit Meaning

Within the crystal curtain, a crystal pillow;
Warm incense induces a dream, under the coverlet
embroidered with mandarin ducks.
On the river bank, willows like haze.
Wild geese fly across the waning-moon sky. 4

Lotus fiber silks, in light autumn hues;
Aigrettes cut in manifold shapes.
(Her) temples adorned with fragrant red flowers;
A jade hairpin in (her) hair, stirring in the breeze. 8

(CTS, XII, 10064)

水精簾裏頗黎枕
暖香惹夢鴛鴦錦
江上柳如煙
雁飛殘月天

藕絲秋色淺
人勝參差翦
雙鬢隔香紅
玉釵頭上風

This poem, one of Wen T'ing-yün's P'u-sa man songs, represents the general tone of tz'u poetry by Wen. What is immediately noteworthy is that the connection between the two stanzas of the poem is not very clear. Each stanza seems to portray a separate poetic scene, so that readers are required to find possible relations between the two stanzas.

Throughout the whole poem we are not told who the speaker is. If we take the speaker to be an omniscient observer, then Stanza 1 may be seen as a description of a lonely woman, who has been induced to sleep by warm incense. And Stanza 2 depicts the dream world in which the woman sees herself standing by a river bank in all her finery. Or else the speaker might be a man looking back upon his parting from a woman in Stanza 1; he remembers that he once slept in a splendid room surrounded by objects suggestive of amorous involvement (lines 1-2), and that he had to leave the place the next day at daybreak (lines 3-4). Then in Stanza 2, the woman saw him off by the river bank with her hair ornaments ruffled by the wind (couplets 3 and 4).[5] Or the speaker may be a woman describing what actually happened to her: in Stanza 1 she recalls how she went to sleep at night in her luxurious chamber amid the coverlet embroidered with mandarin ducks, a symbol of conjugal bliss reminiscent of her absent lover. In the morning she looks out the window and sees the hazy willows and the flying geese against a gray and gloomy background which again reminds her of her dismal situation. Thus, in Stanza 2 she starts to dress herself in silks with lotus patterns and decorates her hair with aigrettes, both suggesting the entanglement of human relations.

Nothing remains for her to do except fondle the ornamented hairpin which continues to hang forlornly in her coiffure.

Whatever interpretation we prefer, it is clear that the two stanzas of the poem are structured by a mere juxtaposition of two separate scenes rather than by a continuous, sequential progression. In this case readers are expected to participate in the act of imagination and to locate possible principles underlying the stanzaic transition. We may perhaps use the term "the rhetoric of implicit meaning" to describe this subtle manner of presentation, in the sense that the reader is forced to turn his attention away from the obvious foreground to the hidden background. The author masks his own face behind the impersonal poetic scenes. Feelings are implicitly rather than explicitly expressed; situations are being shown rather than being told.[6]

This unusual emphasis on the juxtaposition of scenes vaguely linked by the rhetoric of implicit meaning indeed reflects one of the most distinctive features of Wen's style in general. When we look more closely into the poetic structure of Wen's <u>tz'u</u> poems, we will see that the organizing principle which governs his stanzaic transition also underlies the textual linkage between the smaller units of his poetry--i.e., between line and line, and between the segments within a line. Generally, there is in Wen's <u>tz'u</u> a lack of conjunctives or any kind of referential pronouns and demonstratives, a method of organization which is associated with the structure of simple images in Chinese poetry. The lack of "deictics,"[7] and consequently the lack of directly specified import, helps to create

a sense of ambiguity in his tz'u poems. Often his most ambiguous lines are also the ones most admired by critics. In his Keng-lou tzu, for example, there is a passage (lines 4-6) whose meaning has continually puzzled the critics, but which has also become one of his most celebrated lines:

> Willow branches long. 1
> Spring drizzles light.
> Beyond the blossoms, the distant sound of the clepsydra.
> Frontier geese startled, 4
> City crows soaring.
> On the painted screens--the golden partridges.
>
> Fragrant mist thin,
> Penetrating the curtains. 8
> Regrets surround the ponds and pavilions of the Hsieh family.[8]
> Behind the red candle,
> Hangs an embroidered curtain,
> My dream continues, but you do not know. 12
>
> (CTWT, I, 61)

柳絲長
春雨細
花外漏聲迢遞
驚塞雁
起城烏
畫屏金鷓鴣

香霧薄
透簾幕
惆悵謝家池閣
紅燭背
繡簾垂
夢長君不知

The lack of grammatical connectives indeed makes the images of wild geese, crows, and artificial partridges in lines 4-6 seem disjointed from one another. However, this is also where the beauty of Wen's rhetoric of implicit meaning lies. The poem starts with an image of a spring day. The persona, alone amidst the quiet scene, hears nothing except the soft raindrops and the steady drip of the water clock (lines 2-3). Confronted by the sight of the willows (line 1), she is reminded of the fact that she is separated from her lover, a feeling which becomes even more intense as she sees the wild geese flying in pairs outside, the crows rising in flight over the city walls, and the still image of two golden partridges on the

painted screen in her chamber (lines 4-5). Thus, the juxtaposition of these sensory images serves as the necessary setting from which the second stanza of the poem emerges. Such a reading may possibly be intended by the author himself, but no explanation is given by him. It depends on the reader's imagination to make an interpretation. In other words, those seemingly fragmentary lines in the poem became meaningful only when we understand that the mosaic impression of Wen's poetic images often implies feelings submerged in the background.

This impression of dense texture of images in Wen's tz'u poetry is further strengthened by his typical juxtaposition of noun phrases within a single line:

> Curtain of thin silk, golden kingfishers.
>
> 畫羅金翡翠 (CTWT, I, 57)
>
> The bird filigree on her jewel box: golden ducks.
>
> 寶函鈿雀金鸂鶒 (CTWT, I, 58)
>
> Head-dress of kingfisher-feathers, pair of golden ducks.
>
> (CTWT, I, 57)
>
> 翠翹金縷雙鸂鶒

In all of these examples, the second half of the line (i.e., "golden kingfishers," "golden ducks," "pair of golden ducks") seems to serve as a modifier of the first half of the line. Yet this relationship is not specified by any grammatical connectives.

This need for getting at the meaning beyond the words leads us to consider Wen's style in a more theoretical light. His organizing principle is not derived from the linear continuity of a strictly "narrative" sequence, but from a process of interpretation whose object is itself. The more this method is exploited, the more the syntactic units seem to be isolated from one another. The idea behind this is that not every poetic utterance has a sequential structure, and that juxtaposition of poetic images is the message itself. What all this means is that Wen's is a paratactic rather than a hypotactic structuring principle. The terms of classical Western rhetoric "parataxis" and "hypotaxis" have been used more recently by Erich Auerbach in his discussion of Latin grammar,[9] but I find them valuable to the analysis of poetics as well, as they correspond to two basic methods of poetic expression. The former refers to a "side-by-side" arrangement of phrases or sentences, and the latter a structure in which the temporal and logical sequences are specified by various connectives. There is a great deal more to be said about these two distinct rhetorical methods before we attempt to see their ultimate importance in the context of tz'u development as a whole.

Of course, the paratactic arrangement of images is by no means unique in the context of the Chinese poetic tradition. As a matter of fact, it is based upon a general expectation in poetic convention that a poem should be unified and that it should be read as a thematically significant piece even if the author's meaning is not clearly perceived. The convention that poems may be read in this manner is particularly cogent in China after the T'ang, for the simple

reason that readers had already developed an ability to penetrate the highly imagistic language in the *lü-shih*. This explains why traditional critics often struggled to get at the "real" meaning of Wen's *tz'u*. Images, though simply placed side by side in the poem, are assigned meanings. For example, the Ch'ing critic Chou Chi once summed up the essence of Wen's poetry in the kind of highly succinct remark characteristic of Chinese poetry criticism: "Fei-ch'ing's [Wen T'ing-yün's] refinement is most profound."[10]

Modern *tz'u* scholars have also contributed greatly to our appreciation of the paratactic structure of Wen's *tz'u* poetry. Yü P'ing-po observes that Wen T'ing-yün "often takes several harmonious images, and randomly places them together, letting them blend naturally."[11] Yeh Chia-ying talks about the pictorial quality of Wen's *tz'u*, an aesthetic quality which derives its value from the total impression of the sensory images themselves rather than from a "logical," sequential context.[12]

Yet the modern reader may well go on to ask whether there is in actuality a neatly laid-out organizing principle governing the paratactic structure in Wen's *tz'u* poetry. Although Wen's poetic images are often given with a paratactic bluntness that seems to suggest that the images are randomly structured together, one can still see that in almost every one of his *tz'u* poems, the poet has carefully selected an underlying subject around which other images revolve. The following poem to the tune *P'u-sa man* demonstrates this particular technique of Wen's:

Head-dress of kingfisher-feathers, inlaid with a
    pair of golden partridges;
Ripples spreading lightly over the spring pond,
    cerulean blue.
Over the pond, a crab-apple;
Rain-washed, fresh, branches loaded with red. 4

Embroidered sleeves hide the dimples on her face;
Misty grasses adhere to flying butterflies.
The blue-gauze door faces fragrant blossoms;
Yet from the Jade Pass, no words arrive.[13] 8

(CTWT, I, 57)

翠翹金縷雙鸂鶒
水紋細起春池碧
池上海棠棃
雨青紅滿枝

繡衫遮笑靨
煙草黏飛蝶
青瑣對芳菲
玉關音信稀

The image in Line 1 serves as a nucleus from which all the other images in the poem are evolved and developed. The line describes the adornment of the woman--her head-dress inlaid with a pair of golden partridges. This particular image gives rise to a series of other images: from the association of the artificial birds the readers are led to imagine that the birds suddenly became alive and flew over the blue waters of the lovely pond outside (lines 2-4). Then in Stanza 2 we return to the image of the woman whose brocade sleeves block our view of her dimpled cheek (line 5). Suddenly the narrator's eye moves to the natural scene again to view butterflies flitting over the grass (line 6). Clearly line 5 recalls line 1, and line 6 recalls lines 2-4. Yet it is important to note that the images in the poem do not proceed in a linear fashion; rather they use a paratactic ordering of corresponding images. Later the Sung *tz'u* poet Chou Pang-yen was to employ a very similar technique to organize his poetic images.

Compared with Wen T'ing-yün, Wei Chuang uses a very different organizing principle in structuring his poetic elements in *tz'u*, as I shall demonstrate below:

(1) *Nü-kuan tzu*

Last night, around midnight,
In bed, clearly I dreamt
That I conversed with you at length;
Still you came with peach-blossom face, 4
And you tried to hide your willow-leaf brows.

Half bashful, yet half gay;

You were about to depart, but unwilling to leave.

Awake, I realize it was a dream, 8

The sorrow, hard to bear!

(CTWT, I, 110)

昨夜夜半
枕上分明夢見
語多時
依舊桃花面
頻低柳葉眉

半羞還半喜
欲去又依依
覺來知是夢
不勝悲

(2) Ho-yeh pei

I remember (chi-te) that year, beneath the blossoms,

At midnight,

When (shih) I first met Lady Hsieh,

West of the lake pavilion, a painted screen hung ; 4

Hand in hand, in secrecy, we made our rendezvous--

Sadly we watched the morning orioles and the waning moon,

And departed.

Since then, we walk different paths; 8

Now we both wander strange lands--

No cause to meet again.

(CTWT, I, 118)

記得那年花下
深夜
初識謝娘時
水堂西面畫簾垂
攜手暗相期

惆悵曉鶯殘月
相別
從此隔音塵
如今俱是異鄉人
相見更無因

The persona in both of these poems tells us in one breath what has happened to him. Wei Chuang is not interested in providing two separate scenes in two stanzas as Wen T'ing-yün might have done, but instead ignores the boundary line between the first stanza and the second and simply follows an unbroken sequence. In other words, the author attempts to portray phenomena in a sequential manner, making everything connected as in a straight chain of thought.

In so doing, Wei Chuang represents a release from restraint in explicit expression. His poetic style is more explicit, more direct, and syntactically more hypotactic than Wen's tz'u. Of course by definition all good poetry is more or less implicit in its expression, or in Susanne Langer's words, "there is no direct poetry."[14] However, the contrast between the implicit and the explicit here merely serves as a convenient way of analyzing different manners of expression in poetry.

The question of what is sequential and explicit is not at all simple. Yet we are not now dealing with syllogistical methods, but rather with the technical devices of hypotaxis, continuous lines, and deictics in poetry. When grammatical connectives such as "if . . . then . . . ," "because . . . ," "since . . . ," "when . . . " are used in a poem to bring out the logical or temporal sequence the reader will get an impression that there is an underlying order governing the poem. The reason is that, as Barbara Smith rightly puts it, "the occurrence of one part will cause us to expect the occurrence of the corresponding parts."[15] The effect of a sequential structure may also be achieved through the employment of continuous lines, for it is a device in which a series of lines are connected to form an integral statement. If deictics are further used to specify place, time, and person, then poetic expressions will appear to be externalized, and thus explicit.

Take, for instance, the second poem Ho-yeh pei cited above. In the poem one witnesses an abundant display of hypotaxis, continuous lines, and deictics. The word shih ("when," line 3) is a temporal

hypotaxis connecting the thoughts expressed in lines 1 through 5. The poem opens with a verb of thought chi-te ("remember") indicating that this is a first-person recollection of a separation scene from a lover, and the whole statement takes 7 continuous lines (i.e., lines 1-7) to complete. The adverbials of time (e.g., "now," line 9; "that year," line 1) and the demonstrative "that" (line 1) all signify a deliberate departure from Wen's rhetoric of implicit meaning to a more deictic mode.

Wei Chuang's hypotactically expressive, rather than paratactically impressive, style also makes it possible for us to see some of his song series as having a continuous "story." For example, unlike Wen's series of songs to *P'u-sa man* where each song seems to remain independent thematically, Wei's *P'u-sa man* songs provide a flowing, "narrative" progression from one poem to another:

Poem #1

The red tower, the night of our departing--
  enough to evoke melancholy thoughts.
By the fragrant lamp, the tasseled curtain half rolled.
As I took leave, I saw the waning moon
And my lady bid farewell with tears. 4

The lute, decorated with golden kingfisher feathers,
And the singing voice of the oriole bouncing off
  its strings,[16]
Urged me to come back soon;
By the green window, she was like a flower. 8

紅樓別夜堪惆悵
香燈半捲流蘇帳
殘月出門時
美人和淚辭

琵琶金翠羽
絃上黃鶯語
勸我早歸家
綠窗人似花

Poem #2

Everyone says the South of Yangtze is lovely,

Wayfarers cannot but stay there till old age.

Spring waters, more blue than the sky;

On a painted boat, I listen to the raindrops as I doze off. 4

The woman in the wine shop is like the moon;

Her two arms are white as snow.

Until you are old, do not (*mo*) return home;

For returning home would (*hsü*) make you broken-hearted. 8

人人盡說江南好
遊人只合江南老
春水碧於天
畫船聽雨眠

壚邊人似月
皓腕凝雙雪
未老莫還鄉
還鄉須斷腸

Poem #3

Now still I recall the delights of the South of Yangtze--

At that time I was young, and my spring garment was light.

Astride my horse, I leaned against the slanting bridge,

From all the towers, red sleeves reached out to greet me. 4

Kingfisher, gold screens;

Dazed with drink, I entered the grove of flowers to
    spend my night.

Today as I see the blossoming boughs,

I vow not to return home until my hair turns white. 8

如今卻憶江南樂
當時年少春衫薄
騎馬倚斜橋
滿樓紅袖招

翠屏金屈曲
醉入花叢宿
此度見花枝
白頭誓不歸

Poem #4

"I urge you to (hsü) get dead drunk tonight,

And in the company of the wine jar not to (mo) worry
    about tomorrow."

I took my host's goodwill to heart;

The wine sinks in and friendship profound. 4

I should (hsü) only lament the fleeting moments of the
    spring night,

And not (mo) begrudge the full cup of wine.

Whenever I drink wine, I laugh and shout "ho! ho!"--

How long can life last? 8

勸君今夜須沈醉
尊前莫話明朝事
珍重主人心
酒深情亦深

須愁春漏短
莫訴金盃滿
遇酒且呵呵
人生能幾何

Poem #5

In the city of Lo-yang the spring scenes are beauteous,

But the talented young man from Lo-yang has grown old

in a strange land.

Willows densely spread over the Prince of Wei's

embankment;[17]

Now my heart is turned into confusion. 4

Beyond the peach blossoms, the spring waters are clear;

Mandarin ducks bathe in the water.

My regrets heighten   as I face the setting sun;

I think of you, but you are unaware.   8

(CTWT, I, 112-113)

洛陽城裏春光好
洛陽才子他鄉老
柳暗魏王堤
此時心轉迷

桃花春水綠
水上鴛鴦浴
凝恨對殘暉
憶君君不知

In Poem #1 the persona recalls a parting scene (perhaps in Lo-yang) in which his lover tearfully begged him to return soon. Poem #2 describes his departure for South of the Yangtze, an area known for its beautiful scenery and women (lines 3-4). He dared not (or could not) go home while still young, for to go home meant to be broken-hearted (lines 7-8). Poem #3 describes that after having left the South for a long time, the persona still looks back upon the happy days he spent there (lines 1-6). Now old and still wandering

from place to place, he has come to realize that it is impossible to return home (to Lo-yang). So with a certain measure of bitterness he vows not to go home until his hair grows white (lines 7-8). Poem #4 is linked closely to the ending couplet of Poem #3; in this poem the persona is advised by his host to get drunk in order to forget about tomorrow (lines 1-4). He accepts the advice of the host, for he knows that life is too short (lines 7-8). Poem #5 starts with a statement corresponding to Poem #1: although the lover in Lo-yang once urged him to return soon, he has become an old man wandering about in a strange place (lines 1-2). He cannot even bear the mere thought of his home (lines 3-4). Surrounded by the peach blossoms and rivers, his nostalgic feeling is beyond description. At last he cries out in a single utterance: "I think of you, but you are unaware."

It would be too one-sided to claim that this is the only interpretation one might give to this series of poems. What is of particular significance is that there is a ring of spontaneous overflow of feelings and an explicit directness in the poems which have encouraged critics to read them as an integral group of songs describing the poet's own experiences during a time of disorder.[18] Wei Chuang's rhetoric of explicit meaning is significantly enhanced by his employment of a particular poetic device--namely, the use of modal words and verbs of thought in all positions of the poem. In these P'u-sa man songs, the two modal verbs hsü ("must") and mo ("don't") which explicitly reveal the speaker's volition and his tone of command can be found in the beginning (e.g., Poem #4, lines 1-2), the middle (e.g., Poem #4, lines 5-6), or the final portion (e.g.,

Poem #2, lines 7-8) of the poem.

This emphasis on the concept of modality recalls the general style of the Tun-huang songs. As has been mentioned in the previous chapter, one of the unique characteristics of Tun-huang songs is the frequent use of modal words and verbs of thought in a head position to state feelings explicitly. It is possible that Wei Chuang made use of this particular rhetorical device of the popular songs in order to express feelings succinctly in _tz'u_. As a result, whenever the poet makes a statement, the words often appear to have a potential of finality.

Yet the fully externalized expressions of strong emotion in Wei's _tz'u_ do not completely destroy the effect of poetic subtlety. This is because his statements, however explicit, often imply a painful realization of the uncompromising discrepancy between wish and reality, so that readers are led to a variety of possibilities for doubt and imagination. For example, almost all the imperative sentences found in his _P'u-sa man_ songs suggest a feeling of extreme helplessness. When he says "until you are old, do not return home" (Poem #2, line 7), he is actually lamenting the fact that he is unable to return home. Thus, this imperative sentence implies something more than a pure command; it serves to reinforce the extremity of the poet's disappointment in life. The situation is so powerfully treated that the poetic utterance produces a highly suggestive quality (typical of any great art)--to the extent that the reader will find it painfully familiar. What we see behind the command is a desirable wish and an undesirable reality; the

tension between the two is striking.

By virtue of their modality, imperative sentences generally call for the attention of the hearer, and in our case, the engaging reader. Of course, Wei Chuang's modal expressions go far deeper than they appear, but the point is that the poet does not hesitate to speak in his own voice. We feel that the poet is interested not only in revealing his own thought but also in guiding the readers. This direct rhetoric, when it is joined with the hypotactic syntax and deictic devices, reveals the author's intent in a clear and explicit fashion.

It will have been noticed that the contrast between the rhetoric of implicit meaning and that of explicit meaning was not unique in _tz'u_ poetry. In _shih_ poetry we can also find examples which contain elements pertaining either to implicit or explicit rhetoric. Both Wen T'ing-yün and Wei Chuang were well versed in _shih_ poetry; it was natural that in composing their poems in the new genre _tz'u_, these poets were influenced by their conception of the old genre. Thus, it is important for us to see how Wen and Wei each seized upon certain aspects of _shih_ poetry and developed them in the _tz'u_ form.

2. From _Shih_ to _Tz'u_: Imitation and Creativity

Before we actually discuss the relationship between the stylization of _shih_ and that of the early _tz'u_, we should make one point clear. The poetic style of Wen T'ing-yün's _tz'u_ is characterized by the use of bright-colored images. Due to the nature of the

subject matter itself, the nouns in Wen's tz'u are mostly descriptions of women's accoutrements. Wen's women almost invariably wear heavy make-up and jewelry, a reflection of the sensuous female milieu which provides him with fertile material for creating sensory images. The accumulated impression of all the adjectives and nouns concerning jewelry, dressing tables, and the like, refers metaphorically to the women themselves. Lines such as the following abound in his tz'u works:

(1) Newly stitched to her embroidered gown of silk--
Pairs of golden partridges.

(CTWT, I, 56)

新帖繡羅襦
雙雙金鷓鴣

(2) The raised pillow hides her painted face;
Green sandalwood, adorned with golden phoenixes.

(CTWT, I, 59)

山枕隱穠妝
綠檀金鳳凰

(3) The kingfisher hairpin's gold pressing my face;
Lonely, closed in the perfumed chamber.

(CTWT, I, 58)

翠鈿金壓臉
寂寞香閨掩

Why did Wen create such colorful images centered on the lives of women? Mention should be made of the fact that the precepts of the *tz'u* school associated with Wen T'ing-yün were later summarized by Ou-yang Chiung in his preface to the *Hua-chien chi*:

> Carved jade, engraved agate--imitating nature's work
> and yet more artful.
> Trimmed flowers, cut leaves--robbing the beauty of
> spring to compete for freshness.

鏤玉雕瓊、擬化工而迥巧
裁花剪葉、奪春豔以爭鮮

For a poet like Wen it was the purpose of *tz'u* to cultivate high artifice, to speak for those women who preferred elaborate robes to plain dress, and heavy cosmetics to natural coloring. *Hua-chien chi* is a living record of this aesthetic or "decadent" movement during the Late T'ang and Five Dynasties, a self-conscious movement which claimed that *tz'u* was a unique literary form whose aim was simply to be beautiful. Being a leading proponent of this aesthetic movement, Wen was regarded by his followers as a model *tz'u* poet.

There is another characteristic of Wen's *tz'u* poetry which is connected with this issue: while the images of women are generally static and pictorial, physical objects are often animated through personification. A woman's billows of hair, for instance, are endowed

with human desire:

> Hair clouds long to cross her fragrant cheeks of snow.
>
> (CTWT, I, 56)
>
> 鬢雲欲度香腮雪

This technique of inversion of animated and inanimated attributes has contributed greatly to the power of Wen's implicit rhetoric. Without having to explain the meaning of the situation, the poet has created, through the personification of objects, an impression that the lonely and lethargic woman lacks the desire to move. She is so passively inactive that the surrounding objects seem to be far more alive than she is. The more luxurious her chamber is, the more helpless she becomes.

Of course the use of bright-colored images and the inner-chamber theme did not start with Wen T'ing-yün. The "palace-style poetry" of the Six Dynasties often used very similar techniques. Yet the autonomy of sensory images, the personification of physical objects, and extended metaphors in poetry did not become prevailingly significant until the Late T'ang period, at which time poets of Recent Style poetry began to favor the use of a new technique which turned human feelings into pieces of artistic abstraction. These poets often concentrated on depicting such delicate and light objects as lamps, screens, raindrops and tears, in sharp contrast to the images of grand objects (e.g., mountains, the long river, huge rocks) in Early T'ang poetry.[19] To the Late T'ang poets the concentrated

essence of these small objects represented the totality of the human world. Even small candles were viewed as possessing feelings:

> The candle shares our sadness at separation,
> Shedding tears for us till dawn.
>
> (Tu Mu, CTS, VIII, 5988)
>
> 蠟燭有心還惜別
> 替人垂淚到天明

The image of candles shedding tears, typical of the Late T'ang Recent Style poetry, can also be found in Wen's *tz'u* poetry:

> Curtain of thin silk, woven with golden halcyon;
> Fragrant candle melting into tears.
>
> (CTWT, I, 57)
>
> 畫羅金翡翠
> 香燭銷成淚

> Incense in the jade censer,
> Tears of red candles.
>
> (CTWT, I, 62)
>
> 玉爐香
> 紅蠟淚

While Wen's *tz'u* poems are almost exclusively about the feelings of women and carry an excessively embellished style, his *lü-shih* poems are characterized by a style that is often stripped of ornament and

is vigorously direct. Rarely do we find so clear an instance of antagonism in one person's poetic style; nowhere could one find better proof for the poet's conscious choice between two literary genres. Many of Wen's lü-shih are about the peaceful and easygoing daily experiences of recluses, fishermen, monks, etc.[20] The poet, like most Chinese poets, often states his lifelong ambition through the depiction of an undisturbed world, a world into which he wishes to retire. In his poems on ancient events he often expresses such conventional ideas as those concerning his failure in his official career and his being unappreciated by his own contemporaries. Thus, unlike his tz'u poetry, Wen's lü-shih is characterized by a broader vision typical of the traditional lü-shih.

In terms of structure, Wen's lü-shih is also in keeping with the ideal model of the conventional lü-shih form--i.e., the two middle parallel couplets are usually paratactic, while the ending couplet is almost wholly hypotactic:

"Morning Walk on Shang Mountain"

Rising at dawn, ringing the cart's bell,
The traveler grieves for his homeland.
The crow of a rooster, moon above a thatched inn;
Human footprints, frost on a wood bridge. 4
Betel leaves falling on the mountain road,
Bramble blossoms brightening the station wall.
So I recall my dream of the mound at Tu,[21]--
Wild ducks and geese flocking around the winding pond. 8

(CTS, IX, 6741)

商山早行

晨起動征鐸
客行悲故鄉
鷄聲茅店月
人迹板橋霜
槲葉落山路
枳花明驛牆
因思杜陵夢
鳧雁滿迴塘

The distribution of the two kinds of syntactic arrangements in this poem, as in most traditional lü-shih poems, corresponds to the movement of the persona's poetic experience. The first couplet introduces the situation of the poem; the second and third couplets, with their strictly parallel structure, together capture a still moment in a succession of images; the final couplet brings the reverie back into a referential context of reality.[22] Such is a poetic experience which comes full circle--an entering into the world of reverie and a turning back from it. It is a world that needs both paratactic and hypotactic orders to guarantee its fullness and integrity.

It has been demonstrated how paratactic structure plays an

important role in Wen's *tz'u* poetry. Might we say that the poet developed his *tz'u* style by imitating the syntactic structure of the parallel couplets in the *lü-shih*? As we can see, the use of parallelism in the two middle couplets has the greatest potential for exploiting the possibilities of parataxis, since parallelism by its very definition signifies a spatial juxtaposition. Yet the crucial point does not lie in the poet's employment of paratactic syntax, but rather in the fact that he turns what is merely a partial stylistic characteristic of the *lü-shih* into a dominant stylistic feature of his *tz'u*. Indeed, without his exercise of such imagination, the *tz'u* might not have become a distinct literary form. In like manner, Wen's contribution to Chinese poetry would have been much less if he merely followed the ornate style of the Late T'ang *lü-shih*. What was unusual about Wen was that after having recognized the limitations of the *lü-shih* form and the great potentiality of the Late T'ang style he turned this accomplishment into a point of departure for his innovations in the new genre--*tz'u*, while remaining unusually conventional in writing his own *lü-shih*.

Like Wen T'ing-yün, Wei Chuang also borrowed significant techniques from *shih* poetry. But unlike Wen, his *tz'u* style seemed to be influenced more by Ancient Style poetry than by Recent Style poetry. It may be that the generally sequential structure of Ancient Style poetry has more to offer to the fluent-connective syntax and the rhetoric of explicit meaning in *tz'u*. In fact it is not difficult to find those common techniques used in both his *tz'u* and his Ancient Style poems.

In creating the illusion of an actual autobiographical account, Wei Chuang often specifies a particular date in the opening line of his *tz'u* poem:

Nü-kuan tzu

The seventeenth of the fourth month;
Exactly a year ago today,
I bade you farewell--
Fighting back my tears, I lowered my face; 4
Bashful, half knitting my brows.

You did not know that my heart was already broken;
In vain the dream follows me.
Except for the moon in the sky, 8
No one understands.

(CTWT, I, 110)

四月十七
正是去年今日
別君時
忍淚佯低面
含羞半斂眉

不知魂已斷
空有夢相隨
除卻天邊月
沒人知

The beginning lines of this tz'u call attention to a referential context (though of an imaginative kind) which contrives to give the whole poem a certain "narrative" significance. It has the effect of reinforcing the truthfulness of a past incident, an experience which seemed more real than the present.

This emphasis on dates and other referential data recalls the famous opening lines of Wei's long narrative poem in the Ancient Style, Ch'in-fu yin ("The Lament of the Lady from Ch'in"):

> In the third month of the year Kuei-mao
> Blossoms were like snow outside the city of Lo-yang.[23]

> 中和癸卯春三月
> 洛陽城外花如雪

Why does Wei show such a respect for the illusion of historicity in his narrative poetry? To be sure, all narrative poetry is to a certain degree associated with an interest in the external world, as there is often a need for verification of reality in this type of literature. The referential context is often provided for the fulfilment of this goal.

Nevertheless, authors of narrative poems in China did not seem to regard historicity as a central issue.[24] The fact is that traditional Chinese readers generally expected a lyrical quality from all forms of poetry. And the solidity of this convention may explain the considerable lack of emphasis on historical facts in

Chinese narrative poetry.

Yet in using the device for providing a date, Wei Chuang has created a dimension of historical authenticity in his narrative poetry. It may be that the incident of the Huang Ch'ao Rebellion had so affected him that the poet hoped to make it known to future generations, as a historian would normally do. But whatever the case, it is most interesting to see that the poet's concern with "historicity" (or at least the art of creating the illusion) should have been reflected in his tz'u writings. As in the Nü-kuan tzu poem cited above, the date given has indeed provided a certain weight of historical detail for its lyrical context.

Of course, this particular device has contributed very different poetic effects to the two types of poetry. As a narrative poem, Ch'in-fu yin focuses on the external world of events (i.e., contemporary affairs); its main purpose is to tell a story. But the density of "historicity" in the tz'u poem serves merely to intensify the complexity of the lyrical experience felt in the present moment.

We have noted that, having inherited the basic structural principles of the tz'u from his predecessors, Wei went a step further to include direct expression of personal feelings and "autobiographical" details in tz'u by means of the device of the persona (as opposed to Wen's exclusive indirect depiction of feminine feelings). This reveals a confidence on the part of Wei Chuang in the potentiality of the new genre. His subject is reflected in his choice of a hypotactically rhetorical style, in which the sequential structure has gained a large place. Any overrefined and extremely sensory

images would be in the way here, where the main purpose is to tell us precisely this and not that. Since Wei was an early *tz'u* poet, almost anything he had added to the *tz'u* genre revealed a reaction against the extremely ornate style established by the Wen school. But, of course, it should also be noted that he did reserve one aspect of his life strictly for his *tz'u* poetry--his delicate sensual feelings and his romantic experiences with women--for these are the essential subject materials with which the *tz'u* form built its ground. By the same token, the subjects of warfare, political incidents and historical events still belong exclusively to the realm of the *shih* form.

The stylistic distinction between Wen and Wei is of course merely a relative one. In some of his *tz'u* poems Wen T'ing-yün exhibits a concern with fluent syntax in poetry. Conversely, Wei by no means excludes bright color images from his poetry. Yet what is worth noting is that traditionally Wen was known as a *tz'u* poet who excelled in writing poems with implicit meaning, and Wei with explicit import. It is in this sense that criticism can condition the aesthetic judgment in a literary tradition.

At this point readers may perhaps think Wei's rhetorical style was not derived from a conscious choice but was itself a reflection of the popular *tz'u* style prevailing during his time. And such an impression is totally justified. The popular *tz'u*, as can be seen in the collection of Tun-huang songs, are almost always characterized by the rhetoric of explicit meaning and hypotactic syntax. Obviously it would be wrong not to consider the impact of popular songs on

Wei's *tz'u* poetry.

3. The Influence of Popular *Tz'u* Songs

Earlier we talked about Wei's five *P'u-sa man* songs as parts of an integral "story." Indeed, in terms of thematic continuity the five songs can be viewed as something similar to the form of the "song cycle" (*lien-chang*), an important formal device employed by the T'ang popular *tz'u* songs. In treating his *P'u-sa man* poems as a song-cycle, Wei did open a new direction for the *tz'u* genre. Later, the device of the song cycle became popular among the literati poets. Liu Yung wrote numerous song cycles which not only in form but also in subject matter approximate the nature of popular songs: e.g., *Wu-shan i-tuan yün* (5 songs), *Shao-nien yu* (10 songs), *Mu-lan hua* (4 songs), *Yü hu-tieh* (5 songs). And Ou-yang Hsiu composed his famous song cycle *Ts'ai-sang tzu* in which each of the 12 songs describes a month of the year (CST, I, 121-122).

In his attempt to capture the vigor of unstylized speech, Wei Chuang sometimes used popular, colloquial expressions which were rarely employed by his contemporary literati *tz'u* poets. A case in point is the expression "ho! ho!" found in his *P'u-sa man* song #4:

> Whenever I drink wine, I laugh and shout "ho! ho!"
>
> 遇酒且呵呵

This demonstrates most fully the poet's effort to turn colloquial usage into literary poetic diction.

If we compare one of Wei's *P'u-sa man* songs (i.e. #3) with a Tun-huang song to the same tune, the similarity of style between the two can be easily seen. The Tun-huang song reads:

> Tomb-Sweeping Day draws near, and the myriad
>   mountains are green.
> Lissome maidens, their waistlines slender.
> Along the wide path fragrant flowers are in
>   full bloom.
> And a youth riding a horse comes into view. 4
>
> His fragrant silk sleeves are light;
> Feigning intoxication, he lets his whip drop.
> Why does he need to turn back?
> Going back will only extend the sorrows of 8
>   spring night!
>
> (THC, #037)

清明節近千山綠
輕盈士女腰如束
九陌正花芳
少年騎馬郎

羅衫香袖薄
佯醉拋鞭落
何用更回頭
謾添春夜愁

The theme of the song is almost completely identical with that of Wei's P'u-sa man song #3. In both of these songs, there is a gallant youth who wears a fragrant garment, rides a horse, meets beautiful maidens, and finally decides not to return home. The only obvious difference between the two is that Wei's persona is recalling a personal experience in the past, but the Tun-huang song is an objective description of a present event. In terms of stanzaic transition, the two songs share a similar structural principle--i.e., they both exhibit such an insistence on sequential structure that the boundary line between the two stanzas cannot be easily detected. This stands in sharp contrast with Wen T'ing-yün's juxtaposition of two distinct scenes in a tz'u poem.

Might we then infer, on the basis of this discussion, that Wen's tz'u is devoid of the elements of popular song style? But this would be an incorrect observation. It is true that in his two-stanza (shuang-tiao) tz'u poems, where the paratactic syntax and the rhetoric of implicit meaning are most predominant, the influence of popular tz'u songs is rather limited. But in his one-stanza (tan-tiao) tz'u poems, we discover a style that is characterized by straightforward and explicit expressions echoing the popular song style:

Nan-ko tzu

In her hand, a golden parrot;

On her breast, an embroidered phoenix.

She steals a glance (hsing-hsiang) at him--

She might as well marry him 4

To form a pair of mandarin ducks.

(CTWT, I, 47)

手裏金鸚鵡
胸前繡鳳凰
偷眼暗形相
不如從嫁與
作鴛鴦

The poem is by no means subtle in rhetoric. Right away the poet directs us to the central issue of the poem without leaving things in the background. The author also uses a colloquial expression *hsing-hsiang* ("to have a look,", line 3) to reinforce the impression of a popular style. The technique of describing one part and then another part of the human body (i.e., "hand" and "breast" in lines 1-2) is similar to a general practice in popular songs, as can be seen in the following Tun-huang song, which is set to the same tune *Nan-ko tzu*:

Like green willow, her eyebrows are drawn;

Like peach blossoms, her face is rouged.

A light silk garment covers her soft breasts--

Her charm unsurpassed, 4

Like a white lotus emerging from the water.

(THC, #120)

翠柳眉間綠
桃花臉上紅
薄羅衫子掩酥胸
一段風流難比
像白蓮出水中

One wonders why Wen T'ing-yün's one-stanza *tz'u* poems exhibit such a completely different style from his two-stanza *tz'u* songs. The question is by no means easy to answer. It is possible that in composing his one-stanza *tz'u* poems, the poet had in mind the poetics of the *chüeh-chü* quatrain. The *chüeh-chü* form had continually served as a popular song form since the Six Dynasties period, and unlike the *lü-shih* verse it generally allowed a certain degree of flexibility in the use of parallelism. That Wen's one-stanza *tz'u* poems often appear to be spontaneous and explicit, rather than ornate and implicit, might have been directly influenced by this general conception of *chüeh-chü* poetry. Such an interpretation is of course tentative, but it suggests relationships between genres that may clarify literary traditions. In any case, Wen was traditionally known rather by his rhetoric of implicit meaning and paratactic syntax in the two-stanza form of the *hsiao-ling*.

The two pioneer poets Wen and Wei can thus be viewed as representing a pair of poetic styles. Despite their differences, however, both poets contributed to the establishment of the essential *tz'u* qualities, chief among them the unique emphasis on the depiction of a sensual and aesthetic world and the structural function of the stanzaic transition. It remained for later *tz'u* poets to synthesize what was done by these two poets and to invent new poetic devices. It was to be a long time before the *tz'u* genre would manifest all its vigor and potentiality.

III. Li Yü and the Full Flowering of the *Hsiao-Ling* Form

Behind the impression of a separation of poetic styles represented by Wen T'ing-yün and Wei Chuang there lies a slow current of synthesis gradually realized in the *tz'u* poetry of the late Five Dynasties. The last monarch of the Southern T'ang (Nan T'ang), Li Yü (937-978), represents the highest achievement of the *tz'u* poets during this period. Before considering his poetry, we may find it useful to look briefly at the general poetic trends at that time. This should offer a broader perspective.

The geographical distribution of the *tz'u* poets during the Five Dynasties period was largely conditioned by the social phenomena of the time. The old capital Ch'ang-an was practically ruined by political upheaval, and the entire territory of the north was ruled continuously by non-Chinese for more than a quarter of a century.[1] In the South where the Chinese found refuge, the only two areas which had considerable economic prosperity were the widely separated upper Yangtze and lower Yangtze regions. The former was the so-called Shu area, and the latter the territory of the Southern T'ang where Li Yü and his predecessors ruled. It was in these two areas that many *tz'u* poets flourished and came to establish a firm tradition in the *hsiao-ling* form.

The poets in the Southern T'ang were very different in approach from those in the Shu area far to the west. When the Shu scholar

Chao Ch'ung-tso collected hundreds of tz'u poems by 18 authors (mostly born in Shu) in the well-known anthology Hua-chien chi,[2] he was promoting both the establishment of a tradition in tz'u and the value of a collective creative effort on the part of the Shu poets. At the time of the compilation of the anthology, the Late T'ang poet Wen T'ing-yün was already dead for about 70 years and the Shu poet Wei Chuang for about 30 years. In collecting the tz'u writings of his contemporary authors, Chao Ch'ung-tso was obviously aware that they must inevitably be judged by the standards of the past, as the works of the two predecessor poets, Wen and Wei, i.e., sixty-six by Wen and forty-seven by Wei, along with eleven by Huang-fu Sung, are given the place of emphasis at the beginning of this collection.

The fact that the anthology starts with 66 tz'u poems by Wen and that its preface by Ou-yang Chiung lays special importance upon Wen's ornate style explains how Wen came to be recognized as the founding father of the "orthodox" tradition in tz'u. Living under the burden of this predominant tradition most of the Shu poets of the time faithfully followed their model poet by composing tz'u poems which can be recognized as the ornate "hua-chien" tz'u style. The general alignment with the Wen style was so pervasive that Wei Chuang's innovative poetic devices, as demonstrated in Chapter II, must have been regarded as an exception to this orthodox tradition. One may say that the contribution of these Shu poets was more in establishing an orthodox critical system than in creating new grounds for tz'u writing.

Contrary to this literary activity was a totally new approach offered by the poets in the Southern T'ang area, in that the poets neither openly professed their allegiance to a certain poetic style nor tried to offer critical theories, but rather indulged in developing new devices. One might almost say that the merit of the Southern T'ang poets lies precisely in their departure from the "hua-chien" school of poetry.

Yet among the Southern T'ang poets, one can still single out Li Yü as a profoundly creative poet who deviated from the usual course by introducing new blood into the tz'u system--as against those authors who more or less remained within the orthodox tradition, despite their poetic inventions. While acknowledging the equal significance of the more orthodox poets, I have chosen to use Li Yü as a standard by which to judge how these poets in the same period (and later periods) adjusted to the major changes in poetic consciousness. By this I do not mean to suggest that the individualistically innovative poets were more significant than the orthodox ones, nor do I wish to imply that poets can be neatly divided into these two categories. My approach is merely based upon the assumption that any obvious interruption of continuity or drastic change of direction can lead us more easily to new insights regarding the development of the tz'u form. We must keep these two kinds of poets continuously in view, although in terms of sheer length of treatment the more orthodox poets may not receive equal attention.

1. The Exploration of Lyrical Sensitivity

Many tz'u critics have called our attention to a significant turning point in the tz'u development brought forth by the works of Li Yü. The often-quoted passage by Wang Kuo-wei is generally regarded as a perceptive evaluation of Li Yü's poetic achievement:

> Not until Li Hou-chu [Li Yü] did tz'u poets expand their field of vision and deepen their feelings. Consequently, the tz'u of the musical performers was transformed into the tz'u of the scholar-officials.[3]

Clearly in the view of Wang Kuo-wei the greatest contribution Li Yü brought to the tz'u tradition was his expansion of the "poetic world." But what does Wang mean by the "tz'u of the musical performers" and the "tz'u of the scholar-officials"? How is this significant to our understanding of the tz'u development?

It seems to me obvious that, in one statement, Wang has attempted to bring to light the most crucial difference between the hua-chien poets and Li Yü. As has been suggested in Chapter II, most of Wen's tz'u, under the influence of the Palace Style poetry, are written from the viewpoint of a female persona (though a few of them are seen as purely descriptive poems). What is striking is that almost none of Wen's tz'u can be viewed as the "pure" lyrical utterance of the poet himself. In other words, when he talks, he often does so under the guise of the voice of a female protagonist. The same technique is also employed by Wei Chuang, although his P'u-sa man series and a few other tz'u poems such as Ho-yeh pei are

read as "autobiographical" poems expressing his personal feelings.[4] We can at least say that with the exception of 8 or 9 poems, Wei's *tz'u* are generally characterized by this "dramatic" point of view.

The device of using the "dramatic" voice was actually in keeping with the performing nature of the early *tz'u*. A *tz'u* poet such as Wen T'ing-yün composed *tz'u* songs primarily for singing girls, and in actual practice a singing girl, who took the role of the "I" of the songs, had to sing to an audience. Of course, the *tz'u* literature in the Southern T'ang area was by no means divorced from this performing function. Nevertheless, one witnesses a drastic change in the use of lyric voice in Li Yü's *tz'u*. Only a few extant poems (i.e., not more than 5) by the poet are explicitly written from the viewpoint of a female persona. Most of his works (except for the narrative ones produced during his early years) are to be taken as direct lyrical expression, revealing the depth of his most private feelings. The "*tz'u* of scholar-officials" in Wang's terminology, may specifically refer to this increasing emphasis on the expression of the poet's personal feelings.

Li Yü's unusual accomplishment in *tz'u* was closely related to his actual personal experiences. We might say that Li Yü was a figure born in the right time and the right place, considered from the perspective of the *tz'u* development. Very few poets have gone through such a drastic change in the circumstances of their personal lives as he did. In his early years (i.e., before he turned 40), as heir-apparent and then reigning emperor, he indulged in an extremely luxurious life at court. After losing his kingdom to the

Northern Sung emperor in A.D. 976 and becoming a political "prisoner" in the Sung capital, he began to live a life of suffering until his death four years later. The striking contrast of these two kinds of life experience provided Li Yü with a need to express his innermost feelings in poetry, with the result that the later Li Yü came to develop a poetic style which was much more intensely lyrical. It was in this period that the poet made a decisive leap forward in using the tz'u form as the major means of expressing his feelings regardless of their subject matter. The poetic world of his lü-shih, by way of contrast, cannot be said to have nearly the same magnitude of scope.[5]

The greatness of Li Yü's poetic world, as revealed in his tz'u, can be accounted for in many ways. The recurrent image of a wide compass of space and time stands out as one of the most effective features of his poetic style. To the poet himself the sweeping expanse of his lost kingdom serves as a symbol of the limitless extent of the universe itself, and the short history of his dynasty as a universal symbol of time past. Time flows from that sweet past to the present, and then rushes onward to the unknown future. In his P'o-chen tzu the poet begins with a couplet that signifies a boundless space and an overflowing fullness of time past:

> This forty-year span, my home and country,
> A thousand miles wide, the mountains and rivers.
>
> (CTWT, I, 231)

四十年來家國
三千里地山河

These lines alone can already show that a significant difference there is between the poetic style of Li Yü and the <u>hua-chien</u> poets. The dominant theme in Li Yü's <u>tz'u</u> is no longer confined to the experiences of the inner chamber, but is extended to embrace the historical dimension of a kingdom and the vast extent of an empire. Through the use of such lines, the poet's individual experiences seem to gain a certain universal importance, in that the images are specific enough to be personal and yet general enough to be all-embracing. These images are usually connected with his remembrance of things past. Such motifs as "lost country," "southern land," "past events" occur again and again in his poems:

> Last night in my small tower, yet again, the
>
> east wind;
>
> I cannot bear to look back to my lost country
>
> in bright moonlight.
>
> (CTWT, I, 221)

小樓昨夜又東風
故國不堪回首月明中

> My idle dream is beyond reach;
>
> The southern country is now colored by fragrant spring.
>
> (CTWT, I, 226)

閒夢遠
南國正芳春

Past events have become illusory;

As though they exist in a dream.

(CTWT, I, 222)

往事已成空
還如一夢中

Li Yü's concern with past and present in *tz'u* poetry is further associated with the predominant moon imagery, which is often used to emphasize his realization of a sharp contrast between the transience of human life and the permanence of nature itself:

The evening is cool, the sky clear, the moon appears--

I can imagine the flickering images of the jade
pavilions and palaces

Reflecting vainly on the water of the Ch'in Huai River.

(CTWT, I, 227)

晚涼天淨月華開
想得玉樓瑤殿影
空照秦淮

Silent, alone, I climb the west tower;

The moon is like a curved hook.

(CTWT, I, 231)

無言獨上西樓
月如鉤

Hidden amid the clustered reed flowers, a lonely
boat anchors;
A flute played in a moonlit tower.

(CTWT, I, 226)

蘆花深處泊孤舟
笛在月明樓

Having experienced a drastic change in his own life, the poet cannot help but look up to the moon as something omnipresent, which symbolizes the quality of permanence. A person's destiny may change many times, but the moon always remains the same moon. It transcends not only time but space. It continues to show up even in times of human vicissitudes, and it shines upon both his lost country and the territory of his cruel conqueror.

Another recurrent motif--the dream--seems to fulfil a similar function:

I dreamt that I returned to my lost country,
At waking my tears run down both my cheeks.

(CTWT, I, 222)

故國夢重歸
覺來雙淚垂

In my dream I did not know I was a stranger;
For one moment I clung to this delight.

(CTWT, 231)

夢裏不知身是客
一晌貪歡

To the poet himself the sweetness of dream is forever associated with his beautiful memories of the past; it is seen as a symbol of the ideal world. The moments of dream in daily life resemble the lyrical moments in the poet's creative life, since they are both brief and beautiful. Without such a momentary but ideal world to escape into, life would indeed be unbearable. Yet, paradoxically, it seems even more unbearable for one to perceive the unbridgeable gap between dream and reality upon awakening from the dream world. What is common to both the dream world and the beautiful past is this quality of evanescence. If the past is equivalent with dream, then the present represents cruel reality.

It seems quite clear that the success of Li Yü's poetic world is largely due to his ability to view his own personal suffering in the light of the destiny of all mankind. Without the highest kind of "unaffectedness" (*chen*), as many critics have pointed out, the poet could not have expressed his feelings nearly as effectively.[6] What, then, is the meaning of poetic "unaffectedness" aside from its obvious meaning of "frankness" and "honesty"?

The "unaffectedness" in the case of Li Yü can be understood in at least two ways. On the first level it refers to the quality of directness in the poet's personality. Historians almost unanimously agreed that the famous line "I cannot bear to look back to my lost empire in bright moonlight" (CTWT, I, 221) was the main

cause that led to the murder of the poet by his conqueror, the Sung emperor T'ai-tsung. Living as a captive, at the mercy of his political enemies, the poet could not even foresee that his poetry might be used as clear evidence that he remained disaffected from the Sung court. In fact, his only concern was to express his genuine feelings in poetry, to the extent that he completely overlooked the possibility that to do so could bring danger in real life. In his praise of Li Yü as the perfect type of tz'u poet, the critic Wang Kuo-wei once said:

> The tz'u poet is a man who has not lost the child within him. Thus, to have lived in the inner court and grown up under the care of women was a weak point for Li Yü as a king, but a good point for him as a poet.[7]

The more one considers the general development of tz'u during the Five Dynasties period, the more one agrees that it was a great fortune for the tz'u tradition to have found a poet such as Li Yü. In retrospect one might even say that the tz'u form and Li Yü found each other in the best possible way. According to the critic Miao Yüeh, one of the basic requirements of a tz'u poet is the maintenance of an ingenuous heart, mindless of clever contrivance.[8] This is because the tz'u genre is built upon the assumption that its poets are to express the subtlest kind of feelings, some of which cannot possibly be expressed in the lü-shih form. That is to say, without maintaining an innocent heart, a tz'u poet would become insensitive to such delicate human feelings and consequently fail as

a poet. Looking into Li Yü's tz'u poetry, we see numerous reflections of the fact that the poet grew up surrounded by the loving care of women. Cruelty and maliciousness were relatively unknown to him. It was the combination of this unusual background and personal temperament that led to the poet's expression of his exclusive concern for court ladies, at the expense of his good name in political history:

> Most unbearable of all was the day when I took
> hasty leave of the ancestral shrine,
> Listening to the farewell songs played by the
> court musicians,
> And shedding tears before my palace women.[9]
>
> (CTWT, I, 231)

最是倉皇辭廟日
教坊猶奏別離歌
垂淚對宮娥

This quality of "innocence" on the part of the poet bears upon another level of significance--i.e., the poetic act of direct personal expression. What do readers really mean when they say that the poet Li Yü is sincere? Some critics believe that the poet is sincere because every expression found in his poetry seems to be an intuitive reflection of his feelings.[10] Such an observation is indeed very perceptive, but it is useful only if we take the word

"sincerity" to mean the general impression of an artistic effect created by an individual poem which gives the illusion of being totally subjective. By definition all artistic expressions are feelings objectified. Even the poet Wordsworth who claimed that "all good poetry is the spontaneous overflow of powerful feelings" would assert the value of objectivity in artistic creation:

> Poems to which any value can be attached,
> were never produced on any variety of subjects
> but by a man who being possessed of more than
> usual organic sensibility had also thought long
> and deep.[11]

Thus Alan Tormey says in The Concept of Expression: "We must distinguish between the artist's activity in constructing a work and the outcome of that activity."[12] When a reader believes that a poet "directly" reflects his intuitive feelings in poetry and thus in that sense is "sincere," he is actually talking, without knowing it, about the poet's "personal style of performance" rather than the poet's creative process.[13] In other words, the concept of "sincerity" here refers to the stylistic devices which the poet employs to create that impression of the "spontaneous overflow of powerful feelings." And this stylistic performance is closely related to the poet's rhetorical effect.

2. Li Yü's Stylistic Development

In terms of rhetorical devices Li Yü seems to have followed

the style of Wei Chuang rather than that of Wen T'ing-yün. In the preceding chapter I have discussed the significance of verbs of thought and modal words used in Wei Chuang's <u>tz'u</u> to heighten the effect of his subjective rhetoric, in sharp contrast to the deliberate creation of an impersonal voice in Wen T'ing-yün's <u>tz'u</u>. Li Yü's use of modal words, however, seems far more predominant than that of Wei Chuang. What is most important here is not simply that the poet continues to use such a device, but that he almost always uses negative modal verbs if he has to employ modal verbs at all:

> Don't (<u>mo</u>) express feelings with tears,
> Don't (<u>hsiu</u>) play the phoenix-flute when people
> are weeping.
>
> (CTWT, I, 223)
>
> 心事莫將和淚說
> 鳳笙休向淚時吹

> If you are looking for spring, you should come
> before spring does,
> If you want to enjoy flowers, don't (<u>mo</u>) wait
> until their branches wither.
>
> (CTWT, I, 228)
>
> 尋春須是先春早
> 看花莫待花枝老

When I return, let not (*hsiu*) candle-light glow,

And let my horse trot in the clear moonlight.

(CTWT, I, 228)

歸時休放燭花紅
待踏馬蹄清夜月

Last year's flowers not yet aging,

This year's moon again full.

Don't (*mo*) just favor the moon and flowers,

Heaven! let youth last long, too.

(CTWT, I, 232)

去年花不老
今年月又圓
莫教偏和月和花
天教長少年

Examples of the use of such negative modal verbs as *mo* and *hsiu* are too numerous to cite. These undoubtedly serve to intensify the personal desires and mental attitudes of the persona in individual poems, as negative modal verbs carry more force than positive modal verbs. This unusual technique constitutes a very special poetic style in Li Yü's *tz'u*. Into those images which would have been treated by Wei Chuang as purely static, Li Yü often projects human wishes, so that the impression created is one

of a conscious poetic self vainly attempting to control external phenomena:

Example 1

Singing orioles scatter,

Leftover flowers jumble together.

Lonely is the hall and the deep chamber.

Don't sweep away the fallen red petals--let them lie.

(CTWT, I, 224)

啼鶯散
餘花亂
寂寞畫堂深院
片紅休掃儘從伊

Example 2

In front of the pavilion the spring drives

away all the red flowers,

Dancing and lingering

In the drizzling rain.

Not for a moment do I let my knit brows relax.

(CTWT, I, 223)

亭前春逐紅英盡
舞態徘徊
細雨霏霏
不放雙眉時暫開

Thus, instead of saying "flower petals are scattered on the ground" (Example 1), the poet emphasizes his personal involvement by turning the image into a command: "Don't sweep away the fallen red petals--let them lie." In like manner, instead of merely describing his knit brows (Example 2), the poet inserts a conscious will into the picture: "Not for a moment do I let my knit brows relax."

The abundance of strong statements of assertion (e.g., "surely," "no doubt") and exclamations in Li Yü's collected _tz'u_ also serves to reinforce this impression of explicit rhetoric:

(1) Strong assertions:

Surely life is full of sorrow, like the river
endlessly flowing east.

自是人生長恨水長東 (CTWT, I, 224)

No doubt you will be broken-hearted.

腸斷更無疑 (CTWT, I, 223)

(2) Exclamations:

Nothing can be done about such long sleepless nights!
The pounding of the mallets and the moon reach
the screens of my lattice.[14]

(CTWT, I, 225)

無奈夜長人不寐
數聲和月到簾櫳

Outside the screen there are two or three banana trees;

The night is long--I can do nothing about it!

(CTWT, I, 225)

簾外芭蕉三兩窠
夜長人奈何

Another characteristic of Li Yü's style is his frequent use of interrogatives:

How can sorrow and regret be avoided in life?

Why do I alone suffer so, and when shall it come to an end?

(CTWT, I, 222)

人生愁恨何能免
銷魂獨我情何限

How much sorrow do I have?

Last night, in my dream. . . .

(CTWT, I, 223)

多少恨
昨夜夢魂中. . . .

How many tears do you have?

They run down your face and across your cheeks. . . .

(CTWT, I, 223)

多少淚
斷臉復橫頤. . . .

It is important to note that like the general practice of many Tun-huang songs, these interrogatives are placed in the opening section of poems. In Wei Chuang the interrogative sentences almost always occur in the concluding part of poems, perhaps due to the influence of the general practice of the <u>chüeh-chü</u> form. Thus, Li Yü's new practice suggests a significant change in both aesthetic values and structural principles of the <u>tz'u</u> form. Where the interrogative sentences in Wei's poems, like their counterpart in <u>chüeh-chü</u>, serve mainly to evoke overtones, Li Yü has broken loose from this aesthetic principle, and instead starts to employ interrogatives in an initial position to call attention to his emotional intensity, though at the same time preserving the basic technique of creating overtones in the ending lines. This also explains why Li Yü's poetry often seems far more subjective in tone than Wei Chuang's. When a persona starts out by asking questions concerning personal feelings such as sorrow and regret without waiting until the concluding section, his poetic voice naturally appears to be more problematic.

Connected with these various rhetorical devices is the poet's use of hypotactic syntax. There are many possible devices one might use in order to establish a sense of continuity between syntactic units. In his discussion of Western stylistics, Auerbach has listed a few possible kinds of hypotaxis--chief among them the "gradation of temporal, comparative, and concessive hypotaxes," and "explanatory connectives."[15] I have found that the major hypotactic device which Li Yü makes use of in his <u>tz'u</u> is quite

similar to the one emphasized by Auerbach--i.e., the "explanatory connective" as a means of emphasizing subjective rhetoric. The persona in Li Yü's tz'u has a tendency to elaborate on his statements, not just providing the temporal sequence which may surround the content of the statement, but revealing the line of thought which may condition his poetic utterance. Here the device of "explanatory connectives" serves as a major means of connecting a statement and its explanation. The following are a few examples of explanatory connectives in the form of simile:

> The past events have become illusory;
> As though they exist in a dream.
>
> (CTWT, I, 222)
>
> 往事已成空
> 還如一夢中

> We may see each other again for a short while,
> But such thoughts are like a dream; it tires me
> when I think of it.
>
> (CTWT, I, 229)
>
> 暫時相見
> 如夢懶思量

It should be noted that the function of similes in the examples cited above is not merely to describe the similarities between two concrete objects, but to establish a relationship

between two consecutive statements which reflects the subjective attitudes of the persona. As a result, Li Yü's sentences often seem hypotactically richer than the poetic lines written by his predecessors. The sequential structure so typical of Wei's hypotactic style is thus extended to embrace more complex means of hypotaxis in Li Yü. At the very least one can say that the poet's use of explanatory hypotaxis has a lot to do with our impression of dynamic and impulsive movement in his poetry. Perhaps this is why the literary historian Liu Ta-chieh holds that Li Yü's greatest achievement lies in his ability to use the simplest kind of sentences to express the most profound and complex emotions.[16]

Yet in spite of this, the poetic "form" itself is not to be swept away by the poet's spontaneous wave of feeling; for he is by no means unaware of the danger of excessive expressiveness. In most of his _tz'u_, we find a symbolic coördination between the rhythm of feelings and the rhythm of language. Form, to the poet, is an organic orchestration of feeling. In Spitzer's terminology this "form" would be an "automatism" of feeling.[17] What is striking about Li Yü as a poet is that he has a tendency toward both continuous expressiveness and a rationalistic control by form. This may be proven by the fact that the rhythms of his poetic lines are often designed to correspond to his wave of feelings. In the light of this fact, we will show in the following section how Li Yü handles two kinds of rhythm in poetry--that of brief, broken lines and that of long, continuous lines.

In his _Wu yeh t'i_, the poet writes:

Silent, alone, I climb the west tower; (6)

The moon is like a curved hook. (3)

The lonely Wu-t'ung trees stand in the (9)

secluded courtyard, locking the clear autumn in.

Cut; it cannot be broken; (3) 4

Arranged; it remains entangled-- (3)

This is the sorrow of separation. (3)

It leaves a very special kind of taste in the heart. (9)

(CTWT, I, 231)

無言獨上西樓 a
月如鈎 a
寂寞梧桐深院鎖清秋 a

剪不斷 b
理還亂 b
是離愁 a
别是一般滋味在心頭 a

Two features stand out: 1) the change from a level-tone rhyme to an oblique-tone rhyme in the opening lines of the second stanza, and 2) the constant expansion and contraction of rhythms (6-3-9 / 3-3-3-9). The first feature could have been easily viewed as a reflection of the general requirement for the tune Wu yeh t'i, were it not for the fact that the change of tone rhymes here

coincides with the introduction of three short breathless lines, followed by a long 9-character line. What is the poetic effect created by such a device? The poet, to be sure, has a particular sensitivity to the acoustic effect. It seems to me that he attempts to juxtapose the disharmonious and the harmonious, a sense of intensity and then the relaxation of feelings.

Looking into the general structure of this poem cited, one can see that following the relatively implicit description of his loneliness in the first stanza, the persona suddenly utters three short sentences which seem to mirror the increasing intensity of feelings and nervousness (lines 4-5). The impression of impatience and helplessness is augmented by the change of tone-rhymes, for it seems to call our attention to the state of disharmony in the heart of the persona. When we proceed to read the ending line of the poem, we find that the symbolizing of feelings by rhythmic structure is achieved in a completely different manner. This 9-character line, changing back to the level-tone rhyme again, reveals a calm and compromising tone through the free flow of its rhythm. The sense of harmonious expansion in form also corresponds to a milder rendering of sorrowful feelings in the choice of diction--the idea "sorrow" in lines 4-6 is here tempered with the expression "a very special kind of taste," which perhaps suggests a calmer attitude.

The same juxtaposition of expansive and contractive lines can be found in many of Li Yü's poems. His _Yü mei-jen_ serves as a typical example:

Spring flowers, autumn moon, when will they come (7)
to a close?
How many past events can anyone know? (5)
Last night in my small tower, yet again, the east wind; (7)
I cannot bear to look back to my lost country in bright (9) 4
moonlight.

Carved balustrades and jade stairs must still be there, (7)
Only the red-cheeked faces have changed. (5)
How much grief can one bear? (7)
About as much as a river full of the waters of spring (9) 8
flowing east.

(CTS, XII, 10047)

春花秋月何時了
往事知多少
小樓昨夜又東風
故國不堪回首月明中

雕闌玉砌應猶在
只是朱顏改
問君能有幾多愁
恰似一江春水向東流

The rhythm of 7-5-7-9 / 7-5-7-9 demonstrates most clearly the systematic alternation of long and short lines. The 9-character line which concludes the poem seems to emphasize the enduring solace of nature itself, in obvious contrast to the more intense and concentrated rendering of feelings in the preceding lines (lines 5-7).

Perhaps no *tz'u* poet before Li Yü was more conscious of establishing the poetics of these 9-character lines. One might almost claim that it was Li Yü who first attempted to employ the 9-character line to express the swelling fullness of the poet's lyrical voice. A brief inquiry into the history of the development of the tune *Yü mei-jen* will make this point clearer. It is of interest to note that all the Five Dynasties poets who wrote in this tune, with the single exception of Feng Yen-ssu (ca. 903-960), continued to use the traditional pattern of 7-5-7-7-3 / 7-5-7-7-3 rather than the new pattern which requires a 9-character line in each stanza.[18] Among the 5 poems to this tune written by Feng, three of them still continue to adopt the traditional rhythmic pattern. And in the two poems which have 9-character lines, one cannot find the same flowing spontaneity suggested by Li Yü's 9-character lines. On the other hand, Li Yü not only completely abandoned the old rhythmic pattern for the tune *Yü mei-jen*, but started to use this new pattern to express a sense of flowing continuity. It is not surprising that most of his 9-character lines remain the most celebrated lines in his *tz'u*:

The flute notes and the crescent moon are just
as they were before.

依舊竹聲新月似當年 (CTWT, I, 228)

My hair is as white as clear frost and unmelted snow--
such memories are hard to bear.

滿鬢清霜殘雪思難禁 (CTWT, I, 228)

Nothing can be done about the cold rain of morning
and the wind of night.

無奈朝來寒雨晚來風 (CTWT, I, 224)

Surely life is full of sorrow, like rivers endlessly
flowing east.

自是人生長恨水長東 (CTWT, I, 224)

The lonely *wu-t'ung* trees stand in the secluded
courtyard, locking the clear autumn in.

寂寞梧桐深院鎖清秋 (CTWT, I, 231)

It leaves a very special kind of taste in the heart.

別是一般滋味在心頭 (CTWT, I, 231)

Of course, not all of his 9-character lines convey a sense of continuity. There is a second type of 9-character lines in

Li Yü's tz'u which serves to capture a sense of discontinuity:

> The east wind is teasing me, that is why it
> brings out in me a heartful of fragrance.
>
> (CTWT, I, 229)
>
> 東風惱我、才發一襟香
>
> We may see each other again for a short while--
> but such thoughts are like a dream; It tires me
> when I think of it.
>
> (CTWT, I, 229)
>
> 暫時相見、如夢懶思量
>
> A clear melody effuses in an instant from her cherry mouth.
>
> (CTWT, I, 221)
>
> 一曲清歌、暫引櫻桃破
>
> Chewing pieces of red silk, and spitting them at
> her lover with a smile.
>
> (CTWT, I, 222)
>
> 爛嚼紅茸、笑向檀郎唾

However, since each of these lines can be seen as two units, one of 4 and one of 5 characters, one should not, in a strict sense, regard them as true 9-character lines. This is because the 5-character line, having enjoyed a long history in Chinese poetry, was often viewed by poets as a basic length in poetry. Thus, when a poetic line can be syntactically divided into 4-5 units or 5-4 units, it is often the case that the author means to write two discontinuous lines rather than a single continuous line.

Since most critics emphasize the enlargement of scope of vision in Li Yü's *tz'u*, his innovations in poetic form are often overlooked. Earlier I suggested that one of the most significant developments of the *tz'u* structure since Late T'ang was its gradual departure from the 4-line *chüeh-chü* and the development of the two-stanza structure. In this respect, Li Yü also made a substantial contribution to the *tz'u* tradition. The tune *Lang t'ao sha*, for instance, was originally a quatrain of 7-character lines, *chüeh-chü* (28 characters), during the T'ang dynasty, and it was Li Yü who first made it into a 54-character *hsiao-ling* with a two-stanza structure (5-4-7-7-4 / 5-4-7-7-4). Compare the one-stanza *Lang t'ao sha* by the T'ang poet Liu Yü-hsi and Li Yü's *tz'u* to the tune:

Liu Yü-hsi:

In the eighth month comes the sound of roaring waves--
The crests, several storeys high, crash against the
hillside and return.
In a flash they reach the Hai-men County,[19]
Sweeping up the sand dunes, transforming them into heaps of snow. 4

(CTWT, I, 30)

八月濤聲吼地來
頭高數丈觸山回
須臾卻入海門去
卷起沙堆似雪堆

Li Yü:

Past events may only be mourned;

Facing the scenery, I find it hard to dissipate my grief.

Autumn winds blow in my courtyard; moss grows on the
    stairs.

I just leave the beaded screen unfurled--I am too lazy to roll it up. 4

Who will ever come?

My golden sword is buried deep,

And my ambition abandoned.

The evening is cool, the sky clear, the moon appears-- 8

I can imagine the flickering images of the jade pavilions and palaces

Reflecting vainly on the water of the Ch'in Huai River.

(CTWT, I, 227)

往事只堪哀
對景難排
秋風庭院蘚侵階
一任珠簾閒不卷
終日誰來

金鎖已沈埋
壯氣蒿萊
晚涼天淨月華開
想得玉樓瑤殿影
空照秦淮

Later, in the Sung dynasty, the poet Liu Yung again changed the rhythmic pattern of this tune into a _man-tz'u_ form: 7-4-4-4-4-8-7-7-6 / 2-4-4-6-5-5-4-4-5-4-4-4-6-8-5-5-4-5 (135 characters). We shall reserve the discussion of that subject for Chapter IV, but at this point it would be helpful to view Li Yü's contribution in the formal structure of _tz'u_ as an important stage in a long, continuous development.

Li Yü's general technique in providing stanzaic transition differs significantly from that of his predecessors. Unlike Wei Chuang who often ignores the boundary line between stanzas, Li Yü's two stanzas in a poem usually represent two lyric moments. Yet his stanzaic transition is also different from Wen T'ing-yün's, since it is generally carried out by an explicit change of tone on the part of the lyrical voice rather than by a mere imagistic juxtaposition:

P'o-chen tzu

This forty-year span, my home and country,
A thousand miles wide, the mountains and rivers.
Phoenix Pavilions and Dragon Towers once reached up
to the skies;
Jade trees and branches formed misty vines;-- 4
Did we ever know the reality of war?

Suddenly (_i-tan_) I have become a slave,
My waist thin and my hair white, I am wasting away.

Most unbearable of all was the day when I took 8
hasty leave of the ancestral shrine,
Listening to the farewell songs played by the
court musicians,
And shedding tears before my palace women.

(CTWT, I, 231)

四十年来家國
三千里地山河
鳳閣龍樓連霄漢
玉樹瓊枝作烟蘿
幾曾識干戈

一旦歸為臣虜
沈腰潘鬢消磨
最是倉皇辭廟日
教坊猶奏別離歌
垂淚對宮娥

The short expression "suddenly" (<u>i-tan</u>) in line 6 of the above poem calls attention to the beginning of a new stanza. We feel that the lyric self is constantly engaged in an active recollection, and in creating a network of lyrical complexity it also serves as the intersection where various dimensions of time meet. The poem moves from distant past (lines 1-5) to the present (lines 6-7), and then to the more recent past (lines 8-10). And

the dramatic turn at the stanzaic transition (line 6) reinforces the impression of an integral body of poetic vision in which recollection of past scenes comes to join the present perception. The movement from one lyric moment to another, emphasized by the two-stanza structure, is an important feature of Li Yü's _tz'u_ style. Very few of his later _tz'u_ are not structured according to this organizing principle. It seems that in his search for a poetic form in which the past and the present can be sharply contrasted, the poet conceived of the _tz'u_ form as the ideal choice.

The significance of the two-stanza structure in Li Yü's _tz'u_ may be further demonstrated through a comparison of this _tz'u_ poem and one of his _lü-shih_ poems on a similar subject:

> North and south of the Yangtze River is my home;
> The past thirty years have been one long dream.
> The inner chamber of the palace in the Wu Garden is
>   now deserted,
> The temple buildings in Kuangling are desolate.[20] 4
> Clouds embrace distant mountain peaks, one thousand
>   faces of sorrow;
> Rain drops on the homeward boat, ten thousand lines
>   of tears.
> We four brothers and the three hundred family members
>   are all imprisoned;[21]
> I cannot bear to sit idle and ponder it. 8
>
> (CTS, I, 72)

江南江北舊家鄉
三十年來夢一場
吳苑宮闈今冷落
廣陵臺殿已荒涼
雲籠遠岫愁千片
雨打歸舟淚萬行
兄弟四人三百口
不堪閒坐細思量

Where in his *tz'u* poem the principle of contrast between past and present serves as the linkage between the two stanzas, the structure of the *lü-shih* is organized by a single act of perception during the lyric moment, without the need for a contrast. Moreover, in the *tz'u* the information provided by the first stanza serves as the basis for the statements made in the second stanza; in other words, the structure represents a transition from one state of mind to another. But this is not the case for the *lü-shih*. There the persona first enters the poetic world by creating a personal, realistic basis (couplet 1)

for the more imagistic, qualitative world of lyric vision (in the two parallel middle couplets), and then comes back to reality again at the end of the poem (though this time with a deeper understanding of reality itself). In the parallel couplets 2 and 3 the focus of perception is realized in the static lyric world where the otherwise referential data have been turned into qualitative images. Thus, the sense of reality is swept away by this heightened vision of timelessness. Only after this momentary world of poetic reverie is over do statements of personal judgment appear (couplet 4). As such, the whole poem represents a cycle of aesthetic experience and no stanzaic transition is required.

The contrast of past and present in the _tz'u_ _P'o-chen_ _tzu_ signifies a continual alternation between the timeless lyric moment and the time-charged world of reality. This seems to suggest that where in the world of the _lü-shih_ a single "journey" is sufficient, here in the poetic world of the _tz'u_ one needs more than one journey to complete the totality of the lyric experience. When the poetic self moves from one journey to another, he turns himself into a probing consciousness, continually exploring the multitudinous reality itself. It is in this sense that the two-stanza structure becomes an effective means of reinforcing the lyric complexity in _tz'u_.

In my previous discussion of the poet's various kinds of rhetorical devices, I have suggested that Li Yü represents the tradition of the rhetoric of explicit meaning, in that his

personal attitudes are often explicitly expressed in one way or the other. However, some readers may wish to ask how his treatment of images differs from Wen T'ing-yün's, since Li Yü's *tz'u* poems are also known for their beautiful images. Are we to simply disregard Li Yü's achievement in imagistic language?

As a matter of fact, one of Li Yü's achievements in *tz'u* is precisely his successful creation of poetic images. There is no doubt that even in those poems where the poetic voice is most explicitly personal, his images are also most striking. A few of his *tz'u* even begin with imagistic descriptions rather than with explicit rhetoric. The following *tz'u* poem to the tune *Yü mei-jen* may demonstrate this:

> The wind whirls around the small courtyard
> overgrown with green weeds,
> Willow sprouts appear spring after spring.
> Leaning against the balustrade for half a day,
> I am all alone and silent.
> The flute notes and the crescent moon are just 4
> as they were before.
>
> I imagine that the pipe songs still continue
> and the goblets are still there,
> And in the pond the ice would be about to melt,
> The candles would burn bright, the incense would be
> subtle, in the secluded decorated chamber.

Now my hair is as white as clear frost and unmelted snow--such memories are hard to bear. 8

(CTWT, I, 228)

風回小院庭蕪綠
柳眼春相續
凭闌半日獨無言
依舊竹聲新月似當年

笙歌未散尊前在
池面冰初解
燭明香暗畫樓深
滿鬢清霜殘雪思難禁

And to be sure, the opening lines of his <u>Tao-lien</u> <u>tzu</u> recall the typical flavor of Wen's imagistic language:

Li Yü:

Deep garden quiet,
Small courtyard empty.

(CTWT, I, 225)

深院靜
小庭空

Wen T'ing-yün:

Willow branches long,

Spring drizzles light.

(CTWT, I, 61)

柳絲長
春雨細

It seems clear that expressive language and imagistic language are not in opposition to each other, and that no poet can produce good poetry without mastering both kinds of language. The real issue here is for us to see how an individual poet manipulates these two essential elements in poetry. In _The Concept of Expression_, Tormey particularly warns us not to hold an "expressive/descriptive dichotomy" in our distinction of artistic methods, as such a contrast "breeds more confusion than it dispels."[22] Nevertheless, he does qualify his statement by saying that such a contrast would be meaningful if it were used for "analysis of functions."[23] In my analysis of poets' stylistic features, I have found it useful to draw a relative distinction between the expression-oriented and the image-oriented, as their "functions" bear upon our discussion of the rhetoric of explicit and implicit meanings.

It appears that, based on the reading of most of his _tz'u_ works, we may claim that Li Yü represents the expression-oriented mode in poetry. Even in the _Yü mei-jen_ poem cited above, one can see that inherent in the imagistic language is the voice of a

poetic "self" constantly comparing past and present. However important the natural images are to the aesthetic value of the *tz'u* poem, the meaning of the poem is determined by the explicit voice of the persona rather than by the association of images themselves. In his treatment of images Li Yü is often quite different from Wen T'ing-yün. Here we shall focus our discussion on two aspects of Li Yü's image-making--the use of simile and that of personification.

In his expression of various shades of emotion, Li Yü often chooses to explain them in terms of concrete images, by means of the simile:

> The sorrow of separation is just like the spring grass,
> The more you walk, the farther you go, the more it grows.
>
> (CTWT, I, 223)
>
> 離恨恰如春草
> 更行更遠還生

> How much grief can one bear?
> About as much as a river full of the waters of spring
> flowing east.
>
> (CTS, XII, 10047)
>
> 問君能有幾多愁
> 恰似一江春水向東流

The novelty of these images lies primarily in the fact that we

normally do not visualize our grief in terms of the infinite growing of spring grass, nor do we compare our sorrows to the endlessly flowing river. To the poet human emotions do not remain static; they grow and flow. Thus, the images of growing grass and flowing river are used here to emphasize the temporal dimension and the changing nature of human feelings. This particular device of Li Yü's, later borrowed by such Sung poets as Ou-yang Hsiu and Ch'in Kuan,[24] indeed forms a striking contrast to Wen T'ing-yün's device of simile where the particular objects chosen almost always represent static and fixed qualities:

> Her look resembles jade,
> Willows are like her eyebrows.
>
> (CTWT, I, 53)
>
> 人似玉
> 柳如眉

> With her embroidered shawl and hair-cloud
> Her beauty in the mirror is like snow.
>
> (CTWT, I, 55)
>
> 霞帔雲髮
> 鈿鏡仙容似雪

As for the device of personification in poetry, both Li and Wen favor this particular method, but for very different purposes. Earlier I have discussed how, through the personification of

inanimate objects, the poet Wen often creates the image of a static, inactive human figure surrounded by "active" and "lively" objects. However, in giving the attributes of a human being to an inanimate object, Li Yü seems to attempt to emphasize the overwhelming significance of human emotion. In other words, it is a device for intensifying the pervasiveness of a subjective attitude. His *Wu yeh t'i tz'u* poem serves as a good illustration:

> The forest flowers have lost their spring red,
> Sooner than their time!
> Nothing can be done about the cold rain of morning
> and the wind of night.
>
> The rouge tears
> Enchant me--
> When shall I see you again?
> Surely life is full of sorrow, like a river
> endlessly flowing east.
>
> (CTWT, I, 224)

林花謝了春紅
太匆匆
無奈朝來寒雨晚來風

胭脂淚
留人醉
幾時重
自是人生長恨水長東

Quite unusually the image of red flowers falling on a rainy day is compared to a woman's "rouge-tears" (line 3). Through this image the poet creates the impression that even the external world shares his personal sorrows. This technique recalls his other _Wu yeh t'i_ poem (CTWT, I, 231) where the _wu-t'ung_ trees are described as being "lonely" (line 3).

This emphasis on human feelings indeed adds a measure of subjectivity to Li Yü's poetic world. Obviously the _tz'u_ genre allows widely ranging possibilities of techniques in creating the lyric world. However, it is important to remember that Li Yü's rhetoric of explicit meaning was considered an exception to the predominant _tz'u_ style during his time. A brief comparison between Li Yü and contemporary poets will perhaps illuminate this point.

Among his contemporaries two authors stood out as important _tz'u_ poets--one was his own father Li Ching (916-961) and the other Feng Yen-ssu. Unfortunately there are only four extant _tz'u_ poems by Li Ching. But since these poems exhibit very similar stylistic features, the lack of material does not seriously hinder our theoretical analysis of his poetic rhetoric.

Again the issue with which we are concerned here is the poets' basic manner of expression--whether it is an attempt to reveal the intent of the lyric self with an effect of directness or to convey the poetic message without directly expressing it. As has been demonstrated, Li Yü's various stylistic features bear upon his essential design of the rhetoric of explicit meaning. On the other hand, neither of his two contemporary poets seemed to have

employed the same rhetorical device as in Li Yü's *tz'u*; their *tz'u* is often characterized by an image-oriented, rather than an expression-oriented, structure. The following two poems represent the typical style of these poets:

Huan hsi sha by Li Ching

The fragrance of the lotus blossoms begins to fade
and the green leaves wither,
The west wind sadly ripples the blue waves.
I, too, am languishing along with the fading spring,
And I cannot bear to see this. 4

In the drizzling rain dreams return from the faraway
Chi-sai,[25]
The cold notes blowing from the small tower
penetrate throughout.
How many teardrops? What will be the end of my regrets?
I lean upon a balustrade. 8

(CTWT, I, 220)

菡萏香銷翠葉殘
西風愁起綠波間
還與韶光共顦顇
不堪看

細雨夢回雞塞遠
小樓吹徹玉笙寒
多少淚珠何限恨
倚闌干

Ch'üeh t'a chih by Feng Yen-ssu

The curved balustrade nestles up against the verdant
    tree;
Willows in the light wind
Unfolding all their golden threads of branches.
Whose hand is adjusting the jade frets on the inlaid   4
    zither?
Through the screens a pair of swallows fly away.

All I see is the airy gossamer and the falling catkins;
When red apricots bloom,
An instant spring rain falls.   8
Awakened from sound sleep to orioles' babble,
Her happy dream is cut short and cannot be retrieved.[26]

六曲闌干偎碧樹
楊柳風輕
展盡黃金縷
誰把鈿箏移玉柱
穿簾燕子雙飛去

滿眼游絲兼落絮
紅杏開時
一霎清明雨
濃睡覺來鶯亂語
驚殘好夢無尋處

In both poems imagistic language plays a major role in the formation of poetic structure. Personal attitude is either implied in the imagistic scene itself or expressed as reflective thoughts inspired by objective phenomenon. In the <u>tz'u</u> poem by Li Ching it is the sense of impermanence in life that the persona seeks to express. But he does not start right at the beginning of the poem to present a subjective statement, as Li Yü might have done. Rather he starts with a natural image: lotus flowers and leaves fading as the west wind sadly ruffles a lake (lines 1-2). Seeing the "wrinkles" of the lake, the persona is reminded of the fact that he, too, is getting old and fading

away in the river of time (lines 3-4). But such a link between the image and its meaning is not provided by any explanatory hypotaxis; the progression is built upon a mere association of images. The reader has to imagine for himself that the "wrinkles" of the lake resembles the old man's face. In the second stanza of the poem, the sense of evanescence continues to dominate; it is now represented by the image of a transitory dream which is accompanied by the "cold" sound of music. At the sight of this perishable world, the persona leans upon a balustrade and begins to shed tears. Clearly the poet's voice in the poem cannot be said to be absent, and in fact, he is always present at the scene. But the poet seems to prefer a device of association based on images, and for that matter, the poetic "I" often appears to be subordinate to the imagistic world.

In Feng's poem we find the same emphasis on images. The first three lines of the poem describe the beautiful picture of a static, harmonious world. The lyrical voice does not intrude into this still picture until a sudden strain of music frightens away a pair of swallows. Then we observe that when the pink apricot-flowers start to bloom, a sudden rain comes to destroy their charm (lines 7-8). Finally another scene comes into view: the persona's dream breaks off because he is suddenly awakened by the orioles' noisy chatter (lines 9-10). What is shared by all these series of descriptions is the idea of the ephemeral quality inherent in the objective world itself. The birds cannot stay permanently in the peaceful world; they are bound to be

driven away. Flowers are not allowed to maintain their full bloom; nor can the happy dream last without interruption. As in Li Ching's poem, the continuity of the poem is based on the principle of association through images.

But in spite of this emphasis on imagistic language, one cannot in fairness hold that these two contemporary poets of Li Yü have completely followed Wen T'ing-yün's stylistic devices. Their techniques of implicit rhetoric are not always the same as Wen's. For one thing, the attempt to blend nature images with subtle human feelings is very different from Wen's typical style of creating rather objective, impersonal images. We should regard this as a significant development in the *tz'u* tradition.

In the history of Chinese poetics, the ideal poetic world has often been defined as one in which objective scenes and feelings are merged. But since Wen's stylistic features in *tz'u* are largely conditioned by the general poetics of the parallel couplets in the *lü-shih* form, he tends to exaggerate the weight of static images in poetry, often at the expense of subjective expression. In the later part of the Five Dynasties period the best of the *tz'u* poets (including those who are obviously image-oriented) seem to have gone beyond that stage, taking advantage of the dual poetic elements (i.e., the objective scene and the subjective feeling) in poetry which were thought for centuries to define the integrity of the poetic world. Clearly, even within the orthodox school of *tz'u* poetry, there were always possibilities for innovation, both in the shaping of the poetic world and the

utilization of new technical devices.

The fact remains that Li Yü's expression-oriented mode in *tz'u* poetry stands in sharp contrast to the more image-oriented *tz'u* poems by his contemporary "orthodox" poets. This is because he basically follows Wei Chuang's rhetorical style, though at the same time adding a dimension of sensory images to his poetic world. Up to this point, the *tz'u* poems I have touched upon were, according to biographical studies by Chinese scholars, written mostly during Li Yü's later years. Although his earlier *tz'u* poems seem to lack the power of lyrical intensity characterizing his later works, they nonetheless remain great in their own right.

3. The Art of Poetic Distance

In real life the earlier and the later Li Yü encountered two radically different kinds of experiences. In poetry Li Yü also employed two distinct kinds of poetics in the two periods. Whereas his later *tz'u* are mostly lyrical, his earlier *tz'u* often appear to be narrative or descriptive. Of course, the terms "narrative" and "descriptive" are used here merely to refer to the poetic structure based on the conception of externalization, as distinguished from that of interiorization characterizing the pure poetic act of lyricism. Viewed in this light, the lyrical tends to focus on the inward absorption of experiences, and the non-lyrical on the objectification of life.

The practice of creating a "narrative" dimension in the literary *tz'u*, in the sense of maintaining a certain story interest, seems to have started with Li Yü. In the following song to the tune *P'u-sa man*, the omniscient narrator describes the meeting scene of two lovers with a view of objectivity:

> Flowers bright, moonlight dim, veiled by faint mist;
> "Tonight I can go to my lover's place."
> Only in her stocking feet she walks the fragrant stairs,
> Her hand carrying gold-embroidered shoes. 4
>
> They meet on the south path to the house,
> Where she trembles for a while in his arms,
> Whispering, "since it is hard for me to have come
> this far,
> Please love me with no restraint."[27] 8

花明月暗籠輕霧
今宵好向郎邊去
剗襪步香階
手提金縷鞋

畫堂南畔見
一向偎人顫
奴為出來難
教君恣意憐

The impression of poetic distance in the poem is achieved mainly because the narrator always remains a mere observer. The narrator is distant from the characters in the poem, so that what he tells may be seen primarily as scenes of a story. The *tz'u* scholar Chan An-t'ai has rightly commented on Li Yü's narrative techniques in his discussion of the poem:

> . . . This can almost be said to have gone beyond the confinement of the lyrical *tz'u*, so as to possess a plot-line and a style approximating drama and fiction.[28]

The effect of the narrative interest in the poem is also reinforced by the interaction between the central character and her lover. And the sense of suspense is built up precisely because the series of actions performed by the central character cannot easily be foretold--to say the least, very few readers would expect that she make such an explicit request to her lover (lines 7-8). This emphasis on the interaction of characters and a plot-line in Li Yü's *tz'u* is relatively absent from the works of Wen and Wei. For example, Wen's *P'u-sa man* #1, which is known to be a successful description of a woman's continual (if not continuous) movements, presents a very different world:

> Painted screens, crenelated;--golden light twinkling.[29]
> Hair clouds long to slide across her fragrant cheeks
> of snow.

Listlessly she gets up, painting her crescent-shaped
eyebrows,
Adorning herself, doing her toilet slowly. 4

Mirrors front and back, reflecting flowers,
Flowers and face shining upon each other.
Newly stitched to her embroidered gown of silk--
Pairs of golden partridges. 8

(CTWT, I, 56)

小山重疊金明滅
鬢雲欲度香顋雪
懶起畫蛾眉
弄妝梳洗遲

照花前後鏡
花面交相映
新帖繡羅襦
雙雙金鷓鴣

Here we see that Wen's woman character, alone and lonely, is slowly doing her routine make-up, and her series of actions are those which can be easily imagined by anyone who is

familiar with the art of adornment. The woman shows no explicit intent, and consequently she does not need to act. The general impression created in the poem is more descriptive than "narrative," more static than active. The poem does not present a story. Its main purpose is to describe the mental state of a deserted woman, whose loneliness is subtly implied by the image of two golden partridges in the concluding line of the poem.

When one looks more closely into Li Yü's narrative art, one can see that his narrative techniques recall the dominant style of the Six Dynasties popular songs known as Tzu-yeh ko:

> She lingers on the decorated bamboo mat,
> The screen and curtain not yet put in order.
> Then she says, "My love, don't come near me
> Until I make myself up." 4
>
> (CHSK, I, 527)

反覆華簟上
屏帳了不施
郎君未可前
待我整容儀

As in Li Yü's P'u-sa man poem, this tzu-yeh song views the movements of the woman character from an objective perspective and faithfully records what she says to her lover. In addition, both of these songs present a main character who explicitly

reveals her feeling by means of a direct request or command, and with a boldness rarely found in literati poetry. One may say that one of the most significant features of Li Yü's early *tz'u* poems is that they frequently carry a popular style. For example, the ending lines of his poem *I-hu chu* clearly recalls the concluding section of an anonymous *tz'u* song *P'u-sa man* which appeals to the popular interest:

I-hu chu by Li Yü

Having completed her morning toilet,
She applies a touch of sandalwood glow to her lips.
Her lilac tongue is slightly revealed,
When a clear melody 4
Effuses in an instant from her cherry mouth.

Her silk sleeves are soiled with dark-red stains,
For her deep cup of fragrant wine spilt over.
She leans against the embroidered bed, so charming 8
and seductive,
Chewing pieces of red silk
And spitting them at her lover with a smile.

(CTWT, I, 221-222)

一斛珠

曉粧初過
沈檀輕注些兒箇
向人微露丁香顆
一曲清歌
暫引櫻桃破

羅袖裛殘殷色可
杯深旋被香醪涴
繡床斜凭嬌無那
爛嚼紅茸
笑向檀郎唾

<u>P'u-sa man</u>　　Anonymous

Peony blossoms laden with pearly dewdrops;

Plucking a flower, she passes the front courtyard

And asks her lover with a smile:

"Which one is more lovely? The flower or me?"　　4

To tease her on purpose

Her lover probably has answered "the flower."

So peevishly she takes offense,

Crushes the flower and throws it at him.　　8

(CTS, XII, 10163)

牡丹含露真珠顆
美人折向庭前過
含笑問檀郎
花強妾貌強

檀郎故相惱
須道花枝好
一面發嬌嗔
碎挼花打人

In both songs the climax of the story is achieved when the main character performs a sudden action. One feels that the effect of suspense is successfully achieved; it would be difficult for readers to imagine that the elegant singer in Li Yü's poem, after chewing a piece of silk in her mouth, would finally spit it at the face of her lover. Very rarely does one find such a description of woman in literati *tz'u* poetry, and this is why Li Yü's *I-hu chu* was severely criticized by some critics as being too vulgar in style.[30]

Yet Li Yü's narrative art goes beyond the mere emphasis on the interaction of characters, and that is one reason why the quality of his *tz'u* surpasses that of the popular songs. In

reading the poem I-hu chu one notices that the poet's skillful manipulation of color images has added another dimension to his characterization: the predominance of the red-color images in lines 5, 6, 9 heightens the impression of a sensuous, and thus captivating woman. Such a careful arrangement of sensory images is often lacking in the popular songs.

Another device to which may be attributed the success of his narrative art is his technique of zooming in to certain unique movements performed by the character. When we again compare the above two songs, we realize that Li Yü's poem is more consistently preoccupied with highlighting the main character's small movements. The entire poem is about the movements of a singer's mouth: when she applies a shade of color to her lips, the charming tip of her tongue reveals itself (line 3). When she sings, her mouth unfolds like a bursting cherry (line 5). It is the same mouth which drinks liquor (lines 6-7), and it is also the same mouth that spits pieces of silk at her lover (lines 9-10).

This technique of the close-up not only brings out the uniqueness of a certain character, but also extends Li Yü's usual method of making the particular stand for the universal,--for the "part" can in fact stand for the "whole" if it is a representative "part." In Western poetic terminology, this practice would be a perfect instance of the use of metonymy. In taking "parts" such as the mouth, or as in the case of P'u-sa man, the feet, as the focus of description, the poet also

opens up a new direction for future *tz'u* poets. This is because the *tz'u* poets prior to Li Yü generally chose to focus on the woman's hair if they had to call attention to a certain portion of a character's attributes. It seems obvious that the general method of characterization employed by such poets as Wen T'ing-yün and Wei Chuang was still confined to the traditional stereotyped image of a woman in the chamber. As Li Yü began to create unconventional images of woman, the impact must have been great.

The achievement of Li Yü's narrative *tz'u* is also reinforced by the unusual effectiveness of his descriptive passages. The poem *P'u-sa man*, for instance, starts with a description of the setting against which the actions are to occur. The descriptive line presents a most striking image: ordinarily flowers cannot shine at night in the dark, but here, in contrast to the dimness of the moonlight, the flowers seem to become quite bright. Most important of all is the function of this particular line in relation to the narrative interest of the poem. The woman dares to visit her lover simply because no one can spy on her adventure on such a cloudy night. It is the psychological state of the woman which is at issue (line 2), yet without the introduction of the opening descriptive line, the effectiveness of the whole poem would have been damaged.

One would expect that because the *hsiao-ling* poem is rather short, the poet might have found it difficult to describe his poetic scenes in detail, particularly in the narrative and

descriptive tz'u where series of external events and scenes are expected to form the major content of poetry. It seems to me that in the case of Li Yü, there is a curious combination of the poet's awareness of the hsiao-ling's limitation in length and a conscious effort to overcome that limitation. And one of the methods which he uses to overcome that problem in a hsiao-ling is to provide opening lines and ending lines which suggest possibilities for temporal and spatial extensions. Consider his 6-line Huan hsi sha:

> The red sun has risen to a thirty foot height;
> The golden furnace is repeatedly filled with animal-
> shaped fragrant charcoal.
> Carpets embroidered in red, wrinkle with dancing steps.
>
> Beautiful maidens dance until their golden hairpins 4
> slip down;
> When I am drunk I pluck a flower and smell it.
> I can hear the music of flutes and drums from a
> remote part of the palace.
>
> (CTWT, I, 225)

紅日已高三丈透
金爐次第添香獸
紅錦地衣隨步皺

佳人舞點金釵溜
酒惡時拈花蕊嗅
別殿遙聞簫鼓奏

The first line implies that the luxurious party has continued all night until the next morning when the red sunlight has fully penetrated into the palace court. And the ending line suggests that there is a similar party held simultaneously in another section of the palace. By using two short lines the author has considerably extended the temporal (line 1) and spatial (line 6) dimensions, while giving the poem a sense of concentrated exactness.

In sharp contrast to his later *tz'u*, his earlier *tz'u* poems generally maintain a continuous, linear progression from the first stanza to the second without a clear-cut transition. It seems natural that in order to create a narrative structure in which all segments of descriptive details are connected, the poet needs to follow a principle of sequential progression in composing his poems. Even in those poems where the narrative elements are not immediately noticeable, the stanzaic transition is carried out through this very principle, as can be seen in the following two *P'u-sa man* songs:

Poem #1

Locked in the garden of the divine,[31] a fairy
Took a nap in her decorated chamber; no human voice
    was heard.
Scattered on the pillow, her beautiful hair was
    adorned with sparkling jewelry,
From her embroidered garment came a waft of rare perfume. 4

I entered secretly into her room but the chain-lock
    stirred--
Startled, she awoke from her dream world enveloped
    by the silver-screen.
Her beautiful face beamed with smiles,
As we gazed into each other's eyes with endless 8
    affection.

(CTWT, I, 226)

蓬萊院閉天台女
畫堂晝寢人無語
拋枕翠雲光
繡衣聞異香

潛來珠鎖動
驚覺銀屏夢
慢臉笑盈盈
相看無限情

Poem #2

The brittle sound of brass reeds, like the clink
    of cold bamboo;
Her slender fingers slowly framed a new tune.
Secretly we exchanged amorous glances,
And the waves of her eyes were ready to flow. 4

Deep in her decorated room, rain and clouds --
But it was hard to express our innermost feelings.[32]
When the banquet was over, all was empty again,
And I was lost in a spring dream. 8

(CTWT, I, 227)

銅簧韻脆鏘寒竹
新聲慢奏移纖玉
眼色暗相鉤
秋波橫欲流

雨雲深繡户
未便諧衷素
讌罷又成空
魂迷春夢中

In one linear, unbroken sequence, the author in each of these poems tells a "story" in which he himself serves as one of the characters. There is a control of poetic distance, as the author describes his own personal involvement with another person in an objective manner. Even when he describes his own feelings, the impression of a poetic distance is carefully maintained, as he is describing feelings felt in the past rather than expressing feelings in the present (e.g., Poem #2, lines 7-8). Thus, the distance is both aesthetic and temporal. The effect of an aesthetic distance is created by the mere fact that the author views his own experience as though it belongs to the hero of a story. The temporal distance is achieved exactly because the poet looks back to the past with a sense of detachment.

The art of poetic distance is characteristic of Li Yü's early *tz'u*, in which the interaction between the self and others in the past, as in the above two poems, often provides narrative elements for his poetry. At this point we may wonder whether the poetic style of the later Li Yü was in some way conditioned by his earlier poetics, although his two styles seem to differ radically.

Contrary to his earlier style, Li Yü's later *tz'u* was grounded in the aesthetics of lyrical sensitivity. Obviously in terms of the poet's point of view, the later Li Yü came to employ a completely new technique. Thus, the impact of his earlier *tz'u* on his later *tz'u* has to be sought elsewhere.

I conclude that the art of lyrical exploration so typically exhibited by his later *tz'u* was greatly influenced by his earlier emphasis on the relation between the self and others. In reading Li Yü's later *tz'u* we often feel that there is a composite picture of the lyric self which embraces but dissolves the accumulated totality of the poet's relations with others in the past. When the poetic self contemplates the meaning of his life-vision in the lyric moment, his spontaneous recollection of his human relations in the past comes to define the ultimate value of the present aesthetic experience. In the lyric moment, the others, though obviously subordinated to his personal experiences, are not treated as mere "objects" of recollection, for their experiences were intermingled with the poet's, and this mutual relationship has also made the experience of recollection more poignantly intense.

The poet's interest in creating a superficial veneer of various connected external events in the context of his lyrical poetry must have been greatly influenced by his narrative techniques in earlier years. What the later Li Yü did mainly was to diminish his control of distance and turn the overwhelming reality of the external world into a mere addition to the lyric self's inner world of perception. In so doing the otherwise objective viewer became one with a lyrical point of view.

Li Yü's lyrical incorporation of external events was crucial to the development of *tz'u* poetry. Later, the Sung poet Liu Yung further developed this technique by using the *man-tz'u* form, and

made this into one of the most important principles of *man-tz'u* aesthetics. Only by viewing it from that broad perspective can we do justice to Li Yü's achievement.

IV. Liu Yung and the Formation of the *Man-tz'u* Form

1. The Rise of a New Sub-genre

Our understanding of the poetic scene during the first part of the eleventh century has undergone a radical change since recent *tz'u* scholars discovered that Liu Yung (987-1053) was an exact contemporary of Yen Shu (991-1055).[1] Before this significant discovery was made, books on Chinese literary history often claimed that, being of a younger generation, Liu Yung did not start to write his *man-tz'u* until after the *hsiao-ling* poetry by Yen Shu and Ou-yang Hsiu (1007-1072) had enjoyed its unquestioned dominance in the *tz'u* world of the early Sung.[2] In recent years, however, scholars have been able to view the two *tz'u* schools represented by Yen Shu and Liu Yung as in real opposition, reflecting sharply the conflict between two different kinds of literary taste.[3]

The fact that both Yen Shu and the other *hsiao-ling* writer Ou-yang Hsiu were born in Kiangsi Province is a significant one. That province was part of the old territory of the Southern T'ang Kingdom during the Five Dynasties period, a region where the *hsiao-ling* form first flourished under the influence of Li Ching, Li Yü, and Feng Yen-ssu. It was only natural that with the Southern T'ang *hsiao-ling* poets (notably Feng Yen-ssu) as their direct predecessors, the early Sung poets should devoutly follow the *hsiao-ling* tradition,

which to them already represented the mainstream literati culture.[4] As a result, these poets preferred to use the hsiao-ling tunes which were prevalent among the Southern T'ang tz'u poets, such as Huan hsi sha, Yü-lou ch'un, and Tieh lien hua (i.e., Ch'üeh t'a chih), so that very few new hsiao-ling tunes were invented during that time.

In sharp contrast to this exclusive concern with hsiao-ling poetry, Liu Yung, in quite a revolutionary step, adopted and invented a large number of new tunes in the man-tz'u form, a form which had been practiced in the popular song tradition (as can be seen in the Yün-yao chi) since the period of the High T'ang (ca. 750), but had obviously not been well received by literati tz'u poets for hundreds of years.[5] A brief survey of Liu Yung's extant tz'u collection makes it clear that most of his tz'u were written in the longer man-tz'u form, and only a few of his works in the shorter hsiao-ling form.[6] Many hsiao-ling tunes such as Nü-kuan tzu (41 characters) and Yü hu-tieh (41 characters) which were popular among the Late T'ang and Five Dynasties tz'u poets were also changed by the poet into the longer man-tz'u form (containing more than 100 characters), leaving no trace of the original metrical patterns. Nowhere can one find a poetic orientation more contrary to the one established by the orthodox tz'u poets.

As a matter of fact, Liu Yung's creative fervor as a poet conformed to, rather than contradicted, the many radical changes taking place in early Sung cultural phenomena. As has been suggested in Chapter I, the two Sung emperors T'ai-tsung (976-997) and Jen-tsung (1023-1063) were extremely interested in new music and continually encouraged the chiao-fang quarters to adopt hundreds of new

tunes, which were said to be quite different from the T'ang and Five Dynasties music. It seems natural that a poet-musician like Liu Yung would take advantage of contemporary musical trends to experiment with unconventional tunes. Moreover, the poet must have drawn his inspiration from the longer *man-tz'u* poems included in the *Yün-yao chi*, such as *Ch'ing-pei lo* (111 characters), *Nei chia chiao* (104 characters) and *Feng kuei yün* (84 characters).

Some traditional *tz'u* critics attributed the development of the *man-tz'u* form in the early Sung to the combined effect of a sudden urban growth and the common need for new music in entertainment circles, as well as to Liu Yung's familiarity with this sub-culture:

> . . . *Man-tz'u* was formed during the Jen-tsung reign [1023-1063] . After the war was over in the Central Plains, Pien-ching became prosperous and flourishing, while the singing clubs and dancing halls competed by creating new sounds. Frustrated and listless, Ch'i-ch'ing [Liu Yung] lingered in the entertainment quarters. Thus, he incorporated the colloquial idioms extensively in his *tz'u* poems so that entertainers could sing them . . . . Later such people as Tung-p'o [Su Shih] , Shao Yu [Ch'in Kuan] , and Shan-ku [Huang T'ing-chien] continued to write in the form, and thus *man-tz'u* became popular.
>
> (Wu Ts'eng, *Neng-kai-chai man-lu*)[7]

Whatever the case, urbanization seemed to have played a major role in Liu Yung's realization of a new conception in tz'u. The longer man-tz'u form must have appeared to the poet an ideal form for elaborate, realistic delineation of scenery, as he wrote in that form on almost all the major newly flourishing cities.[8] Among these was his famous Wang hai-ch'ao on the famous scenery of Hangchow, a tz'u poem which was said to have originally inspired the Emperor of the Jurchen to invade the South China region.[9] The popular interest in the making of the man-tz'u form might have aggravated the literati poets' opposition to Liu Yung's poetic principles. But far more significant than this was the basic structural difference between the hsiao-ling and the man-tz'u form for which the poets found no compromise. The aesthetic value of the man-tz'u structure is the focus of issue in the present chapter, and I shall elaborate on it as my discussions proceed point by point. Yet it is important here to discuss briefly a few crucial differences between the two tz'u forms under consideration, in order to gain a broader perspective as to why a disagreement on poetic forms could create the genuine opposition that existed in the early years of the Northern Sung.

On the most superficial level, a man-tz'u poem is longer than a hsiao-ling: its length ranges roughly from 70 to 240 characters, as distinguished from that of hsiao-ling which usually does not exceed 62 characters.[10] Poems containing 60 to 70 characters are often considered borderline cases. Some traditional scholars further divided man-tz'u into two categories: (1) the "medium-length tune" tz'u (chung-tiao) with 59 to 90 characters, and (2) the "longer tune"

tz'u (*ch'ang-tiao*) with more than 91 characters.[11] Yet to distinguish these *tz'u* forms merely according to the criterion of length does seem not only very arbitrary, but practically speaking, also impossible to apply. Thus, the Ch'ing scholar Wan Shu warned us not to take the convention of length distinction too literally: "What were the bases for the so-called law? There is absolutely no reason to regard a *tz'u* as being short simply because it is short one character or a *tz'u* as long simply because it has one more character."[12]

Wang Li is perhaps one of the few modern *tz'u* scholars to be concerned with the underlying principles behind the structural differences between *hsiao-ling* and *man-tz'u*. He believes that although the traditional practice of form distinction based on length is quite arbitrary, it is nevertheless a very reasonable one.[13] The fact that a *hsiao-ling* poem usually turns out to be a shorter poem with 58 characters or less reveals its certain connection with the structure of Recent Style poetry (which has a maximum of 56 characters). On the other hand, the *man-tz'u* form displays divergent principles from those assumed by Recent Style poetry, and thus often possesses a greater length for that reason.

A more profound analysis along these lines is provided by Shuen-fu Lin. He conceives of the *hsiao-ling* form as one which usually contains four strophic units, with two units to one stanza.[14] In other words, a *hsiao-ling* is composed of strophes which are structurally comparable to the couplets in Recent Style poetry. If the numbers and patterns of strophes (understood broadly as the

syntactic units which end in rhyme) grow to the point where traces of the structure of Recent Style poetry can no longer be found, then the form may be called a man-tz'u.[15] This explains why a strophe of a man-tz'u poem generally contains more lines than that of a hsiao-ling does.

Of course, from the beginning of the formation of hsiao-ling, the tz'u poets already revealed an attempt to move away from the basic structural principles of Recent Style poetry. One of the accomplishments of the hsiao-ling poets was that they began to use diverse rhythmic patterns for the two stanzas of a hsiao-ling poem (e.g., 2-2-3-6-7-2-5 / 7-3-5-3-3-2-5 in Ho ch'uan), thus revealing their attempt to move away from the lü-shih poetics where a repetition in rhythmic patterns is the rule. But we can still find a great number of hsiao-ling poems with identical rhythmic patterns in the two stanzas. It was the longer man-tz'u form which finally went beyond the principle of metrical repetition.[16] Of the numerous man-tz'u tunes whose song words exceed 90 characters, there are only a few tunes that prescribe identical patterns in the stanzas.[17] It seems obvious that the man-tz'u poems are characterized by diverse stanzaic patterns, and such a striking feature has to be understood as a decided shift from a structure associated with Recent Style poetry to that of an independent poetic form, although historically one should view the man-tz'u accomplishment as a continuous, further development of the hsiao-ling.

Perhaps the most important feature of the man-tz'u form is its use of the device called ling-tzu (literally "lead-in words"),

which functions as a lyrical directive for a group of lines in the poem. This technique was promoted by Liu Yung, and it marked a significant turning point in the history of *tz'u*. We shall focus on the analysis of this important device in a later section of this chapter; at this point we may simply remember that *ling-tzu* is a special device employed in the *man-tz'u* through which a series of lines in the poem are connected.

Liu Yung's epoch-making contribution to the *man-tz'u* form was by no means unrecognized by his contemporary poets and later critics. Yet his political career was seriously impeded by the liberalism of his *tz'u* poetics. What had really baffled his contemporary *hsiao-ling* poets was perhaps not so much his revolutionary invention of many *man-tz'u* tunes as his apparent advocacy of a "popular" (or vulgar) poetic taste which came to be associated with the new form he was creating. It was in this context that the *hsiao-ling* poet Yen Shu (then a prime minister) dared to condemn Liu Yung's *tz'u* openly. A story has it that, being continuously denied an official post because of the nature of his *tz'u*, the poet became depressed by his failure. He dauntlessly appealed to Yen Shu, but was in turn ridiculed by the prime minister:

> Yen Shu said: "Sir, do you compose *tz'u* songs?" San-pien [Liu Yung] answered: "Like you Prime Minister, I also write *tz'u* songs." The Prime Minister said, "Although I write *tz'u* songs, I have never produced a line like 'Idly sewing, I would cuddle up to him.'" So Liu withdrew.[18]

Liu Yung's tz'u style was no doubt influenced by the growing popularity of colloquial literature in his time. The use of colloquial expressions merely reflected one of the common trends in Sung literature. Even the esteemed classical essayist and poet Ou-yang Hsiu was known to have produced some 73 quite "vulgar" tz'u poems, but since they form merely a small proportion of Ou-yang's literary works, the "refined" image of the poet was not shattered in spite of the various criticisms he received.[19] Later the Sung poet Huang T'ing-chien also produced many erotic and "vulgar" tz'u, but since this was at a time when colloquialism became more and more common to the literati tz'u, he did not suffer similarly harsh ridicule from his fellow poets.

2. Liu Yung and the Popular Tradition

The sharp contrast between the literati and the popular tradition can be best demonstrated by the fact that those tz'u poems by Liu Yung which seemed to most baffle his fellow poets were also the ones most welcomed and celebrated by the popular audience. A case in point is the man-tz'u poem Ting feng-po:

> Since spring has brought the gloomy green and
> sorrowful red,
> My heart takes no interest in anything.
> While the sun climbs up to the tips of the
> flowers
> And the orioles fly through the willow branches, 4

I am still in bed, embracing my fragrant coverlet.

My face haggard,

My hair disheveled,

The whole day I am languid, too lazy to make my toilet. 8

What can I do (wu-na)?

How unfair, since my heartless husband has left

Not a single (wu-ko) message has come from him.

If only I knew that things would turn out this way (jen-mo)! 12

I regret in the beginning I did not have his tooled-
leather saddle locked up.

All I had to do was bring paper and pen to his study,[20]

Encourage him to chant poetry and read.

Then we could have accompanied each other all day 16

And never have had to be separated.

Idly sewing, I would cuddle up to him,

If he were with me,

The prime of our life 20

Would not have been wasted.

(CST, I, 29-30)

自春來、慘綠愁紅
芳心是事可可
日上花梢
鶯穿柳帶
猶壓香衾臥

暖酥消
膩雲嚲
終日厭厭倦梳裹
無那
恨薄情一去
音書無箇

早知恁麼
悔當初、不把雕鞍鎖
向雞窗、只與蠻箋象管
拘束教吟課
鎮相隨
莫拋躲
針線閑拈伴伊坐
和我
免使年少
光陰虛過

As has been mentioned, the line "Idly sewing, I would cuddle up to him" (line 18) was singled out by Yen Shu as an example of vulgar expression, which in his opinion represents poor taste and thus deserves contempt. On the other hand, this same _tz'u_ has become a classic in colloquial literature. A play by the famous Yuan

dramatist Kuan Han-ch'ing (ca. 1200-1270) was based entirely on this *tz'u* poem.[21] It is important to note that no literati poet other than Liu Yung has enjoyed so great a position in the popular tradition. Fictional accounts growing out of his *tz'u* work, such as the song cycle *Mu-lan hua*, can be found in Lo Yeh's *Tsui-weng t'an-lu*, Hung P'ien's *Ch'ing-p'ing shan-t'ang hua-pen*, and Feng Meng-lung's *Yü-shih ming-yen*.[22] The title of the one-act play *Ch'iang-t'ou ma-shang* in the Yuan dynasty might actually have been taken from a line of his *Shao-nien yu* song cycle (CST, I, 32).

The reasons for Liu Yung's popularity among the general audience are not difficult to find. As James J. Y. Liu has said, the poet's innovation lies for the most part "in his introduction of a new realism in the expression of emotion, a much freer use of colloquial languages. . . ."[23] As in the *Ting feng-po* song cited above, the "new realism" can be best seen in the depiction of a female persona (perhaps representing a low-class woman) who explicitly expresses her bitter regrets as well as sincere love for her "husband" in language most suitable to her status. The colloquial expressions *wu-na* ("what can I do," line 9), *wu-ko* ("none," line 11), and *jen-mo* ("like this," line 12) all serve to reinforce this aspect of realism. Viewed in this light, it was not surprising that Liu Yung's *tz'u* should have been sung, in the words of Yeh Meng-te (1077-1148), "by people in every corner of the land."[24]

Thus, for the first time in the history of literati *tz'u* we see a poet use extensively those colloquial expressions which were popular earlier in the *Yün-yao* songs or current in contemporary

daily conversation, but rejected by other literati *tz'u* poets: *i* ("that man"), *shei* ("who"), *tsen sheng* ("how"), *tsen jen te* ("how can I"), *cheng k'o* ("how can I"), *huai le* ("spoiled"), *shih le* ("correct"), *hsiao te* ("can endure"), etc. This is why traditional critics expressed almost unanimous admiration for the poet on the one hand and disappointment on the other:

> (1) Liu T'un-t'ien [Liu Yung]. . . transformed old music into new music. He published *Yüeh-chang chi* which won great acclaim everywhere. Although the musical tones of his *tz'u* are harmonious, his language is as low as dust. . . . (Li Ch'ing-chao, 1084--?)[25]

> (2) Liu Ch'i-ch'ing's [Liu Yung's] *Yüeh-chang chi* has been admired and acclaimed often. . . but his poems are shallow and vulgar. . . . (Wang Cho, d. 1160)[26]

> (3) . . . As for Liu Ch'i-ch'ing, his musical tunes were harmonious, and his sentence structures were often quite good. But it must be admitted that he uses vulgar language. (Shen I-fu, fl. ca. 1247)[27]

The impression of a popular style in Liu Yung's *tz'u* may also be created by the fact that the poet's treatment of love differs from that of his predecessors. We find that Liu Yung explores and

expresses love in a straightforward manner, almost to the point of being histrionic. As a result, the traditional value of maintaining an aesthetic distance in literati poetry between the self and the feeling of love is completely abandoned. In the Late T'ang and the Five Dynasties period the "inner chamber" theme (kuei-yüan) in tz'u poetry was almost always written from the viewpoint of a deserted woman. But in Liu Yung we witness a peculiar change in perspective: the deserted one, more often than not, assumes the male role (i.e., the poet himself):

Man-chiang hung

A thousand regrets, ten thousand sorrows
Drag on my youthful heart.
My dream unfinished--in the lonely mansion
    I awoke from drunken sleep;
The night is long and dull. 4
What a pity! We shared so many tender feelings in bed,
Yet today our love does not endure.
Alone, all I have gained is this sleeplessness,
And I'm getting weak and pale. 8

My distress deepens,
What shall I do?
I cannot help it, I just go on like this,
Listlessly-- 12
Alone, lost in thought,

I often shed tears.

I do not know why these things keep coming back,

Why until death I cannot cast them aside. 16

Eventually, then, I'll ask you

Why it is.

(CST, I, 42)

滿江紅

萬恨千愁
將年少、衷腸牽繫
殘夢斷、酒醒孤館
夜長無味
可惜許枕前多少意
到如今兩總無終始
獨自箇、贏得不成眠
成憔悴

添傷感
將何計
空只恁
厭厭地
無人處思量
幾度垂淚
不會得都來些子事
甚恁底死難拚棄
待到頭、終久問伊看
如何是

Aside from the abundance of colloquial expressions in the second stanza and the explicit elaboration of the love theme, the poem also appears to carry a popular style because of a lack of proper distribution between outside scenes and inner feelings. Yet _tz'u_ poems such as this represent only one of the poetic styles Liu Yung mastered. Some scholars have made a suggestion that these more or less "popular," or "unrefined" _tz'u_ poems were written by the younger Liu Yung during the period when he spent days and nights with courtesans in the capital at K'aifeng, the economic and cultural center in China during that time.[28] And the "refined" _tz'u_ poems, in which natural scenes are merged into lyrical feelings, were by the more mature poet who became a wanderer in faraway regions as a result of his failure in the civil service examinations.[29] However artificial and however historically unrealistic such a distinction seems to be, it is nonetheless a heuristically useful one for the purpose of our analysis. It seems that these two separate categories represent neatly the two life-styles the poet experienced, and the two kinds of audience his _tz'u_ works appealed to.

It should be recalled that the development of the literati _tz'u_ form had always been closely related to the popular song tradition even before the time of Liu Yung. Wei Chuang and Li Yü, for example, adopted many important techniques from popular songs. In reality, one can never wholly separate the literati from the popular _tz'u_ tradition. The demarcation between the two was never so keenly realized until the _tz'u_ critics in Sung times found themselves

puzzled by the large number of "colloquial" tz'u produced by Liu Yung. Of course, Li Yü did use some colloquial expressions, such as hsieh-erh ko ("a little") and chiao wu-na ("very charming"), but these constituted only a very small portion of his total work. It was Liu Yung who, as a literary tz'u poet, first boldly adopted a colloquial style and a set of subjects generally associated with popular literature.

Liu Yung was no doubt the first literati poet to have been influenced to this degree by the popular style of the Yün-yao chi and other Tun-huang songs. His adoption of the man-tz'u form was partial proof of such a connection. This assumed connection between Liu Yung and the Tun-huang songs caused the later dramatic ch'ü writers and colloquial fiction writers to look up to him as a pioneer figure in their tradition. The Ch'ing critic K'uang Chou-i compared the style of a ch'ü song in Tung Chieh-yüan's Hsi-hsiang chi to the poetic style of Liu Yung's tz'u:

> Liu T'un-t'ien's [Liu Yung's] Yüeh-chang chi represents one of the authorized styles of tz'u poetry. And the ch'ü vocabulary since the time of the Chin and the Yuan have also stemmed from it. . . . This song [by Tung Chieh-yüan] expresses feelings in splendid language, is properly structured, and is easy to understand. Its style is close to the style of Yüeh-chang chi. . . . Tung was the forerunner of Northern ch'ü, but his songs were written in the same vein of T'un-t'ien.

The *ch'ü* form has evolved from the *tz'u* form,

and that is its origin.[30]

Moreover, the descriptive verse in Yuan and Ming fiction might also have been influenced by Liu Yung's numerous travelogue *tz'u*, in its detailed delineations of natural scenes:

Liu Yung:

As a beautiful spot in the Southeast,

As a great city in the Three Wu area,[31]

Ch'ien-t'ang has been prosperous since times of old.

(CST, I, 39)

東南形勝
三吳都會
錢塘自古繁華

Chiao-hung chuan:

Szechwan is a prosperous land since times of old--

At this moment flowers are blooming, the scenery is bright and charming.

(CST, V, 3897)

四川自古繁華地
正芳菲、景明媚

"Yüeh Hsiao-she p'an-sheng mi-ou":

Since times of old, the beauty of the Ch'ien-t'ang River
is unsurpassed,

Throngs of tourists come to view the tides. . .

(CST, V, 3899)

自古錢塘難比
看潮人、成群作隊

Yet in spite of all these facts one can still say that there are significant points that distinguish Liu Yung's *tz'u* from popular literature. Whereas the Tun-huang songs were an antecedent to the Northern dramatic *ch'ü* (*pei-ch'ü*) both stylistically and structurally,[32] Liu Yung remained an epoch-making figure in the literati *tz'u* tradition. The poet indeed drew many insights from popular songs and in turn exercised a powerful impact on that tradition, but he never departed from the mainstream of the literary *tz'u*. For this we have several explanations.

In sharp contrast to the Tun-huang songs where a great many themes were dealt with, Liu Yung's *tz'u* poems were mostly on his emotional experiences with singing girls and his personal feelings encountered during his "wandering" years. Clearly in this respect Liu Yung was carrying on the poetic tradition long established by the *hua-chien* poets. His involvement with singing girls was indeed quite similar to Wen T'ing-yün's style of life, and like Wen, he was a pioneer poet in an important *tz'u* form. They shared a basic

poetics in _tz'u_ in their "exclusive" treatment of emotional experiences in that form. The difference between the two may be simply one of perspective: Wen preferred to see the world objectively from the viewpoint of the singing girl, while Liu often expressed his own subjective personal feelings.

As a true pioneer in the _tz'u_ tradition, Wen T'ing-yün came to be known respectfully in _tz'u_ circles by his official title "Wen, the Teaching Assistant" (Wen _chu-chiao_) despite his notorious involvement with singing girls. Yet as a "revolutionary" figure working against an orthodox tradition, Liu Yung was often casually referred to as "Liu the Seventh" (Liu Ch'i). The real difference between them may be that in his _tz'u_ writing Wen generally avoided colloquialism while Liu intentionally borrowed it in the shaping of a new _tz'u_ language. Thus, despite their similar familiarity with the popular song tradition, the one attempted to create a totally separate literati tradition while the other hoped to bring together a number of poetic features from the two traditions.

The revolutionary aspect of Liu Yung's poetics, however, should not be seen as an opposition to the literati tradition, but rather as an attempt to broaden the poetic horizons of _tz'u_. True, Liu Yung's _tz'u_ poems appealed to a popular audience, because they seemed so easy for almost everyone to appreciate. But the poet always considered himself as a member of the intellectual elite[33]--his collected work _Yüeh-chang chi_ was meant to be read by other literati poets.

In fact Liu Yung never borrowed poetic methods "literally"

from the popular songs. What he saw in them was only a potentially rich source of inspiration, but never a set of rules to follow. There are only 16 *tz'u* tunes out of the total of 127 tunes in Liu Yung's collection which we know to have been previously used by Tun-huang songs. Among these 16 tunes employed by Liu Yung, only 3 bear identical metrical patterns with those known from the Tun-huang songs, and 5 were changed from the *hsiao-ling* form to the *man-tz'u* form.[34] Most of the Tun-huang songs (65%) have level-tone rhymes, and only 18% of them carry strictly oblique-tone rhymes (the rest of the 17% having mixed rhymes).[35] In contrast to this, Liu Yung used mostly oblique-tone rhymes, which was to become a common, though not the absolutely exclusive practice among the later Sung *tz'u* poets. Thus, Liu Yung still remained in the mainstream of the literary *tz'u*, and so his contribution to *tz'u* can be best understood in this light.

3. The Poetics of Liu Yung's *Man-tz'u*

It would be inaccurate to claim that Liu Yung was the first literati *tz'u* poet ever to have written in the *man-tz'u* form. The extant *tz'u* collections reveal that before the time of the Sung dynasty there were a few poets who occasionally composed *man-tz'u* poems, i.e., the Late T'ang poets Tu Mu and Chung Fu and the Five Dynasties poets Yin O, Li Ts'un-hsü, and Hsüeh Chao-yün (CTS, XII, 10059, 10071, 10113, 10041, 10097). Many *tz'u* scholars refused to believe that these poets ever wrote any *man-tz'u*, since it was their assumption that the *man-tz'u* as a form was not started until

the time of the Northern Sung.[36] However, the discovery of the early popular _tz'u_ songs in the Tun-huang Caves has gradually forced scholars to reconsider their previous views. There seems no apparent reason for scholars to continue to doubt the authorship of the pre-Sung literary _man-tz'u_, since it has been proven by the _Yün-yao chi_ that the form indeed had existed in the popular song tradition since the time of the High T'ang.

Yet the fact remains that Liu Yung was the first literary _tz'u_ poet to have consciously practiced in the _man-tz'u_ form. At that time no other poet, including his contemporary Chang Hsien (whose work will be discussed later in this chapter), was as wholeheartedly committed to the promotion of this new form as Liu Yung. In addition, the few _man-tz'u_ poems written by the Late T'ang and Five Dynasties poets can be considered merely occasional experiments. In many respects, these early _man-tz'u_ were not as fully developed as Liu Yung's. For example, where the _Ch'iu-yeh yüeh_ by Yin O has a structure made of two identical stanzas, Liu Yung's _tz'u_ to the same tune has materialized into quite an unbalanced stanzaic structure (4-9-10-6-6-6 / 4-5-5-6-4-4-5-4-4). Some of these poems were basically _hsiao-ling_ poems in structure--for instance, Li Hsün's _Chung-hsing yüeh_ (84 characters) merely doubled the length of the original _hsiao-ling_ form. Thus in length the poem resembles a _man-tz'u_, but its structure more or less functions like that of a _hsiao-ling_. Most important, these poets had not yet employed the device of _ling-tzu_, a linguistic device which came to characterize the _man-tz'u_ poetry of the Sung.

What is the device of ling-tzu, and how did it become a structural principle in man-tz'u? A ling-tzu (composed of one, two, or three characters) may be defined as a directive for a series of consecutive lines (or phrases) in a poem. It may be a verb, an adverb, an adjective, or a conjunction. Liu Yung first used ling-tzu extensively in his man-tz'u poems, and it became a conventional requirement only after later poets consciously followed his practice. Generally in composing a man-tz'u a Sung poet observed carefully how former poets structured the ling-tzu segments in their poems to the tune, so that he could follow the set pattern accordingly, though occasionally not without variations. The following ling-tzu words are some of the examples proposed by the Sung critics:

(1) One-character ling-tzu:[37]

k'an ("see")

p'a ("worry")

liao ("imagine")

tsung ("even if")

shen ("very")

tan ("but")

(2) Two-character ling-tzu:[38]

mo-shih ("is it. . . ?")

huan-yu ("again")

na-k'an ("how can I bear?")

(3) Three-character ling-tzu:

keng neng hsiao ("again how can I bear. . . ?")

tsui wu tuan ("most unthinkable")

yu ch'üeh shih ("but again. . . ")

Further investigation has suggested to me that those of Liu Yung's more "refined" man-tz'u poems which were praised continuously by traditional critics over the centuries are exactly those poems in which the ling-tzu words are employed most skillfully. The following two poems, Yü lin ling and Pa-sheng kan-chou (henceforth YLL and PSKC) will demonstrate this point:

(1) Yü lin ling

The autumn cicadas are chirping sadly,
As I face (tui) the pavilion in the evening--
The sudden rain has just passed.
At the banquet near the city gate I am preoccupied; 4
I linger, but the orchid boat is ready to go.
Hand in hand, we look into each other's tearful eyes;--
Not a single word is said, for we were choked with tears.
I think of (nien) the place where I will go--a thousand 8
miles of misty waves ahead of me--
A scene of evening haze enveloping the boundless Southern
sky.

From of old, tender natures grieve at separation;
But how, then, can I bear (keng na k'an) this in this

desolate autumn season?

Tonight when I awaken from drunken sleep, where shall I be? 12

A willow-bank, the breeze at dawn, the fading moon.

This time I'll be gone for a few years,

All the pleasant days and beautiful scenes set before us will surely be in vain.

Even if (pien tsung yu) I should experience a thousand kinds of romantic feelings, 16

To whom shall I express them?

(CST, I, 21)

寒蟬淒切
對長亭晚
驟雨初歇
都門帳飲無緒
留戀處、蘭舟催發
執手相看淚眼
竟無語凝噎
念去去、千里烟波
暮靄沈沈楚天闊

多情自古傷離別
更那堪冷落清秋節
今宵酒醒何處
楊柳岸、曉風殘月
此去經年
應是良辰、好景虛設
便縱有、千種風情
更與何人說

(2) *Pa-sheng kan-chou*

I face (*tui*) the scene of a downpouring evening rain,
splashing on the river and sky,--
The clear autumn is washed clean.
Gradually (*chien*) the frosty wind brings a chilly
current of air,
The mountain-pass and the rivers become desolate, 4
And the fading sunlight falls on the tower.
Here the red blossoms wither, the green leaves decay--
One by one the beautiful scenes in nature fade away.
Only the water of the Yangtze River 8
Flows east, without a word.

I cannot bear to view the distance from a high point,--

Gazing upon (wang) my homeland faraway

Would arouse all my homesick thoughts. 12

I sigh over (t'an) my straying steps these years,

Why do I suffer these endless wanderings?

I imagine (hsiang) my fair lady now looks out earnestly
from her chamber--

How many times did she take the boat on the horizon 16
for mine?

How would she know that I, leaning here against my
balustrade,

Am bursting with grief?

(CST, I, 43)

對瀟瀟暮雨灑江天
一番洗清秋
漸霜風淒緊
關河冷落
殘照當樓
是處紅衰翠減
苒苒物華休
唯有長江水
無語東流

不忍登高臨遠
望故鄉渺邈
歸思難收
歎年來蹤迹
何事苦淹留
想佳人、妝樓顒望
誤幾回、天際識歸舟
爭知我、倚闌干處
正恁凝愁

In these two poems one finds a variety of *ling-tzu*:

YLL:

tui ("face ," line 2) verb

nien ("think of," line 8) verb

keng na k'an ("how can I bear," line 11) adverbial conjunctive

pien tsung yu ("even if," line 16) adverbial conjunctive plus verb

PSKC:

tui ("face," line 1) verb

chien ("gradually," line 3) adverb

wang ("gaze upon," line 11) verb

t'an ("sigh," line 13) verb

hsiang ("imagine," line 15) verb

What is immediately noteworthy here is that the multi-syllabic words, keng na k'an and pien tsung yu, serve as conjunctives through which an impression of hypotactic syntax is enhanced. Because of its sheer length, a man-tz'u poem, when compared with the shorter hsiao-ling, seems to need more function words to maintain the effect of continuous flow. By the same token, a strophe in man-tz'u generally contains more lines or line segments than does a hsiao-ling strophe, the reason being that the lines are often integrated and connected by these ling-tzu conjunctions. This is why Liu Yung's innovation in the device of ling-tzu marked a significant turning point in the history of tz'u. The syntactic flexibility resulting from the use of ling-tzu is another radical feature of the man-tz'u form which should not be overlooked. In PSKC, for instance, the syntactic position of the adverb chien ("gradually," line 3), which precedes both subject and verb, must seem quite inappropriate to those who are familiar with Chinese grammar, for as a rule a monosyllabic adverb cannot precede the subject of a sentence.[39] In man-tz'u poetry, however, a poet was not only permitted but also encouraged to place such ling-tzu adverbs in this otherwise ungrammatical position.

At this point readers may wonder how such a small linguistic

feature as ling-tzu can contribute to the overall artistic merit of YLL and PSKC. I believe that the crucial function of ling-tzu lies in its skillful blending of a few varied elements which are directly responsible for the greatness of the poems: (1) the colloquial and the literary language; (2) multiple layers of poetic act; and (3) the expressive and the imagistic counterparts. Upon closer scrutiny, one realizes that the multi-syllabic ling-tzu conjunctives just mentioned above are mostly colloquial expressions. On the one hand, these words serve as mere function words upon which the rhythms of the syntactic flow are based. On the other hand, these ling-tzu remind readers of a kind of colloquialism that corresponds to the rhythm found in common, conversational language. Yet most important, we find that mingled with these colloquial ling-tzu conjunctions is the employment of the literary language which brings to mind the poetic style of an intellectual elite. The way in which the colloquial expressions and literary diction are intermingled seems to have produced an entirely new poetics during the time of Liu Yung. The poet of course adapted this interplay of styles to his own temperament and purposes. He seemed to have attempted to give the notion of poetic style a new meaning. To him the so-called "literary" language appropriately presented but one aspect of human ideas; he needed a new form of language to deal with his poetic world. To tempt readers out of their conventional way of reading poetry, it was important to provide them with a new form of language based upon the manipulation of varied linguistic expressions. And it was through the device of

ling-tzu that this goal was properly realized.

It may have been noted that many of Liu Yung's monosyllabic *ling-tzu* are also verbs of thought (e.g., *nien* "think of," *hsiang* "imagine") which are combined to reveal the various mental attitudes the persona wishes to express. And the multi-syllabic *ling-tzu* conjunctions often occur in the interrogative sentences through which the poet's doubts and hesitations are clearly brought forth (e.g., lines 11-12 and lines 16-17 in YLL). It seems obvious that the poet wishes to combine in a single poem multiple kinds of feelings, and in order to do this in a coherent way he has used the device of *ling-tzu* as a structural principle upon which aspects of poetic act may be connected and integrated. Thus, by taking advantage of *ling-tzu* in conjunction with his overall explicit rhetoric, the poet has established a new poetic convention in *man-tz'u* which distinguishes it from *hsiao-ling*.

We may recall that in the tradition of *hsiao-ling* poetry Wei Chuang and Li Yü also preferred to employ verbs of thought in such a way that these verbs function almost like the *ling-tzu* words in *man-tz'u*:

Wei Chuang:

I remember (*chi te*) that year, beneath the blossoms
At midnight,
When I first met Lady Hsieh. . . .

(CTWT, I, 118)

記得那年花下
深夜
初識謝娘時....

Li Yü:

I can imagine (hsiang te) the flickering images of the jade
pavilion and palaces
Reflecting vainly on the water of the Ch'in Huai River
(CTWT, I, 227)

想得玉樓瑤殿影
空照秦淮

The two verbs chi te ("remember") and hsiang te ("imagine") would have been treated as ling-tzu in man-tz'u poetry, as both serve as "lead-in words" preceding a series of lines. But these cannot be called ling-tzu, for the simple reason that the ling-tzu device never became a prescribed structural principle in the context of hsiao-ling poetry. Whereas the verbs of thought are used merely to establish the impression of explicit rhetoric in Wei Chuang's and Li Yü's poetry, these same verbs are employed by Liu Yung specifically as ling-tzu tags to express the multiple dimensions of the poetic act in man-tz'u.

While Liu Yung invented *ling-tzu* primarily for the purpose of expressing various layers of poetic act, he also created another type of *ling-tzu* (i.e., *tui* "face," chien "gradually") to refer to perceptual impressions of natural images. As has been suggested, Liu Yung's greatest artistic achievement lies in his careful blending of expressive and imagistic language. Even in the single *tz'u* poem PSKC, one can see that the poet has employed two kinds of *ling-tzu*: the kind which expresses feelings in a straightforward manner, and the kind which describes perceptual experiences through imagistic presentation:

(1) *I* *sigh* *over* my straying steps these years, (1-4)
Why do I suffer these endless wanderings? (5)

歎年來蹤迹
何事苦淹留

(2) *Gradually* the frosty wind brings a chilly current of air, (1-4)
The mountain-pass and the rivers become desolate, (4)
And the setting sun falls on the tower. (4)

漸霜風淒緊
關河冷落
殘照當樓

Often the first type of _ling-tzu_ initiates a group of continuous, irregular lines, while the second type is followed by parallel lines, or at least lines of equal length. When these two types of _ling-tzu_ are used in the same poem, the intermingling of continuous and discontinuous syntax strikes a balance between expressive rhetoric and imagistic language. This is because the continuous flow of syntax can often convey the impression of unrestrained feelings. On the other hand, the symbolic significance of complementary, parallel scenes leads us to believe that the persona alone faces the whole of the universe in a single vision.

Liu Yung's device of _ling-tzu_ in _man-tz'u_ made it possible for him to develop a sequential structure in which elaboration of feelings and detailed delineation of images are combined to give an effect of endless expansiveness. We feel that the poet attempts to describe everything, and painstakingly express his various shades of emotion in an exhaustive manner not frequently encountered in Chinese poetry. While in the _hsiao-ling_ tradition a poet had to employ the form of song cycles in order to present different aspects of a poetic situation, the _man-tz'u_ poet could now include the whole of the complex situation in a single poem by using _ling-tzu_ words to establish a sequential principle in structural progression. Thus, according to traditional critics, one of Liu Yung's artistic merits was his skillful arrangement of structural parts and the transitions between them:

> In Liu Ch'i-ch'ing's [Liu Yung's] Yüeh-chang chi . . . the narration progresses naturally; there is a beginning and there is an end[40]. . . .

> Liu's tz'u poetry has always been noted for its straightforward narration. In the opening section, in the ending part, or in the stanzaic transition, there are one or two words which attract one's attention with an enormous power.[41]

In asserting the importance of ling-tzu, Liu Yung also set up a particular rule for the man-tz'u versification--i.e., his insistence on the use of the "falling tone" (ch'ü-sheng) for the monosyllabic ling-tzu (the so-called "i-tzu tou"). As we can see, most of his monosyllabic ling-tzu in YLL and PSKC (e.g., tui, nien, chien, wang, and t'an) carry the falling tone. As a poet-musician, Liu Yung insisted on a clear distinction of the so-called "four" tones in poetry, and this unusual musical sensitivity, unprecedented in tz'u history,[42] may have affected the poet's conscious choice of a phonemic tone which, in his opinion, could best bring out the significance of ling-tzu. Later tz'u poets faithfully followed Liu Yung in using this particular device. According to such traditional critics as Shen I-fu and Wan Shu, the "falling tone" generally tended to be expressive of emotion, so that it was an ideal means of bringing forward the ling-tzu words--the key elements--in a poem.[43]

In most cases the appearance of a <u>ling-tzu</u> signifies the beginning of a new strophe, and thus in that sense <u>ling-tzu</u> may be viewed as a crucial device through which different strophes are combined. From this we come to consider the overall structural principle of <u>man-tz'u</u> poetry. Since the sheer length of a <u>man-tz'u</u> immediately calls for careful planning in poetic composition, there has been a great concern on the part of traditional critics with structural arrangement in <u>man-tz'u</u> poetry. One of the structural principles in <u>man-tz'u</u>, as proposed by some critics, is the technique known as the "Ch'ang-shan snake" principle.[44] Just like the legendary Ch'ang-shan snake whose head and tail are always in coordination, so should the beginning and concluding parts of a <u>man-tz'u</u> be in perfect coordination. The term "Ch'ang-shan snake" was originally taken from an ancient tactical deployment of troops, and after it became current in <u>tz'u</u> criticism, some fiction critics began to recognize it as a guiding principle in narrative literature in general.

In <u>hsiao-ling</u> poetics, the stanzaic transition is a major structural concern, and this same issue becomes even more important in the <u>man-tz'u</u>:

> At a stanzaic transition in a <u>chung-tiao</u> [medium-length tune] and a <u>ch'ang-tiao</u> [longer tune] <u>tz'u</u> one does not want to make a complete break; nor does one want to link the sections explicitly.[45]

> Most important is that the second stanza should not break away from the theme of the poem; it should connect what precedes it and what proceeds from it.[46]

If the rule of stanzaic transition is already important in the *hsiao-ling* form, it is the *man-tz'u* which actually brings it into full play. The *man-tz'u* form is not only longer than the *hsiao-ling*, but often has more than two stanzas in a poem, which would naturally complicate the process of organization. As a pioneer poet in the *man-tz'u* tradition, Liu Yung contributed greatly to the establishment of this structural dimension; he employs various techniques in a very creative way. His art of explicit rhetoric often creates the wrong impression that the poet merely says what he wishes, without consideration for structural integrity. But if one explores the various techniques which the poet uses to organize his stanzas in *tz'u*, one can see what great attention he has paid to matters of organization and composition.

The beginning lines of the second stanza in a *tz'u* poem appear to be a key point from which the poet extends his line of thought or continues his sequential flow. One of Liu Yung's most favored techniques is the kind employed in YLL, where the first strophe of the second stanza serves as a conclusion to what has previously been said:

> From of old, tender natures grieve at separation;
> But how, then, can I bear this in the desolate autumn

season?

多情自古傷離別
更那堪、冷落清秋節

As such, time moves all in haste,

I think of our fleeting life--not lasting a hundred years.

(CST, I, 34)

似此光陰催逼
念浮生、不滿百

Often such lines are delivered in the form of interrogatives or hypothetical statements, perhaps for the purpose of emphasis:

This experience of loneliness, to whom shall I express it?

(CST, I, 15)

一場寂寞憑誰訴

After all is said and done,

To whom shall I air my grievances?

(CST, I, 16)

算到頭、誰與伸剖

If only I knew that things would turn out this way. . . .

(CST, I, 29)

早知恁麼 . . . .

In like manner, a new stanza often begins with verbs of thought which serve as *ling-tzu*:

> I *ponder* our toilsome life, what a pity that in our
> blossoming youth and prime years
> Separations are many and joy is rare.
>
> (CST, I, 35)

念勞生、 惜芳年壯歲
離多歡少

> *I secretly ponder* the past,
> How many happy secret meetings and joyous gatherings. . . .
>
> (CST, I, 17)

暗想當初
有多少、 幽歡佳會. . . .

To heighten the expressive function of such verbs of thought, the poet often adds to them various kinds of intensifiers (e.g., *chi* "very," *nan* "difficult"):

> Intensely (*chi*) sad!
> Again and again I recall
> The depths of our inner chamber. . . .
>
> (CST, I, 26)

愁極
再三追思
洞房深處. . . .

Hard (*nan*) to forget!--

The literary gatherings and banquets,

How many times did I let the beautiful scenery pass by?

One after another the years change.

(CST, I, 40)

難忘
文期酒會
幾孤風月
屢變星霜

Another technique which Liu Yung often uses is one which approximates Wei Chuang's sequential progression, whereby the boundary between the two stanzas is seemingly ignored. Such *tz'u* poems as *Ying hsin-ch'un* (CST, I, 17), *Wang hai-ch'ao* (CST, I, 39), *Ju yü shui* (CST, I, 40), *Ch'iu-yeh yüeh* (CST, I, 23), *Pa-liu tzu* (CST, I, 39) are all organized according to this particular structural principle. Very often this type of stanzaic transition is deliberately emphasized by hypotaxes (either temporal or explanatory) placed at the beginning of the second stanza. This particular device may be seen as an extension of Liu Yung's general tendency to create *ling-tzu* and hypotactic syntax:

Temporal hypotaxis:

At this moment my heart is burdened with ten

thousand threads of feelings

My sad countenance bursts with grief,

My broken heart--not a single word is said.

(CST, I, 26)

此際寸腸萬緒
慘愁顏
斷魂無語

At this moment I look back in vain,

I gaze upon the capital,

My tearful eyes are hard to control.

(CST, I, 28)

此際空勞回首
望帝里
難收淚眼

At that time,

Although of all the beautiful girls

I knew your name for a long time,

Yet how late it was when I first met you.

(CST, I, 40)

當時
綺羅叢裏
知名雖久
識面何遲

Explanatory hypotaxis:

So I think of the "colorful phoenix" in the
Ch'in tower,
And the "morning cloud" of the Ch'u house,[47]
In the past I was enchanted by their singing
voices and smiles.

(CST, I, 17)

因念秦樓彩鳳
楚觀朝雲
往昔曾迷歌笑

So at this point I ponder:
Her decorated chamber was too easily deserted,
Floating duckweeds are hard to stop drifting.

(CST, I, 37)

到此因念
繡閣輕拋
浪萍難駐

The most innovative technique developed by Liu Yung is perhaps that which may be called the progression of the camera-eye view. Many of his travel poems start with a description of autumn landscape seen from a constantly moving boat. The account often

seems more of a continuous visual experience than an instantaneous perception, as in _Yeh-pan yüeh_ (CST, I, 37):

Frozen clouds, gloomy weather,
On a fragile leaf of boat
I left the river islet at the spur of the moment.
I pass thousands of valleys and crags, 4
And sail across the deep waters of the Yüeh River.
Roaring waves are gradually subdued,
But forest winds suddenly rise,
And then I hear the traveling merchants hail one another. 8
With my sail hoisted,
I let drift the painted boat, swiftly passing the
Southern Shore.

(1st stanza)

凍雲黯淡天氣
扁舟一葉
乘興離江渚
渡萬壑千巖
越溪深處
怒濤漸息
樵風乍起
更聞商旅相呼
片帆高舉
泛畫鷁、翩翩過南浦

Then the poet begins the second stanza with the phrase *wang-chung* ("within my sight") to emphasize the significance of a panoramic view and the conscious act of seeing on the part of the persona:

> *Within my sight* the banner of a wineshop
>   glistening,
> A cluster of misty villages,   12
> A few rows of frosty trees.
> Under the fading sun
> Fishermen bang their boats and return home.[48]
> Dying lotus--desolate and scattered,   16
> Withered willows--reflecting back and forth.
> On the bank-side, in twos and threes,
> Young girls at ease, after washing their silk gauze,
> Shy away from travelers; bashfully they laugh and   20
>   chatter with one another.

(2nd stanza)

望中酒旆閃閃
一簇煙村
數行霜樹
殘日下
漁人鳴榔歸去
敗荷零落
衰楊掩映
岸邊兩兩三三
浣沙遊女
避行客、 含羞笑相語

One feels that with the introduction of the act of perception, the camera-eye slowly moves and begins to view a series of pictures as close-ups. It attempts to comprehend something beyond the range of the immediate vision. The sense of progression in the poem is thus carried out in both a "temporal" and a "spatial" manner.

Finally one realizes that beneath all these layers of description is a sensitive soul which turns all the perceptual experiences into a truly introspective expression in the third stanza:

> So at this point I ponder:
> Her decorated chamber was too easily deserted,
> But the floating duckweeds are hard to stop drifting. . . .

> 到此因念
> 繡閣輕拋
> 浪萍難駐 . . . .

The unifying power of the lyric self prevents the poem from being purely descriptive. Yet its artistic value would not seem as great if the descriptive parts were not as skillfully handled. The poet's ability to combine expressive and descriptive elements in this relatively long poem (containing as many as 144 characters) is indeed a marvel. What the poet uses here is a technique of "mirroring" which, in Ralph Freedman's terminology, refers to the lyric self's capacity to become "an aesthetic image of nature."[49]

Freedman's interpretation of this particular technique, though in the context of the European "lyrical novels," may be borrowed to explain the meaning of Liu Yung's poetic art, as the lyrical self here is confronted with a wide range of reality which may be stretched to embrace the world of fiction:

> He is the center and the receptacle. Mirroring the novel as a whole, he is caught in miniature in an equally slow-moving picture.
>
> Since the self is the point at which inner and outer worlds are joined, the hero's mental picture reflects the universe of sensible encounters as an image. The "world" is part of the hero's inner world; the hero, in turn, mirrors the external world and all its multitudinous manifestations.[50]

The idea of the self as "lyrical par excellence" which absorbs all images of the external world may be best demonstrated by a very long poem by Liu Yung: _Ch'i shih_ (212 characters). Its unusual length immediately demands a well-organized network of feelings and images:

> Late Autumn day,
> A momentary light shower splashes on the garden balcony.
> At the threshold, chrysanthemums are desolate and sparse,
> By the well, the _wu-t'ung_ trees are in confusion, 4
> provoking the fading haze.

Sorrowful (ch'i-jan),

I gaze into the River Pass.[51]

Flying clouds are gloomy in the evening sun.

In those days when Sung Yü felt sad, 8

He came here to view the waters and to climb the hills.

The distant roads--faraway

The traveler grieved,

Tired of listening to the gurgling of the Lung River. 12

At this moment the cicadas cry amid the decaying leaves,

Crickets chirp in the withered grasses.

They call to one another noisily.

In this desolate house, the days pass as if they were years. 16

The elements slowly change,

And quietly it becomes late at night.

The wide sky is pure,

The Milky Way clear and transparent, 20

The bright moon fair.

My thoughts are endless (ssu mien-mien).

Night after night I face this scene,

How can I bear (na-k'an) to count the years on my fingers 24

And silently contemplate that past?

With no fame, no official post,

In luxurious quarters and in red towers,
Too often, I passed the years loitering. 28

In the capital the scenery was fine.
In those days, when I was young,
At night, I feasted; in the morning I made merry;
Not to mention the experiences with my wild friends and strange companions-- 32
When we watched a musical performance, we drank to each other, all trying to linger a little longer.
Since we parted time has passed as swiftly as a flying shuttle--
The good times of old are now like a dream.
Blocked by mists and water, my journey is far--without end. 36
I contemplate (nien) wealth and fame, long fettered by my worn looks.
I look back on (chui) past events;--in vain, my sad face bursts with grief.
As hours pass, I sense a slight chill.
Gradually I sob, I hear a few notes of a bugle fading away. 40
Facing the idle window lattice,
Putting off lights and awaiting the daybreak,
I embrace my own shadow, without sleep.

(CST, I, 35)

晚秋天
一霎微雨灑庭軒
檻菊蕭疏
井梧零亂惹殘煙
淒然
望江關
飛雲黯淡夕陽間
當時宋玉悲感
向此臨水與登山
遠道迢遞
行人淒楚
倦聽隴水潺湲
正蟬吟敗葉
蛩響衰草
相應喧喧

孤館度日如年
風露漸變
悄悄至更闌
長天淨
絳河清淺
皓月嬋娟
思緜緜
夜永對景
那堪屈指
暗想從前

未名未祿
綺陌紅樓
往往經歲遷延

帝里風光好
當年少日
暮宴朝歡
況有狂朋怪侶
遇當歌、對酒競留連
別來迅景如梭
舊遊似夢
煙水程何限
念利名、憔悴長縈絆
追往事、空慘愁顏
漏箭移、稍覺輕寒
漸嗚咽、畫角數聲殘
對閒窗畔
停燈向曉
抱影無眠

Unlike Yeh-pan yüeh where the descriptive (stanzas 1, 2) and the expressive elements (stanza 3) can be rather neatly distinguished, this poem achieves a better effect in fusing the various kinds of poetic elements. It is almost impossible for us to find a single stanza where the lyrical voice is not present. And yet at the same time the

descriptive and narrative components in the poem have poetic value in their own right. No doubt Liu Yung was one of the very few Chinese poets who had the competence to manage long lyrical poems. In view of this fact, we can also understand why he should be recognized as the first great poet in the man-tz'u form.

Generally the uniqueness of a man-tz'u poem lies in its multi-dimensional structure. In reading Ch'i shih, one gets the impression that poetic expressions and images emerge in layer upon layer without end, like peaks rising one upon another. Some traditional critics have specified methods by which Liu Yung manages to maintain the integrity of his lyrical structure despite the great length of his man-tz'u. Cheng Wen-cho, for instance, gives the following explanation by means of a simile:

> I have probed deeply into where the meaning of his [Liu Yung's] tz'u poems lies. Indeed there are layers and layers of meaning. It is like painting pupils on the eyes of a dragon: the dragon's spirited appearance is so lively that with one or two more strokes it will rush out of the wall and fly away.[52]

What does Cheng mean by the "one or two more strokes" with which the poet brings life to a poem? I believe that the "one or two more strokes" refers to the various lyrical expressions added to the non-lyrical elements in Liu Yung's poems. As in Ch'i shih, almost all the descriptive and narrative components are interrupted by some sort of expressive statements, without which the whole poem would lose its

lyrical impact. Such expressions as ch'i-jan ("sorrowfully," line 5), ssu mien-mien ("my thoughts are endless," line 22), na-k'an ("how can I bear," line 24), as well as the many monosyllabic ling-tzu (e.g., nien "think of," line 37; chui "recall," line 38), all help to build up the intensity of a lyrical voice, which is at times hidden to the ordinary view.

The process of establishing this quality of the "lyrical par excellence" in the poem is also based on its lack of time-bound narrative continuity. Obviously the so-called "narrative continuity" is displaced by the lyrical exploration of a few broken episodes. True, a linear time sequence is provided by the poem: it moves from sunset (stanza 1) to twilight (stanza 2) to the dead of night. But the truly narrative elements in the poem are those about the past rather than the present. When the persona sets out to tell the story of the historical figure Sung Yü in stanza 1, he does not mean to let historical facts interfere with his lyrical consciousness. Rather, through the act of narration, the persona reinforces the awareness of an inner self, for he is in fact identifying himself with the lonely poet in the past. Then silently facing the twilight, he begins to regret his uninhibited experiences in younger days (stanza 2), and so gradually he brings together, in his own recollection, a few fragments of the bygone scenes. It seems that all the narrative passages serve only to register the impact of external realities upon the inner consciousness.

Quite evidently it is this skillful fusion of the extended narrative-descriptive passages and the concentrated lyrical expressions that is responsible for the greatness of Liu Yung's poetic art. The

Five Dynasties poets Wei Chuang and Li Yü reveal a similar tendency to maintain lyrical integrity in a poem containing narrative elements. Yet the grandeur of the narrative section is often limited by the very nature of the hsiao-ling form itself. Because of its brevity in length, a hsiao-ling poem normally has to compress ideas and images into a few lines. While this may often heighten the lingering effect of a lyrical voice, it also constrains the scope of the non-lyrical elements. For example, in his frequent attempts to recall his past glory, Li Yü often employs the general term "past events" to refer to the total aggregate of his previous experiences:

> How many past events can anyone know?
>
> 往事知多少 (CTWT, I, 221)
>
> Past events may only be mourned.
>
> 往事只堪哀 (CTWT, I, 227)

What exactly were these "past events"? The poet does not and cannot describe them fully in the hsiao-ling, obviously due to the lack of space allowed in that poetic form. On the other hand, when Liu Yung has a chance to talk about his past experiences as in Ch'i shih he can always project a very elaborate picture of the past events in question:

> In the capital the scenery was fine.
>
> In those days, when I was young,

At night, I feasted; in the morning I made merry;
Not to mention the experiences with my wild
friends and strange companions--
When we watched a musical performance, we drank to each
other, all trying to linger a little longer.
(lines 29-33)

帝里風光好
當年少日
暮宴朝歡
況有狂朋怪侶
遇當歌、對酒競留連

The length of a man-tz'u no doubt leads to the possibility of a perfect balance of the varied poetic elements. Of course Li Yü's art of lyrical exploration was unsurpassed in its own right, but in terms of the complexity of lyrical incorporation of narrative and descriptive elements it was Liu Yung who finally brought it into full play in tz'u poetry. Nevertheless, one should view Li Yü as an antecedent to Liu Yung. In many ways one can see a continuous thread of development linking these two poets;--Li Yü's interest in the narrative tz'u and popular songs might have given some inspiration to the later poet.

4. A Revaluation of Liu Yung's Achievement

There is no denying that two of Liu Yung's most significant innovations, the use of *ling-tzu* conjunctions and the lyrical exploration of the details of external events seem to be closer in origin to the popular than to the elite tradition. Yet his *tz'u* poetry represents such a mixture of the refined and the colloquial that it almost violates both of these styles. This is why for most critics it is quite difficult to place Liu Yung's work in a particular stylistic category. What Liu Yung represents is indeed an intermediate style--virtually unknown in the history of the literary *tz'u*. Through this intermediate style, which combines the refined and the popular, Liu Yung changed the direction of the *tz'u* development.

I have tried to analyze the most distinguishing characteristics of Liu Yung's *tz'u* above. Yet without a comparison between Liu Yung and other *tz'u* poets the meaning of his contribution cannot be fully elucidated.

I have mentioned that a few *man-tz'u* poems were produced before Liu Yung's time, and that in terms of overall structure they are more akin to the *hsiao-ling* form than to the *man-tz'u* form. The device of *ling-tzu* and the sequential structure are practically undeveloped in these poems. There is yet another important area that should not be overlooked--that is, the problems of image-making and syntactic construction. I have found that in the *man-tz'u* poems by the Late T'ang and Five Dynasties poets the 3-character lines tend to be independent lines that represent isolated images, while the

3-character units in Liu Yung often cannot stand by themselves, because they function merely as introductory segments to longer lines:

Li Ts'un-hsü (Five Dynasties):

I enjoy the fragrant spring; (3)
Warm breezes blow the curtains.
Orioles sing in the verdant trees;
Light mists veil the pavilion at night. 4
Apricots and peaches grow pink; (3)
Numerous calyxes bloom. (3)
By the Ling-ho Palace, (3)
One thousand rows of imperial willows, 8
Their golden silky branches slanting. . . .

(CTWT, I, 95)

賞芳春
暖風飄箔
鶯啼綠樹
輕烟籠晚閣
杏桃紅
開繁萼
靈和殿
禁柳千行
斜金絲絡. . . .

Liu Yung:

When we first met and then parted

I thought I would never see you again. (3-6)

Recently we encountered by chance and once again (3-7)

dined together.

Over our wine goblets, lingering, (3-3) 4

You frowned and sighed deeply

Evoking endless sorrow over the past. . . .

(CST, I, 23)

當初聚散
便喚作、無由再逢伊面
近日來、不期而會重歡宴
向尊前、閒暇裏
斂着眉兒長歎
惹起舊愁無限. . . .

This would not have been an important issue were it not for the fact that it leads us to a significant observation about Liu Yung's poetry: where his three-character line-segments are gradually incorporated into long, continuous sentences, his 4-character lines begin to serve as isolated, independent lines representing a juxtaposition of images. Most important, such 4-character lines

often, though not always, employ strict parallelism:

(1) The river maples gradually grow old
The islet orchids half wither.

江楓漸老 (CST, I, 26)
汀蕙半凋

(2) The Milky Way is clear and faint,
The bright moon is fair and beauteous.

絳河清淺 (CST, I, 35)
皓月嬋娟

(3) To the Ch'u valley the clouds return,
At the Kao-yang balcony people have departed.

楚峽雲歸 (CST, I, 51)
高陽人散

(4) Roaring waves are gradually subdued,
Forest winds suddenly rise.

怒濤漸息 (CST, I, 37)
樵風乍起

Thus, by making the 3-character lines part of continuous, hypotactic sentences, the poet has reserved the 4-character lines to produce a balancing effect in forming juxtaposed, paratactic phrases. Of course, the practice of producing 4-character parallel lines was by no means Liu Yung's invention. Poets such as Yen Shu and Ou-yang Hsiu all employed this method in writing their hsiao-ling

poems. But Liu Yung's innovation lies in his ability to incorporate such lines successfully into the context of hypotactic syntax. Moreover, he appears to be the one who invented the structure of parallel lines preceded by *ling-tzu*. To be able to maintain a balance between continuous lines and discontinuous lines, between non-parallel structure and parallel structure, is certainly one of Liu Yung's highest achievements in many of his *man-tz'u* poems.

Another important area concerns the problem of metrical patterns in *tz'u*. What baffled the traditional critics most was that in Liu Yung almost no two *man-tz'u* poems to the same tune have identical metrical patterns. For instance, the three poems to the tune *Tung-hsien ko* range from 119-126 characters; the two poems to *Lun-t'ai tzu* have a discrepancy of 27 characters; the two poems to *Feng kuei yün* have 102 and 119 characters respectively; and all seven *tz'u* poems to *Ch'ing-pei lo* are quite different in length. Many *tz'u* critics who wrote prosodic manuals in the Ch'ing dynasty simply assumed that each of these poems represented a "variant form" of the tune. Commenting on one of Liu Yung's poems to the tune *Yü-chieh hsing*, the *Tz'u-p'u* says: "The lines and phrases are mixed up . . . It is considered a variant form."[53]

The problem is that the critics were wrong in their presupposition. What they were not aware of was that, as with his many other innovative devices, Liu Yung's handling of metrical patterns had its origin in the popular song tradition. If one examines the Tun-huang songs, one finds that in many cases two songs to the same tune are different in rhythm and length. The reason is that since the beginning

of the popular song tradition (including the Hsiang-ho ko-tz'u in yüeh-fu), it was a general practice to add ch'en-tzu or even ch'en-chü (literally, "additional words or sentences") to individual songs. Unlike the so-called ling-tzu segments whose length and position in a particular tz'u pattern were prescribed in the prosodic manuals, the ch'en-tzu words could be added to any poem without restriction. And as a result, two songs to the same tune often turn out to be quite different in length. Obviously the differences in the metrical patterns of those songs to the same tune did not refer to different "forms" of the tune, for there was only one identical musical tune. It was the device of ch'en-tzu which created such variations. This practice was never discontinued in the popular song tradition, and later in the dramatic ch'ü (especially the "series form," the so-called t'ao-shu) it was exaggerated to the point that the "added words" are often longer in length than the main text.

In their conscious attempt to create a poetic genre distinguished from the popular tz'u songs, Wen T'ing-yün and his other contemporary tz'u poets avoided using the device of ch'en-tzu. As a result, their hsiao-ling poems, if they belong to the same song-series, are bound to have identical metrical patterns and length. This represents the literati poets' effort to emphasize the concept of uniformity in poetry. This practice was so unanimously observed that even Liu Yung, whenever he wrote in the hsiao-ling form, faithfully followed this unwritten rule set up by his predecessors.

On the other hand, Liu Yung was quite revolutionary in dealing with the man-tz'u form. It may be that as a fine musician the poet

could afford to be more flexible in composing his individual tz'u poems, as he paid more attention to the musical notes than to the actual length of the poems. The use of ch'en-tzu in the popular songs must have appeared to him a perfect device to borrow in order to establish a "new" concept in poetic rhythm. The poet might have attempted to free himself from the traditional value of uniformity in form by viewing each of the tz'u poems he wrote (regardless of their identity in tune patterns) as a unique piece of creation. However, later tz'u poets, conditioned by the traditional belief in metrical uniformity, developed the practice of "filling in words" (t'ien-tz'u) and the concept of the "standard form" (cheng-t'i) versus the "variant form" (pien-t'i). They gradually paid more attention to the number of characters and the metrical patterns said to be prescribed by orthodox poets than to the original musical notes. And this later tendency was largely responsible for the ultimate separation of music and tz'u poetry.

The fact that Liu Yung was a fine musician only partially explains his readiness to employ unconventional techniques. His predecessor Wen T'ing-yün and the later poets Chou Pang-yen, Chiang K'uei and Wu Wen-ying were all accomplished musicians. But they did not exhibit Liu Yung's metrical flexibility; rather they set out to establish in tz'u the unshattered tradition of "filling in words." Indeed it was a different concept of form that prompted Chou Pang-yen and his followers to deviate from Liu Yung's practice.

Nevertheless, as a pioneer-poet in the man-tz'u form, Liu Yung must have had a great impact in terms of a broader sense of rhythmic

flexibility on many later poets despite their differing views. I have suggested that one of the characteristics of a _man-tz'u_ poem is its increasing emphasis on stanzas with different patterns. Might this be seen as a direct influence of Liu Yung's notion of flexibility in metrical patterns? We do not have sufficient support to prove this point. But since it was Liu Yung who seemed to insist first on this particular structure in _man-tz'u_, there are grounds for us to believe that the two issues are actually two sides of the same coin. Of course, it should be noted that while later poets gradually accepted and valued the notion of diversified stanzaic patterns in _man-tz'u_, the practice was never carried out as far as Liu Yung might have wished. This fact is clearly reflected in many of the comments made in traditional prosodic manuals:

> The tune [_I-ts'un chin_] originated with this _tz'u_ [by Liu Yung]. But in the latter part of the poem, the sentences and phrases are mixed up. . . . For this tune, we take [Chou Pang-yen's] poem as the standardized form.[54]

> In [Liu's _tz'u_ to _Ch'iu-yeh yüeh_] there are many irregularities and inaccuracies. Check the following poem [by Yin O], and it will be clear that there are errors and omissions in [Liu's poem]. Yin's _tz'u_ poem is more regular in form and is easier to imitate than the previous poem.[55]

> Liu's *tz'u* has contained many errors. This *tz'u* poem [by Liu] differs greatly in sentence structure from poems by others [set to the same tune *Fa-ch'ü hsien-hsien-yin*]. There are mistakes in it; one should not imitate it. . . .[56]

In spite of these criticisms, the fact remains that Liu Yung's great contribution to the formation of the *man-tz'u* structure was unsurpassed. The shaping of a new poetic form takes a revolutionary spirit like Liu Yung to bring it into full play. There was, of course, another *tz'u* poet--Chang Hsien--who, as an exact contemporary of Liu Yung, helped to somewhat promote the *man-tz'u* form. In many ways Chang Hsien was a poet who remained basically in the orthodox tradition and yet was open-minded enough to experiment with new forms. Aside from the several *man-tz'u* tunes he composed, he wrote to five *tz'u* tunes which were also used by Liu Yung (i.e., *Kuei-ch'ao huan*, *Pu-suan-tzu man*, *P'o-chen yüeh*, *Man-chiang hung*, *T'ien-hsien tzu*).

It is worth noting that where Liu Yung was at his best in *man-tz'u*, Chang Hsien excelled in the *hsiao-ling* form. Chang Hsien's *man-tz'u* poems often lack the dimension of sequential progression, the uninterrupted flow of syntax, and the fully-expressed poetic voice so characteristic of Liu Yung's *man-tz'u*. Most of Chang Hsien's lesser poems in *man-tz'u* are basically descriptive of the flourishing cities and emotional relations with women. At his best the poems achieve a similar effect of imagistic elegance typical of his *hsiao-ling*. The following two poems by these two authors were set to the

same tune, <u>Kuei-ch'ao</u> <u>huan</u>:

Chang Hsien:

The sound of the revolving pulley is heard from the
    uncovered well,
At dawn people carry silver bowls, pull white ropes,
In the Western Garden they chat; at night the wind blows.
Dense flowers blow down--the red ones form a path. 4
In the censer, ashes not yet cold,
On the Lotus Pedestal the residue of fragrant candles
    congeals.
Even with gold equal to one's size
Who could be so lucky 8
As to buy such a beautiful scene?

Powder falls from her light make-up,--the red jade
    shines.
The moon-shaped pillow, the loose hairpins--her hair
    falls down to her collar.
Having feelings, there are no animals that don't form 12
    pairs;
Mandarin ducks should always be together.
The day is long, but can its merriment be steady?
How can it compare to a day which transforms into an
    endless spring night?
In the dim light before sunrise, 16

Softly and gently, she lazily gets up,

By the curtain ballast--shadows of fallen flowers.

(CST, I, 64)

聲轉轆轤聞露井
曉引銀瓶牽素綆
西園人語夜來風
叢英飄墜紅成徑
寶猊煙未冷
蓮台香臘殘痕凝
等身金
誰能得意
買此好光景

粉落輕妝紅玉瑩
月枕橫釵雲墜領
有情無物不雙棲
文禽只合常交頸
晝長歡豈定
爭如翻作春宵永
日曈曨
嬌柔懶起
簾押殘花影

Liu Yung:

At the ferry bank, two or three small boats.
Reeds move with a whistling sound, as the wind
    blows gently.
On the sand islet nesting geese dash out from the
    haze and fly,
By the bridge over the stream, the fading moon   4
    blends with frost--white.
Gradually the light at daybreak comes to view,
The road is distant, the mountain far,--all full of
    travelers.
Those who are coming and going,
In lone carts and in two-oar boats   8
Are all seekers of profit and fame.

I gaze toward my hometown, but it is separated from me
    by mists and waters.
Suddenly I feel as if home-sickness gives me wings.
Depressing clouds and sorrowful rain, our two hearts   12
    are bound together,
The beginning of this year, the end of last year,
    one comes right after the other.
This season slips away in a twinkling of eyes,
What use, after all, is my wandering around like the
    drifting weeds and plants bending in the wind?
Go home!   16

In the depth of the jade tower

There is a person who thinks of me.

(CST, I, 22)

別岸扁舟三兩隻
葭葦蕭蕭風淅淅
沙汀宿雁破煙飛
溪橋殘月和霜白
漸漸分曙色
路遙山遠多行役
往來人
隻輪雙槳
盡是利名客

一望鄉關煙水隔
轉覺歸心生羽翼
愁雲恨雨兩牽縈
新春殘臘相催逼
歲華都瞬息
浪萍風梗誠何益
歸去來
玉樓深處
有箇人相憶

The contrast between these tz'u poems is clear. The first poem is composed of static pictures occasionally interrupted by comments (i.e., lines 8-10, lines 12-15). In the second poem, the descriptive, narrative and lyrical elements, in all their multifariousness, are meant to be comprehended as a multi-layered experience which progresses in time. The ending statements of the two poems also reveal sharply their differences in nature: Chang's poem is basically image-oriented and Liu's poem expression-oriented.

Following the traditional hsiao-ling poetics associated with Wen T'ing-yün, Chang Hsien values above all the lingering quality of imagistic language. His nickname "Three-shadows Chang" (Chang San-ying) refers specifically to his three refined images of the "shadow," one of which is found in the ending strophe of his Kuei-ch'ao huan above. Later critics have sufficiently observed the similarity between his man-tz'u and hsiao-ling styles in terms of both structure and diction:

> In his ch'ang-tiao poems [Chang Hsien] used only the hsiao-ling method of composition; they demonstrate a unique style.[57]

> [Chang Hsien] could only write hsiao-ling poems. His ch'ang-tiao poems are too elegant and refined; they are not really of good quality.[58]

This supports the point that the poetics of man-tz'u over the centuries has been conditioned to a large measure by Liu Yung's

sequential structure and subjective rhetoric, qualities which would have been considered exceptional according to the *hsiao-ling* aesthetics. Reading through the present chapter, the reader may perhaps think for a moment that since the device of *ling-tzu* and continuous syntax was to become a general characteristic of the *man-tz'u* form, it is no longer possible for us to see the two styles, the explicit and the implicit, in opposition. But this would be a mistake. Generally as *ling-tzu* became a conventional method of expressing mental attitudes, and as hypotactic structure became a generic feature, the differences in the poetic styles tended to lie elsewhere. Within the limits of the present chapter, an exploration of this problem is not necessary. We shall go into the later changes in poetic conceptions when the occasion arises.

V. Su Shih and the Elevation of the *Tz'u* Genre

1. From Liu Yung to Su Shih: An Enlarged Perspective

Liu Yung's innovation in the formal aspects of the *man-tz'u* form has a parallel in Su Shih's unusual achievement in the extension of poetic scope in *tz'u*. Where Liu Yung derived his poetic inspiration mainly from the popular song tradition, Su Shih drew his imaginative insight from other poetic genres. As a versatile master of almost all literary forms, Su Shih brought to *tz'u* poetry a totally new perspective. As the traditional critic Liu Hsi-tsai put it, "there is no idea which cannot be expressed, and there is no subject which cannot be treated" in the *tz'u* poetry of Su Shih.[1] Su's poetic diction ranges from mundane colloquialism to classical expressions. The *tz'u* form, in the hands of the poet, has now become a medium for writing farewell poems as well as elegies. It may be used to express political ambition, patriotism, and philosophical ideas, or even to describe the life of farmers.

Of course, all these subjects were considered common in both Ancient Style and Recent Style poetry. But what is significant here is not that the poet wrote about such subjects, but that he did it through the *tz'u* form, a form which was previously thought to depict mainly the sensual or emotional aspects of life. Perhaps Li Yü's achievements in the *hsiao-ling* were somewhat comparable to Su Shih's,

but in terms of the breadth of scope for lyrical expression Su Shih was far greater. For example, in mourning the deaths of his wife and son, Li Yü wrote exclusively in the Ancient Style and Recent Style forms, but never in the _tz'u_ form. Obviously in his discrimination of poetic genres Li Yü considered this particular subject unfit for the new poetic form--_tz'u_. On the other hand, Su Shih's ability to express was so great that he broke through this generic limit. This seems to imply that the _tz'u_ genre, in all its potentiality, could by then rank equally with the securely established _shih_ poetry.

Where Li Yü was still confined by the limitations of the _hsiao-ling_ form, Su Shih could choose to use either the shorter _hsiao-ling_ or the longer _man-tz'u_ depending on the kind of poetic world he wished to represent through the creative process. Unlike Liu Yung who mainly expressed love for women, Su Shih's concept of love was enlarged to include his affection for male friends. He consciously wished to avoid being associated with the particular _tz'u_ style popularized by Liu Yung. To him Liu Yung represented a very narrow vision in poetry. Even for the performance purposes of his _tz'u_ poetry the poet deliberately devised a method quite opposite to Liu Yung's--where Liu Yung would ask gentle courtesans to sing his songs, Su Shih had strong men sing his _tz'u_. This transfer from the effeminate to the manly in the performance aspect is indeed striking. In a letter to a friend, he wrote:

> . . . Recently, however, I wrote some short _tz'u_.

> Though not carrying Liu Ch'i's [Liu Yung's] style, they do represent a school of their own. Ha-ha! Some days ago . . . having composed a song, I asked some big, strong men from Tungchou to clap their hands and stamp their feet while singing it . . . it was quite a grand spectacle.[2]

This is why traditional critics often claimed that Su Shih was the founder of the school of "heroic abandon" (hao-fang) in tz'u poetry. The term hao-fang generally refers to Su Shih's stylistic tendency to be vigorous and unrestrained, but it may also be taken as a criticism of his lack of attention paid to the musical aspect of tz'u writing. The poet Li Ch'ing-chao (1081-1140?) criticized Su Shih particularly for ignoring the musical function of tz'u poetry, since in her view the two artistic forms, tz'u and music, should be inseparable.[3] Of course, Su Shih was by no means ignorant of the musical arts. According to letters he wrote to his friends, he worked very hard on music during his Hangchow years.[4] As he became increasingly involved in the career of tz'u writing, his knowledge of music also increased. Nevertheless, it is true that he was not a musician like Liu Yung or Chou Pang-yen (1056-1120). And because of his limitations in this area, he often had to follow the ready-made tz'u tunes instead of composing new ones.[5] Ironically Su Shih's limitations exercised an important impact on later tz'u practice. The notion that a tz'u poem was primarily a literary creation and only secondarily a musical composition indeed helped the

promotion of the literary value of tz'u. Gradually the practice of "filling in words" became the general procedure in tz'u writing.

One often finds in Su's tz'u poetry the awakening of a new spirit and a profound concern with larger issues in life, a poetic style radically different from that of Liu Yung. To the tune Pa-sheng kan-chou, for example, Su Shih writes as though he has penetrated into the secrets of life itself (in obvious contrast to Liu's exclusive concern with emotional experience in his own Pa-sheng kan-chou):

> The wind comes rolling up the tide from ten thousand
> miles away, perhaps with feeling,
> It sends back the tide, perhaps unfeelingly.
> I ask: On the Ch'ien-t'ang River,
> In the bay at Hsi-hsing, 4
> How many times have we seen the slanting beams of
> the setting sun?
> Don't contemplate present and past--
> In one instant the ancients are all gone.
> Who is like the old Tung-p'o[6] 8
> With a hoary head, yet remaining carefree? . . .
>
> (CST, I, 297)

有情風、萬里卷潮來
無情送潮歸
問錢塘江上
西興浦口
幾度斜暉
不用思量今古
俯仰昔人非
誰似東坡老
白首忘機. . . .

The image of an old man standing aloof from the troubled world (lines 9-10) is a familiar one in both his *shih* and *tz'u* poetry. Connected with this transcendental aloofness is a genuine love for the simplicity of Nature itself (e.g., lines 1-2). In Chinese poetry, this is considered the highest poetic world, as it represents the ideal state of human existence in Chinese philosophy. The two literary giants in the *shih* tradition, T'ao Ch'ien (372-427) and Wang Wei (701-761), both attempted to capture this very conception of life in poetry. As Su Shih began to express this traditionally esteemed lyrical vision through the *tz'u* form, a great change necessarily took place.

It was no accident that Su Shih should take T'ao Ch'ien as his ideal model in poetry, as they shared a very similar philosophical

outlook on life. Su composed about 120 shih poems following the rhyme schemes of verses written by T'ao Ch'ien. In his tz'u poetry, he often expresses his admiration for T'ao Ch'ien,[7] and even considers himself to be a reincarnation of the poet:

Chiang-ch'eng tzu

Alert in my dream, wide-awake in drunkenness
It is only because Yüan-ming [Tao Ch'ien]
Was my previous incarnation.
Having traveled all places, 4
I still plow the fields myself.
Last night at the Eastern slope the spring rain
was abundant;
Black magpies were joyous,
Announcing the new clear day. 8

By the west side of Snow Hall, an underground
spring murmurs.
The North Mountain stands vertical,
The small stream flows by horizontally.
Southward I gaze upon the hill with a pavilion, 12
In solitude and elegance, the Tseng-ch'eng Hill
rises up high.[8]
These are the same scene of the ancient-day Hsieh Brook.[9]
Ah, I am getting old,
I'll consign my remaining years to this place. 16

(CST, I, 298)

夢中了了醉中醒
只淵明
是前生
走徧人間
依舊卻躬耕
昨夜東坡春雨足
烏鵲喜
報新晴

雪堂西畔暗泉鳴
北山傾
小溪橫
南望亭丘
孤秀聳曾城
都是斜川當日境
吾老矣
寄餘齡

Su's imaginative power is also influenced by the philosophy of Chuang-tzu. His familiar image of drifting to the limits of the universe in a light boat recalls the philosopher's ideal of "easy-wandering" (*hsiao-yao yu*) in life.[10] His visionary perception of dreaming and reality also echoes Chuang-tzu's famous butterfly dream:

In my dream there was a butterfly flitting joyously,
Whose whole body was light.

(CST, I, 293)

夢裏栩然蝴蝶
一身輕

The *tz'u* form has become for the poet a perfect tool for visualizing aesthetic experiences in life. The poet allows his imagination free play in poetry, and through this creative process he combines life and art in one. This self-realization through poetry indeed marks the most unique function of lyric poetry.

Su Shih's general manner of presentation is in keeping with his emphasis on personal feelings on the one hand and universally shared knowledge on the other. Within this framework, there is a constant endeavor to establish certain interpretations of life in general. The poet expresses the most varied phenomena and subjects with a philosophical perspective:

Don't say that all things will become empty
after we turn our heads;
Even before we turn our heads, all things are a dream.

(CST, I, 285)

休言萬事轉頭空
未轉頭時皆夢

The worldly events are like a long dream,
How many times has the autumn turned cold
in our life-span?

(CST, I, 284)

世事一場大夢
人生幾度秋涼

Life is like an inn,
And I am a traveler.

(CST, I, 286)

人生如逆旅
我亦是行人

This sense of self-realization associated with the writing of *tz'u* is again enhanced by the author's frequent addition of prefaces to his poems. It should be recalled that for each completed *tz'u* poem the earlier *tz'u* poets had merely included the name of the *tz'u* tune, which did not usually correspond with the poem's subject matter. That a *tz'u* poem, in these cases, was thought to be primarily a musical composition is quite clear. During the early years of the Northern Sung, poets such as Chang Hsien began to add short titles to their *tz'u* poems. But Su Shih was the first *tz'u* poet to include long prefaces revealing his serious intent behind the act of composition. In view of the overall development of the *tz'u* genre, this marks the beginning of a new poetic era.

As Shuen-fu Lin has pointed out, the preface to a poem is an

introduction to the poetic act.[11] If the moment of lyrical experience must be frozen in time (symbolized by the frame of the poetic form itself), then the preface must point to the external reality which moves with a flow of time. In practice, the preface aims at providing a biographical dimension which the poem itself lacks--for the poem is an autonomous, self-contained structure reflecting the visionary movement of a lyrical consciousness. By combining the preface and the poem, the poet can achieve a harmonious unification of the real and the imaginative, the prosaic and the poetic. The preface to the Chiang-ch'eng tzu cited above clearly establishes this point:

> T'ao Yüan-ming traveled to Hsieh Brook on the fifth day of the first month. He sat with his friends by the river, and gazed upon the Southern Hill. Charmed by the special elegance of the Tseng-ch'eng Hill, he wrote the Poem on Hsieh Brook. Even today we are inspired to imagine his experience. This is the spring of 1082; I farm the Eastern slope, and have built a Snow Hall in which I live. To the south of it are the hills behind the Four-view Pavilion; to the west of it are small streams in North Mountain. Moved, I sigh: "This is also 'An Outing on Hsieh Brook.'"
>
> (CST, I, 298)

陶淵明以正月五日遊斜川，臨流班坐，顧瞻南阜，愛曾城之獨秀，乃作斜川詩，至今使人想見其處。元豐壬戌之春，余躬耕於東坡，築雪堂居之。南挹四望亭之後丘，西控北山之微泉，慨然而歎，此亦斜川之遊也。

Evidently this preface serves as a realistic counterpart to the poem's lyric act of self-realization. And the poem in turn represents a lyrical version of the external reality.

What is most significant here is that by writing such prefaces the poet has at the same time attached a sense of tradition to the *tz'u* poetry. The fact is that traditional *shih* poets had often used prefaces to bring forth a biographical dimension for their poems, a convention well established from the time of T'ao Ch'ien. Thus by introducing an old device to a new form, Su Shih has recreated what had already been in existence.

This recalls another poetic device of his which also exercised a great impact on later *tz'u* poets--that is, the use of historical allusions. In many ways the use of historical allusions reflects the poet's general tendency to transcend both time and space.

Allusion in poetry functions like metaphor, as both devices are grounded on the same principle of equivalence, except that the former concerns human events and the latter imagistic qualities.[12] Allusion is a "historical archetype" which signifies the sense of timelessness amidst the changes of human action in the course of history.[13] It is a device for viewing time in a time-free perspective. By using allusions the poet is able to place historical instances and his present situation side by side, as though they belong to a certain set category which is in its signification a-historical. Such a way of viewing history has a long tradition in *shih* poetry. It performs a special function in emphasizing the quality of lyric poetry, as it reveals most effectively the power of the lyric self to see history and reality as timeless visionary images.

The general concern with history marks a unique feature of Su Shih's *tz'u*, which no *tz'u* poet before him had sufficiently developed. Sometimes the poet includes quotations in his *tz'u* poems, a device borrowed from his Ancient Style poems, to direct attention to historical incidents:

> West of the ancient rampart, they said, was
> "The Red Cliff of Master Chou of the Three Kingdoms."[14]
>
> (CST, I, 282)

故壘西邊 人道是
三國周郎赤壁

The quotation is effective in enhancing the impression of historical significance, as it represents the desire to fathom the basis of information by tracing it back to its source.

Why did Su Shih borrow most of his essential techniques from the *shih* tradition? It may seem rather peculiar to many readers that a versatile man like Su Shih, who excelled in *shih* poetry already in his 20's, should have waited until his late 30's to write his first *tz'u* poem. No doubt, the poet, like most of his elite contemporaries, did not at first look up to *tz'u* as a "respectable" literary genre. As has been mentioned in Chapter I his writing career in the *tz'u* form did not start until his first year as a local official at Hangchow (1072). By that time Liu Yung and Yen Shu had been dead for almost twenty years, and Ou-yang Hsiu had just passed away. When he started to develop this new interest in *tz'u* poetry, the old poet Chang Hsien was already in his 80's.

It was only natural that a poet who had already fully mastered the *shih* poetry would apply some of the *shih* technique to writing poems in a new form. Because of the many similarities between his *shih* and *tz'u* techniques, critics have used the famous phrase "treating *tz'u* as *shih*" (*i shih wei tz'u*) to describe Su Shih's *tz'u* poetics.[15] This statement is correct in some ways, but incorrect in others. It is true that the status of the *tz'u* form in the hands of Su Shih was elevated to the level of *shih* tradition. But there are important generic distinctions between them which should not be overlooked. These differences became increasingly obvious in the Sung dynasty as there gradually emerged a striking

exchange of generic roles: the *tz'u* poetry became a perfect form for pure lyricism as the Recent Style poetry had been in the T'ang dynasty, while it slowly pushed the *shih* poetry out of the domain of that pure lyricism.[16] In other words, as time went by the *tz'u* form established itself as "the lyric par excellence," while *shih* poetry began to touch on other levels of experience. This interesting transition was no doubt enhanced by the lyrical quality of Su Shih's *tz'u* poetry.

2. *Shih* and *Tz'u*: Generic Distinctions

The gradual shaping of the *tz'u* form may have posed several important problems for the poet. I believe that in his discrimination of poetic genres, Su Shih either consciously or unconsciously had a certain set of rules to follow. That was because the different poetic structures often represented different poetic conceptions. The poet seemed to reserve the *tz'u* form for expressing complex innermost feelings while having his *shih* poetry deal with miscellaneous types of expression (e.g., argumentation, social comment, occasional writing), often without a concentrated lyrical framework.

This observation can be well supported by the fact that while the poet wrote so many elegies in the *tz'u* form which revealed most poignantly his lyrical feelings, he did not write any such pieces in the *shih* form. In like manner, his aesthetic experience of music was mostly expressed through the *tz'u* form.[17] On the other hand, some of his *lü-shih* poems were written to present arguments, and a

great number of his <u>chüeh-chü</u> poems were composed for colophons on paintings. Where his Ancient Style poems often include long narrative passages, few of his <u>tz'u</u> poems were written in that fashion. The narrative elements in his <u>tz'u</u> poetry are mostly free from a temporal sequence, as they are the momentary reflections of his lyrical consciousness. It is the instantaneous lyrical expression that forms the center of Su's poetic experience in <u>tz'u</u>. All is turned inward and refashioned into aesthetic vision. Before we explore the poetics of his <u>tz'u</u> poetry in their own right, it will be necessary for us to compare his <u>shih</u> and <u>tz'u</u> in a more thorough manner.

The word <u>shih</u> is, of course, a very broad term. It includes both the Ancient Style poetry and Recent Style poetry, and within the Recent Style poetry there are again the <u>lü-shih</u> form and the <u>chüeh-chü</u> quatrain. The Ancient Style poem usually turned out to be longer than the Recent Style poem, because its length was not prescribed. This fact bears on an interesting phenomenon I have noted: in composing his longer <u>man-tz'u</u> poems Su Shih borrowed a number of poetic devices from his own Ancient Style poetry, whereas his shorter <u>hsiao-ling</u> poems were often influenced by the poetic of Recent Style poetry. This leads us to suspect that length did play an important role in the poet's generic consideration. Only in light of this fact can we find it meaningful to further distinguish between his <u>man-tz'u</u> and Ancient Style poems, and between his <u>hsiao-ling</u> and Recent Style poems.

One of the most characteristic features of Su Shih's <u>man-tz'u</u>

poetry is its tendency to provide a condensed view of natural settings in support of the lyrical voice. This technique of highlighting the essential elements presents a more concentrated poetic world than Liu Yung's, as all is focused on the poet's lyric vision. In his Nien-nu chiao (CST, I, 282), for instance, the general outlook of the setting is described in a few words:[18]

> Chaotic stones pierce through the sky,
> Startling billows slap the riverbank,
> Whirling a thousand heaps of snow.
>
> (lines 5-7)

亂石穿空
驚濤拍岸
捲起千堆雪

And the victory of the heroic but cool Chou Yü is described in a short sentence:

> While he was holding a feather fan, wearing silk headgear, talking and laughing,
> The mighty foe disappeared like ashes, vanished like smoke.
>
> (lines 13-14)

羽扇綸巾 談笑間
強虜灰飛煙滅

When we examine one of his Ancient Style poems on a similar subject, the differences in the descriptive method are striking:

"Seeing off Mr. Cheng, the Financial Officer"

Waters surround the P'eng-tsu Tower,[19]
Mountains encircle the Racing-horse Platform.[20]
Since of old, this is a place of heroes,
For a thousand years, there have been remnants of sorrow. 4
The hero with a prominent nose already ascended to
heaven,[21]
The warrior whose eyes had double pupils was also
turned into ashes.[22]
At the White Gate Lü Pu was defeated,[23]
The Great Star fell on Lin-huai.[24] 8
And imagine Liu Teh-yü[25]
Once gave a feast and lingered here.
Lately I suffer from loneliness,
The deserted garden is filled with dark green moss. 12
The sounds of the river comes to us from Pai-pu,
The mountain reaches as far as Chiu-li and then
turns around.
Mountain and water collide with each other,
The sound at night turns into wind and thunder. 16
On this vast field of Ch'ing-ho,
A Yellow Tower was built by me
The autumn moon sinks to the corner of the city wall,

Spring wind tosses my wine-cup. 20

As I entertain you, my guest,

I write new poems, like beautiful jasper.

When the tower is completed, you will have already left.

Human affairs indeed often contradict our wishes. 24

In future years when you are tired of traveling,

And with white hair, sing "Home Again,"

You will climb up the tower and heave a long sigh:

"Sir, where can you be?" 28

(STP, I, 140)

送鄭户曹

水繞彭祖樓
山圍戲馬台
古來豪傑地
千歲有餘哀
隆準飛上天
重瞳亦成灰
白門下呂布
大星隕臨淮
尚想劉德輿
置酒此徘徊

爾來苦寂寞
廢圃多蒼苔
河從百步响
山到九里回
山水自相激
夜聲轉風雷
蕩蕩清河壖
黃樓我所開
秋月墮城角
春風搖酒杯
遲君為座客
新詩出瓊瑰
樓成君已去
人事固多乖
他年君倦游
白首賦歸來
登樓一長嘯
使君安在哉

Quite evidently in this poem the descriptive passages (e.g., lines 1-2, lines 13-20) are so elaborate that they almost resemble an endless catalogue of scenes. Besides, the historical allusions

(lines 5-10) also create the impression of encyclopedic breadth. The poem is only nine lines longer than the tz'u poem Nien-nu chiao (19 lines), but it has presented a poetic world which is far more oriented toward historical facts and scenic description, in sharp contrast to the lyrical density found in his tz'u poem.

When the poet has a statement to make in his tz'u poetry, he also has a tendency to summarize it, rather than to dally with it. For example, his own solution to the problem of separation from loved ones is expressed in a few lines in his tz'u poem Shui-tiao ko-t'ou (CST, I, 280):

> For human beings there are sorrows and joys,
> separations and unions,
> For the moon, there are cloudy and clear skies,
> waxing and waning phases,
> These things can never be perfect since of old.
> I only wish that we could live long enough
> To share this beautiful moon across a thousand miles.
>
> (lines 15-19)

人有悲歡離合
月有陰晴圓缺
此事古難全
但願人長久
千里共嬋娟

Yet the same idea is elaborated into a rather long discourse in one of his Ancient Style poems:

> . . . How sad at heart, we four people are!
> When we share this moonlight across a thousand miles.
> The bright moon does not understand the sadness of
> growing old.
> Even on this pleasant day it is hard for us to have
> a reunion.
> As I look back, the guests
> Have gathered and separated like floating weeds.
> I once heard that under the moonlight in this night,
> Even across ten thousand miles, people can experience
> the same cloudy or clear day.
> Heaven itself has so designed it,
> How can we make light of such a meeting of minds?
> Next year let us all watch the moon,
> And contemplate our feelings of present and past.
>
> (STP, I, 144)

...悠哉四子心
共此千里明
明月不解老
良辰難合并

回顧坐上人
聚散如流萍
嘗聞此宵月
萬里同陰晴
天公自著意
此會那可輕
明年各相望
俯仰今古情

Clearly, these very different poetic devices all reflect the fundamental differences between man-tz'u and Ancient Style poetry.

The hsiao-ling form in tz'u is distinguished from Recent Style poetry for different reasons. As has been suggested, because of the weight of parallelism in the two middle couplets, a lü-shih poem cannot have the same stanzaic transition as in tz'u poetry. As a result, a lü-shih poem is strangely devoid of the dimension of progression, whether it is a lyrical expression or a discursive point at issue. On the other hand, the use of irregular lines in tz'u makes it free from an insistence on parallelism. Su Shih must have welcomed this possibility offered by the tz'u form, which the lü-shih form could not have offered. Perhaps this was why he often changed existing lü-shih poems (either by previous authors or by himself) into irregular-lined hsiao-ling poems. For instance, two

of his *hsiao-ling* poems to the tune *Ting feng-po* were composed in this manner.[26] When one compares his original *lü-shih* poem and its new version in the *tz'u*, one can see how a new verbal structure can represent a new structure of consciousness:

Lü-shih: "Red Plum"

Fearful of sorrow, fond of sleep, alone she blooms late. (7)
Herself afraid that her icy face may not be becoming. (7)
So she appears light red, in the color of peach-and-apricot, (7)
Yet she maintains her lonely, slim posture like snow-and-frost. (7) 4
Her cold heart does not want to adopt a spring-like attitude. (7)
Dizzy with wine, her jade-complexion becomes flushed for no reason. (7)
The old poet does not know where the spirit of the red plum lies,[27] (7)
Still looking for its green leaves and fresh branches. (7) 8

(STP, I, 180)

紅梅

怕愁貪睡獨開遲
自恐冰容不入時
故作小紅桃杏色
尚餘孤瘦雪霜姿

寒心未肯隨春態
酒暈無端上玉肌
詩老不知梅格在
更看綠葉與青枝

Hsiao-ling: Ting feng-po

Fond of sleep, too lazy to bloom, she does not mind being late, (7)
She pities herself because her icy face is not becoming. (7)
Occasionally she appears light red, in the color of peach-and-apricot; (7)
Easy and graceful, (2) 4
She still maintains her lonely and slim posture like snow and frost. (7)

Don't let your idle heart follow the manner of others; (7)
But why (2)
Did the wine make you somewhat dizzy, causing your heart to reshape your complexion? (7) 8
The senior poet does not know where the spirit of the red plum lies, (7)
As he chants (2)
He still looks for green leaves and fresh branches. (7)

(CST, I, 289)

定風波

好睡慵開莫厭遲
自憐冰臉不時宜
偶作小紅桃杏色
閑雅
尚餘孤瘦雪霜姿

休把閑心隨物態
何事
酒生微暈沁瑤肌
詩老不知梅格在
吟詠
更看綠葉與青枝

Clearly the integrity of the imagistic world represented by parallelism in couplets 2 and 3 of the original *lü-shih* poem is immediately destroyed by the structure of irregular lines in the new *tz'u* version. What is more striking is that the static pictorial world represented by couplet 3 of the *shih* poem has been turned into an imperative sentence followed by an interrogative sentence in strophe 3 (lines 6-8) of the *tz'u* poem. Thus, the new strophe in the *tz'u* version has the function of moving away from the world of parallelism on the one hand, and reinforcing the

stanzaic progression on the other. This reflects the general style of Su Shih's tz'u to highlight the transition from the first stanza to the second. Often the second stanza begins with words that suggest a sudden change in mood for emphasis:

> Suddenly I hear someone on the river playing
> the sad notes of a stringed instrument,--
> Sorrowful, full of feeling. . . .
>
> (CST, I, 299)
>
> 忽聞江上弄哀箏
> 苦含情

> I turn my head toward the foot of the mountain,
> and then turn my head backward to look.
> The road is extending endlessly. . . .
>
> (CST, I, 299)
>
> 轉頭山下轉頭看
> 路漫漫

> I stop drinking to listen to the sound of the lute;
> Softly plucking with fingers, she strums the
> instrument lightly. . . .
>
> (CST, I, 301)
>
> 停杯且聽琵琶語
> 細撚輕攏

Of course, it is easy to see how the structure of irregular lines in *tz'u* represents a departure from the world of parallelism. Yet the crucial point is that, even in his *hsiao-ling* poems to the *Mu-lan hua* tune which formally look like 7-character *lü-shih* poems, the poet has in all cases avoided the device of parallelism. Often the poet employs such function words as *keng* ("even more") and *yu* ("still") in strophes 2 (lines 3-4) and 3 (lines 5-6) to build up the illusion of a more hypotactic syntax:

> Falling upon the leaves of the *wu-t'ung* tree
> midnight rain
> Startles and breaks up my dream world, there is
> no place to find it.
> From the cool-night pillow and mat, I already know
> it is autumn,
> Even more (*keng*), I hear the cold crickets urging the
> shuttle of the loom. 4
>
> In my dream I vividly saw the road I took when I came,
> And still (*yu*) we were in the river pavilion, drinking,
> singing, and dancing.
> At your place now there must be someone through whom I have
> sent my regards
> To tell you about my feelings since our separation. 8
>
> (CST, I, 283)

梧桐葉上三更雨
驚破夢魂無覓處
夜涼枕簟已知秋
更聽寒蛩促機杼

夢中歷歷來時路
猶在江亭醉歌舞
尊前必有問君人
為道別來心與緒

However, Su Shih's Mu-lan hua poems represent only one instance of tz'u structure. Parallelism by no means disappears from tz'u poetry--in fact, it is often used as an important poetic device to balance the generally more hypotactic syntax. For example, 5-character parallel lines are found in many of Su Shih's hsiao-ling poems, and 4-character parallel lines in many of his man-tz'u poems.[28] What is significant, then, is not the disappearance of parallelism from the tz'u poetry, but the flexibility of its occurrence. In composing a tz'u poem, a poet creates parallelism only when he wishes, as it is no longer considered a formal requirement.

This notion of flexibility concerning the use of parallelism may be partially responsible for the relatively more hypotactic syntax in tz'u. It should be mentioned that in this area, as well as in others, hsiao-ling bears more resemblance to the chüeh-chü than to the

lü-shih. Like the lü-shih, the chüeh-chü lacks the stanzaic transition and the structure of irregular lines, the two things which came to define the uniqueness of the tz'u form. Yet it shares with the tz'u form a similar flexibility in the use of parallelism, in contrast to the rigid pattern of parallelism in the lü-shih. This is because chüeh-chü has a poetic structure which allows this freedom. Generally there are four possible kinds of organization for a chüeh-chü poem:

(1) parallelism for both couplets

(2) parallelism for the first couplet

(3) parallelism for the second couplet

(4) no parallelism for any couplet

Clearly the wide possibility of choices has made chüeh-chü free from the rigid structure of parallelism. Moreover, among all these choices, the fourth remains the most common one for poets.[29] This may account for the general impression of having a more flowing syntax than the lü-shih. In a typical 8-line lü-shih poem, the two parallel middle couplets can afford to form a pure imagistic center, as they are comfortably surrounded by the two non-parallel couplets. But in the 4-line chüeh-chü poem, there is no possibility for forming such a center--even when both couplets contain parallelism they cannot be purely imagistic, as the poem needs some non-imagistic elements to lend it vigor.[30] It is quite possible that in composing his hsiao-ling poems, Su Shih often had the poetics of the chüeh-chü form in mind, as there are striking similarities between his techniques used in these two forms. Traditionally, one of the major techniques of composing a chüeh-chü is to employ a method of contrast (e.g.,

between two points in time).[31] Su Shih was one of those poets who favored such a device in constructing the poetic world in chüeh-chü:

This year I plant it myself,
Wondering when I shall depart.
Some year in the future when I come back again,
Its leaves may have fallen, and that would break my heart.

(STP, II, 68)

今年手自栽
問我何年去
他年我復來
搖落傷人思

In youth I worked hard at farming,
At that time I was tired of the green mountains
surrounding my old residence.
In old age, I find luxurious rooms uninteresting,
And often I need to visit the hermit's hut.

(STP, I, 117)

少年辛苦事犁鋤
剛厭青山遶故居
老覺華堂無意味
卻須時到野人廬

A similar, or perhaps more exaggerated, insistence on the technique of contrast can be found frequently in his *tz'u* poetry:

> Above the city wall, rows of towers and stacks of
> mountain peaks,
> Below the city wall, the clear River Huai and the
> ancient River Pien.
>
> (CST, I, 323)
>
> 城上層樓疊巘
> 城下清淮古汴

> That year we met in eastern Hsü-chou for a horse-race,[32]
> Today desolation surrounds the Southern Shore.
>
> (CST, I, 284)
>
> 當年戲馬會東徐
> 今日淒涼南浦

> Last night, a small boat in Ching-k'ou,[33]
> This morning the head of my horse facing Ch'ang-an.
>
> (CST, I, 285)
>
> 昨夜扁舟京口
> 今朝馬首長安

Indeed the connection between his *hsiao-ling* and *chüeh-chü* poetics is not an accidental one. As a versatile poet who was familiar with all the existing poetic conventions, Su Shih must have seen the

necessary connection between the structure of hsiao ling poetry and that of chüeh-chü. His general tendency to favor the style of fluidity in the chüeh-chü form may have been partially responsible for his sudden conversion to tz'u writing. This theory can be supported by the fact that in the early period of his tz'u career (i.e., 1077-1078), the poet composed a number of tz'u poems to the tune Yang-kuan ch'ü, which were in fact prosodically identical to chüeh-chü poems. But, of course, this does not mean that we should disregard the generic differences between the two forms merely because they share some similar aesthetic and structural principles.

In terms of structure the tz'u form may be viewed as a median between Ancient Style and Recent Style poetry; it has both a structure of progression (emphasized by the stanzaic transition) and an insistence on the concentrated effect of lyrical voice. The present comparison between Su Shih's tz'u and shih poetry is merely to bring to light some of the crucial structural principles in tz'u which were obviously neglected by those traditional critics who claimed that Su Shih's tz'u poetry was written exactly like his shih poetry. In our study of generic development, Su Shih provides us with a perfect context for discussing various poetic forms--not only does his tz'u poetry represent a climax in the overall development of the tz'u genre, but the corpus of his shih poems remains one of the chief glories of Chinese literature. Since the structure of the tz'u form is so complex, I have merely attempted to deal with its most essential qualities here through a comparative approach in the hope that we may locate it as a distinct verbal structure. In the following section I shall focus on

Su Shih's _tz'u_ style and his important breakthroughs in the _tz'u_ tradition.

3. The Lyrical Consciousness and Its Imaginative World

The structure of lyricism in Su Shih's _tz'u_ poetry has not been sufficiently studied. Many critics have seemed reluctant to attach the word "feelings" to the context of his _tz'u_, as there is often an impression of aloofness or indifference in his poetic world. I believe that this is because certain critics confuse the meaning of objectification in poetry. Not only is the general scope of Su's _tz'u_ enlarged, but various forms of feelings are explored and refashioned into a new artistic integration by the poet's imaginative power.

One of the characteristics of Su Shih's _tz'u_ style is his frequent projection of feelings onto other human beings. He often imagines what others would feel in the particular poetic situations he creates, but he never tries to hide the truth that all is in his own imagination. Such is the general impression one gets in reading those _tz'u_ poems which have some historical interest. A case in point is the famous _Nien-nu chiao_:

> The big river flows east,
> Its waves swept away the dashing heroes of a thousand ages.
> West of the ancient rampart, they said, was
> "The Red Cliff of Master Chou of the Three Kingdoms." 4
> Chaotic stones pierce through the sky,
> Startling billows slap the riverbank,

Whirling a thousand heaps of snow.

The river and mountains are like a picture-- 8

At that time how many heroes were there?

I can imagine the Chou Yü in those ancient days:

The younger Ch'iao had just married him,

His brave appearance was sparkling. 12

While he was holding a feather fan, wearing silk
headgear, talking and laughing,

The mighty foe disappeared like ashes, vanished like smoke.

To the ancient Kingdom my spirit now wanders,--

The sentimental one must laugh at me 16

For growing white hair at this early age.

The world of mortals is like a dream--

Still I make a libation to the river moon.

(CST, I, 282)

大江東去
浪淘盡、千古風流人物
故壘西邊 人道是
三國周郎赤壁
亂石穿空
驚濤拍岸
捲起千堆雪
江山如畫
一時多少豪傑

遙想公瑾當年
小喬初嫁了
雄姿英發
羽扇綸巾談笑間
強虜灰飛煙滅
故國神遊
多情應笑我
早生華髮
人間如夢
一尊還酹江月

In the poet's conception, all the noble spirits of a thousand years are instantly swept away by the towering waves of the Great River (lines 1-2). The poet knows that he, too, will soon vanish into the historical past. For the truth is, Nature endures, but mortals do not. If past heroes are bound to disappear, why should one become sentimental about the inevitable changes in history? Obviously the poet, whose hair had already turned gray by his mid-40's, is posing such a question to himself. But he artificially places himself in a situation where he confronts the long-dead hero Chou Yü (A.D. 175-210) who is supposed to laugh at Su's gray hair. In fact, the poet is the one who is sentimental. Yet in his imagination Chou Yü has been transformed into the "sentimental" one who comes to meet him across the boundary of history (lines 15-17).[34]

The transference of feelings to others can also be found in many of his other *tz'u* poems, chief among them the well-known *Yung yü lo,* in which the poet imagines that poeple in future generations will sigh for him at the sight of his Yellow Tower, just as he now laments over the cold, deserted Swallow Tower:

. . . The Swallow-Tower is empty,[35]
Where is the beautiful lady now?
To no purpose, the swallows in the tower are locked up.
Past and present are like a dream;
Have we ever awakened from the dream?
All we have is old joys and new grievances.
In the future, when facing
The Yellow Tower in a night scene,
Someone will heave a deep sigh for me.

(CST, I, 302)

...燕子樓空
佳人何在
空鎖樓中燕
古今如夢
何曾夢覺
但有舊歡新怨
異時對
黃樓夜景
為余浩歎

This reveals the poet's general attitude toward acquiring a broader perspective. While the story of the Swallow Tower itself merely points to a particular historical incident, the poet has added a universal significance to it through sheer imagination.

This particular technique may be properly called "the projection of feelings." What is most striking is that the poet also makes use of this technique in dealing with inanimate objects. In his Shui-tiao ko-t'ou (CST, I, 280), the moon acts like a conscious being, circling around the pavilion and lowering itself to peep into the chamber, with its light shining upon the lonely poet:

> It circles around the vermilion pavilion,
> Lowers itself to the decorated door,
> And shines upon the sleepless one.
>
> 轉朱閣
> 低綺户
> 照無眠

To this bright moon, whose fullness itself seems to represent an ironic reflection on the imperfection of the human condition, the poet asks whether it has any reason to bear a grudge against mankind:

> It should not have any grievances;
> But why does it always become full when we are separated?
>
> 不應有恨
> 何事長向別時圓

In the poet's imagination, not only is the moon conscious of feelings, but the sun, the wind, and waters are also endowed with human emotions:

> The setting sun, full of emotion, still shines upon the seat.
>
> 落日多情還照坐 (CST, I, 300)
>
> Only the emotional, flowing water accompanies us on our journey.
>
> 只有多情流水、伴人行 (CST, I, 292)
>
> The wind comes rolling up the tide from ten thousand miles away, perhaps with feeling.
>
> 有情風、萬里卷潮來 (CST, I, 297)

In Su's _yung-wu tz'u_ poetry (i.e., _tz'u_ poems on objects) numerous kinds of flowers, plants, and birds are treated as human beings.[36] Such a method of perception no doubt enhances the sense of communication between human awareness and external objects. It reflects a personal wish to move beyond the individual world to embrace universal values. In his famous _Shui-lung yin_, the poet dramatizes the feelings of the willow catkin in terms of its feminine qualities, and thus broadens the scope of poetic perception:

> It looks like a flower, but still not like a flower.
> And no one cares for it; we just let it fall.
> Forsaking home, it clings to the side of road.
> When we come to think of it; although

Heartless, it has thoughts.

Its tender heart, twisted and broken,

Its lovely eyes overwhelmed by sleepiness,

About to open, but closed again. 8

In a dream it follows the wind for ten thousand miles,

To search for where its lover has gone,

Yet again it is awakened by the oriole's cry. . . .

(CST, I, 277)

似花還似非花
也無人惜從教墜
拋家傍路
思量卻是
無情有思
縈損柔腸
困酣嬌眼
欲開還閉
夢隨風萬里
尋郎去處
又還被、鶯呼起....

Even more significant than this method of personification is the poet's constant insistence on his role as an observer. Yet he is by no means a silent viewer of the external object; in almost all cases, as in <u>Shui-lung yin</u>, he explicitly tells the readers his personal reflections, which often reveal the most intense aspect of

his mental attitudes:

I do not regret that the flowers have all flown away,
But this I regret--in the Western garden, the fallen red
ones are hard to reassemble.

不恨此花飛盡
恨西園、落紅難綴

Such an emphatic statement is actually in keeping with Su Shih's general style of explicit rhetoric. It is a way of saying "not A but B"; it is an act of active interpretation. The effectiveness of this technique as a means of stating strong assertions cannot be overemphasized:

I do not see the residents;
I see only the city.

(CST, I, 290)

不見居人
只見城

I remember only when the song was sung;
I do not remember the time when I returned.

記得歌時
不記歸時節

The affection remains, but the person does not.

(CST, I, 304)

恩留人不留

This device of explicit rhetoric joins with the poet's frequent attempt to create the impression of doubt on the part of his persona. Doubt and uncertainty suggest the continuous working of an active mind. In *Shui-lung yin* and in other poems, the poet seems to consciously employ this device to achieve a certain effect of paradox:

> It looks like a flower, but still not like a flower.
>
> 似花還似非花
>
> The sun comes from the Western mountain where it is raining,
> The sky is not clear, yet is clear.
>
> (CST, I, 292)
>
> 日出西山雨
> 無晴又有晴
>
> You are about to part, but still do not part.
>
> (CST, I, 296)
>
> 欲去又還不去

Ironically, in *Shui-lung yin* the persona who expresses doubt is also the one who attempts to describe things in terms of quantitative proportion. The poet attempts to act like an alert reporter and commentator who constantly reasons and reflects on his own views. Under his imaginative power of observation, the willow catkins seem to be gradually transformed into a well-proportioned mixture of "spring colors," dust, and water (3:2:1):

Spring colors: three parts.

Two parts dust.

One part flowing water.

春色三分
二分塵土
一分流水

Although Su Shih was not the first poet to have developed the concept of quantitative proportion in _tz'u_ poetry,[37] he was responsible for making it a new important poetic device. The device has a function of enhancing the illusion of numerical "precision." When it is applied to those abstract entities which cannot in reality be so precisely quantified, the comparative ratio comes to serve as an effective means of exaggeration:

Three parts spring color, one part sorrow.

(CST, I, 286)

三分春色一分愁

Ten parts wine,

With one part singing.

(CST, I, 288)

十分酒
一分歌

In establishing the rhetoric of explicit meaning in the _tz'u_ context, Su Shih borrowed a useful technique from his own Ancient Style

poetry. I have noticed that one of the characteristics of his Ancient Style poetry is the frequent use of a formulaic expression, chün pu-chien ("Don't you see"):

> Don't you see that during the Yüan-kuang and
>
> Yüan-feng periods of the Former Han,
>
> The river overflowed the Hu-tzu area for twenty years,[38]
>
> The water of Chü-yeh Lake poured eastward to fill the
>
> rivers Huai and Ssu,[39]
>
> And the Ch'u people indulged in eating the Chan fish
>
> coming from the Yellow River?
>
> (STP, I, 131)

君不見西漢元光元封間
河決瓠子二十年
鉅野東傾淮泗滿
楚人恣食黃河鱣

And in his man-tz'u poetry, we find the occasional use of a similar pattern:

> Don't you see that there was a purification celebration
>
> held at the Orchid Pavilion[40]
>
> During which all the guests were heroic and talented?
>
> (CST, I, 281)

君不見蘭亭修禊事
當時坐上皆豪逸

The Southern Sung poet Hsin Ch'i-chi also adopts this method, obviously under the influence of Su Shih:

> Don't you see that both Yü-huan and Fei-yan have now turned to dust?[41]
>
> (CST, III, 1867)
>
> 君不見、玉環飛燕皆塵土

The expression "don't you see" was originally the standard opening for the yüeh-fu ballads bearing the title Hsing-lu nan.[42] This technique is particularly powerful in calling attention to a certain historical fact. Su Shih's artistic merit here lies in his ability to transform a common formulaic expression from its original "narrative" context into a lyrical one. In his Ancient Style poetry, the expression merely serves as a tag to begin a long narrative passage, but in the tz'u poetry it has become a convenient device for adding short comments to the lyrical situation, and thus functions like a ling-tzu segment. In other words, the old device has been turned into a new effective means in tz'u for reinforcing the effect of poetic act.

The artistic effect of explicit rhetoric in Su Shih's tz'u is significantly heightened by a few conventional devices developed by earlier tz'u poets, chief among them the use of modal verbs and interrogatives. Yet the combination of the poet's imagination and

temperament gives them a greater dramatic impact than in previous *tz'u* poetry. There seems to be a higher degree of dynamism through which the consciousness of the poetic act is expressed. For example, the modal verb *mo* ("don't") was frequently employed by Wei Chuang and Li Yü, but it did not occur at the head position of the poem as often as in Su's *tz'u*. As one can see, many of Su's *tz'u* poems begin with this modal verb:

> Don't (*mo*) listen to the rain, piercing the forest,
> hitting the leaves,
> Why not sing, whistle and walk leisurely?
>
> (CST, I, 288)
>
> 莫聽穿林打葉聲
> 何妨吟嘯且徐行

> Don't (*mo*) sigh that the plains are desolate,
> You should just leave Lu slowly.
>
> (CST, I, 284)
>
> 莫歎平原落落
> 且應去魯遲遲

> Don't (*mo*) be surprised that her sash embroidered with
> a pair of ducks is too long,
> Her waist is so small that even a dancing gown
> is heavy to wear.
>
> (CST, I, 289)

莫怪鴛鴦繡帶長
腰輕不勝舞衣裳

The flexibility of placing interrogatives in all positions of the poem also makes Su's tz'u poetry appear to be spontaneously direct:

Interrogatives:

(1) at the beginning of the poem:

Since when did the bright moon come to existence?
With a cup of wine in hand, I ask the blue sky.

(CST, I, 280)

明月幾時有
把酒問青天

(2) near the beginning of the poem:

I ask: On the Ch'ien-t'ang River
In the bay of Hsi-hsing,
How many times have we seen the slanting beams
of the setting sun?

(CST, I, 297)

問錢塘江上
西興浦口
幾度斜暉

(3) near the end of the poem:

When am I going to return,

And become a leisured man?

(CST, I, 302)

幾時歸去
作箇閒人

(4) at the end of the poem:

Let me ask: Among my various friends in South Yangtze,

Who is like me,

So enchanted in Yangchow?

(CST, I, 320)

試問江南諸伴侶
誰似我
醉揚州

Interrogative followed by answers:

(1) at the beginning of the poem:

There are weeping willows on all sides, and
ten miles of lotus flowers.

Let's ask: At what spot are the flowers most abundant?

The south side of the painted tower where the setting
sun is gentle.

(CST, I, 317)

四面垂楊十里荷
問云何處最花多
畫樓南畔夕陽和

(2) toward the end of the poem:

Let me ask: How is the night?

The night has reached its third watch.

(CST, I, 297)

試問夜如何
夜已三更

(3) at the end of the poem:

If you ask: This man's abilities and skills,

How about them?

He stands first in the world, an utter fool.

(CST, I, 291)

試問使君才與術
何如
占得人間一味愚

On top of these devices of explicit rhetoric Su Shih developed a flowing syntax through the use of continuous lines (i.e., the device of using a series of lines to complete an integral statement). This contributes

greatly to the vigorous effect of his poetic utterance:

Ultimately I should let my boat go
And reside in the deep fragrant place
To look at her beauty.

(CST, I, 320)

終須放、船兒去
清香深處住
看伊顏色

Or, is it because
When the east wind chases after you,
It blows away a few spring wrinkles
Between your eyebrows?

(CST, I, 297)

又莫是
東風逐君來
便吹散眉間
一點春皺

Often the impression of continuous lines is forwarded by the repetition of a key word in two consecutive lines. Perhaps inspired by the linking device used in the ancient <u>yüeh-fu</u> poems, the poet employs this new method for building up the sense of syntactic continuity in <u>tz'u</u> poetry:

Tomorrow there are fallen flowers and flying catkins

The flying catkins will accompany my sailing boat

As waters flow east.

(CST, I, 296)

明日落花飛絮
飛絮送行舟
水東流

After all, I do not envy this world

In this world days are like years.

(CST, 304)

終不羨人間
人間日似年

Sometimes a certain word is repeated so many times that it achieves an impression of incantational recurrence as well as one of semantic continuity:

Much emotion, much feeling, and yet much illness,

Inside of the Tower of Much-scenery (To-ching lou).

(CST, I, 301)

多情多感仍多病
多景樓中

Don't say that the lunatic does not understand lunacy

In his old age, the lunatic becomes even more lunatic.

(CST, I, 296)

莫道狂夫不解狂
狂夫老更狂

It seems being in command of the unlimited potentiality of *tz'u* poetry, the poet is ready to experiment with all kinds of devices. Here we witness an abundance of the most varied kinds of hypotaxis. For example, the spontaneous overflow of his continuous syntax is often enhanced by his use of concessive hypotaxis (e.g., *sui* "although"):

The snow is like my old friend, and my friend
    resembles the snow;
Though (*sui*) lovable,
They are rejected by some.

(CST, I, 299)

雪似故人人似雪
雖可愛
有人嫌

Although (*sui*) I excel in literary skill,
When I open my mouth who comes close?

(CST, I, 302)

雖抱文章
開口誰親

One of Su's most interesting innovations was his employment of classical function words in some of his *tz'u* poems, a device whose intended effect was opposite to that of colloquialism. By this time colloquialism had already been accepted by *tz'u* poets, and it was only natural that Su Shih would look elsewhere for linguistic innovation. The function words such as *yi* and *i* which would otherwise be used exclusively in classical prose can be found in some of his *tz'u* where the main purpose is to reason rather than to express. A case in point is his *tz'u* poem to *Shao p'ien* in which the poet retells T'ao Ch'ien's story of retreating to the farmland:

> . . . *Yi*! "Let me go home!" . . .
> Seeing grasses and trees flourishing,
> The recluse is stirred within himself:
> "Our life is going to end, *i*!" . . .
>
> (CST, I, 307)

...噫，歸去來兮...
觀草木欣榮
幽人自感
吾生行且休矣....

The effect of a prosaic rhythm created by the classical function words in this type of tz'u must have posed a problem for Su's fellow poets, in whose view tz'u poetry was supposed to represent nothing but the intrinsic value of pure lyricism. The use of classical function words in this case indeed seemed an ironic twist to the tz'u's insistence on the poetic and the emotive. Some later poets followed Su's footstep by imitating the themes and styles of ancient prose works in their tz'u.[43] Yet such a practice was never fully accepted into the mainstream of tz'u poetry, for it was often viewed with disfavor by traditional critics. However, the critics' continuing objection to the use of classical function words in tz'u reassures us that whereas colloquialism played a determining role in the formation of tz'u poetics, the inclusion of classical usage proved to be relatively insignificant in the development of tz'u.

The fact remains that Su Shih's work marks a milestone in the evolution of tz'u poetry. Earlier I mentioned that he was the forefather of the school of "heroic abandon" in tz'u. This may be due to the fact that his tz'u poetry carried a style that was often disapproved by critics. Yet I believe that the achievement of Su's imagistic language also has a great effect in shaping his particular poetic style, although this is an area which is often overlooked.

The image of turbulent waves reaching to the sky is a familiar one in Su Shih's tz'u poetry. Like Li Yü who often uses the images of the moon and the flowing waters to signify the meaning of eternity, Su Shih perceives the river-and-wave image as conveying the universal quality of things permanent. To us these images also represent most effectively

the totality of the poet's inner visions. One finds that when Su attempts to capture the larger-than-self vision within himself, he often uses this powerful device to achieve a dimension of imagistic immediacy:

> I dream that a small boat drifts on Chen Lake,[44]
> Snowy billows are tossed up into the sky,--one thousand
> acres of white. . . .
>
> (CST, I, 281)
>
> 我夢扁舟浮震澤
> 雪浪搖空千頃白

> In a small boat I shall disappear from here,
> And spend my remaining years on the rivers and the sea.
>
> (CST, I, 287)
>
> 小舟從此逝
> 江海寄餘生

To Su Shih rivers and waves symbolize an extension of his own impulse toward liberation. If the reality in life is one of cares and restrictions, it is the flowing rivers that free the self from this world. In those poems where such an idea of self-expansion is lacking, the poet also prefers to use the river-and-wave image in the opening lines to serve as a poetic setting:

> The Yangtze and the Han River come from the West,
> Below the high tower, dark water like grapes.

It carries the snowy billows from Mt. Min and Mt. Omei,--
On the Chin River,[45] spring colors.

(CST, I, 280-281)

江漢西來
高樓下、葡萄深碧
猶自帶、岷峨雪浪
錦江春色

Startling as it must have appeared to his contemporaries, Su Shih's introduction of such grand images is hardly less admirable to us today. The correspondence between lyrical consciousness and imagistic perception is nowhere more appropriate. The poet parallels his enlargement of *tz'u*'s thematic scope with a broadening of imagistic functions. This is why when we compare Su Shih's and Liu Yung's worlds, the latter seems rather narrow despite its richness in realistic depiction.

Viewed from a different perspective, however, Su Shih's technique of creating images was significantly conditioned by the *tz'u* style of his predecessors. Despite his open attack on Liu Yung's "effeminate" style, he praises the unsurpassed quality of the following strophe by Liu:[46]

Gradually the frosty wind brings a chilly current of air,
The mountain-pass and the rivers become desolate,
And the fading sunlight falls on the tower.

漸霜風淒緊
關河冷落
殘照當樓

In one of Su's earlier man-tz'u poem Ch'in-yüan ch'un, one witnesses the strong traces of Liu Yung's influence, as can be seen in the combined use of ling-tzu and parallelism in an imagistic context:[47]

> Gradually the brightness of the moon dims,
> The frost at daybreak is shining.
> Clouds and mountains are grand and splendid,
> The morning dew lies thick.
>
> (CST, I, 282)

漸月華收練
晨霜耿耿
雲山摛錦
朝露漙漙

Liu Yung's man-tz'u poetry must have exercised a considerable impact on Su Shih's early experiments with tz'u poetry. Early in his

Hangchow years Su Shih wrote mainly in the _hsiao-ling_ form, and occasionally in the middle-sized _man-tz'u_ form (e.g., _Hsing-hsiang tzu_, _Chu ying-t'ai chin_, _Chiang-ch'eng tzu_, _I-ts'ung hua_). Only in his third year (i.e., 1074) there did he start to experiment extensively with the longer man-tz'u form; tunes such as _Yung yü lo_, _Yü-chung-hua man_, _Shui-lung yin_, and _Man-chiang hung_ gradually became the major medium for his lyrical expression. It may be that the device of _ling-tzu_ as well as other structural principles of the _man-tz'u_ form provided him with a new inspiration for poetic experiments. In any case, the popularity of the _man-tz'u_ form at that time must have contributed greatly to this literary endeavor, and so unconsciously the poet became a "faithful" follower of Liu Yung.

Yet unlike Liu Yung's typical elaboration of descriptive details, Su Shih's images of natural settings appear to be larger in scale and more expressive in function. In a way, he combines Liu Yung's _man-tz'u_ structure and Li Yü's archetypical images in constructing his poetic world. The result is a new emphasis on the total impression of natural images and a much more elaborately stratified strophic structure. There is no longer the camera-eye view which moves gradually from one natural setting to another, but the immediate comprehension of the grand scene in focus. Where the natural images in Liu Yung may be compared to very fine, delicate drawings, Su turns them into large pieces of impressionistic painting. And behind such an archetypal and abstract version of natural images, we witness a sequential structure by which the poet organizes fragmented poetic reflections into complex trains of expression. All this echoes the fullness of a

lyrical consciousness and the power of poetic imagination.

If Su Shih's tz'u appear to be more intellectual than emotional, it is only due to an illusion created by the poet's artistic devices. Everything in his poetry has a double function: each expression or image is at once a spontaneous reflection of his lyrical voice, and an objective rendering of that voice. And he creates most strikingly a poetic situation which approximates this artistic process. This is why when he establishes a metaphorical relation between an external object and human feeling, he also must leave himself as an outside observer who delivers philosophical statements.

In her definition of lyric poetry, Langer emphasizes the importance of the "illusion" of experience.[48] She believes that since events in actual lives are fragmented and indefinite, the poet's business is to create "the semblance of events lived and felt."[49] In other words, "all poetry is a creation of illusory events, even when it looks like a statement of opinions, philosophical or political or aesthetic."[50] If one views Su Shih's poetic world in this light, one realizes how the discursive elements in his poetry are indeed non-discursive in function, since they all belong to a symbolic context which is supported by the art of illusion. All philosophical statements are the reflection of the present moment, which are not meant for arguing but for expression. Langer's comment on the general function of poetic thought reads like a pertinent interpretation of Su Shih's poetic art:

> Poetic reflections, therefore, are not essentially

> trains of logical reasoning, though they may incorporate fragments, at least, of discursive arguments. Essentially they create the semblance of reasoning; of the seriousness, strain and progress, the sense of growing knowledge, growing clearness, conviction and acceptance--the whole experience of philosophical thinking.[51]

The abundance of poetic reflections reveals the poet's personal attitude toward the external world in general. It is significant to see that the poet, through the rhetoric of explicit meaning, constantly calls the reader's attention to his own thoughts. His voice conveys the spirit of the "heroic abandon" and his vast and expansive world.

In conclusion I should mention that after the device of ling-tzu and continuous syntax became a conventional practice for man-tz'u, later poets (especially in the Southern Sung) began to develop a metaphorical dimension in tz'u which became a means for sustaining the rhetoric of implicit meaning. The poet Chou Pang-yen at the end of the Northern Sung represents the beginning of this new poetic movement. Yet I believe that without Su Shih's enlargement of poetic scope and his exhausting of almost all the possibilities of rhetorical method, Chou Pang-yen could not have had the basis for his profound metaphorical explorations.

In many aspects, Su Shih represents both the logical conclusion to the long, continuous efforts to broaden the vision of the poetic

world in the tz'u tradition, and a significant step in anticipation of the later poets' explorations of the imagistic dimensions. Where Su Shih remains an observer in creating a metaphorical relation between external objects and universal human feelings, Chou Pang-yen develops a situation of poetic empathy in which the lyric self seems to establish a symbolic correspondence with external objects. In his Lan-ling wang, Liu ch'ou, and Hua fan (CST, II, 609-611), Chou Pang-yen reveals a new poetic sensitivity whose empathic involvement with the external has become so real that it does not need to dissociate itself from its objects. As a result, the poetic voice makes few explicit statements to assert its own independent existence. Later this growing complexity in the direction of symbolism was to characterize the school of "delicate restraint" (wan-yüeh) in the Southern Sung tz'u.

It seems that it is this device of symbolism which accounts most for the impression of implicit rhetoric in Chou Pang-yen and in such Southern Sung poets as Chiang K'uei (ca. 1155-ca. 1230) and Wu Wen-ying (ca. 1205-ca. 1270).[52] These poets often begin a poem with images of seemingly independent objects or events, which in their conception function as metaphorical extensions of their private feelings. It is this symbolic dimension which is responsible for the general impression of ambiguity, or in James J. Y. Liu's terminology, the "opaque" quality of their poetry.[53]

It is important for us to see that this poetic conception associated with Chou Pang-yen was merely one step beyond Su Shih's "transference of feelings" in poetry, but it brought about a new poetic mode. The strange combination of hypotactic syntax and the rhetoric

of implicit meaning became possible only when this new dimension of symbolism was gradually realized. For however hypotactic the syntax is, and however expressive the _ling-tzu_ segments are, if the symbolic dimension is meaningful only to private perception, the general impression of the poetic voice would appear to be implicit rather than explicit.

Thus, the orthodox school of "delicate restraint" in _tz'u_ poetry was to develop into something quite different from the one originally advocated by Wen T'ing-yün. The basic aesthetic value of implicit rhetoric was likewise maintained, but the syntactic feature was bound to be significantly different, as a result of the cumulative contribution made by Su Shih and other individualistically innovative poets.

Concluding Remarks

Both the *hsiao-ling* and the *man-tz'u* forms in *tz'u* share a common divergence from Recent Style poetry. Their similar emphasis on lines of unequal length and the principle of stanzaic transition have significantly contributed to the gradual formation of *tz'u* as an independent poetic genre. Yet it was the longer *man-tz'u* form which represented the ultimate achievement of *tz'u* poetry in its realization of a complex structure of lyrical interiorization.

The lyrical exploration of narrative and other non-lyrical elements remains one of the most significant features of *tz'u* poetry. Its uniqueness, however, does not lie in its mere emphasis on lyricism, as such has been the general phenomenon in the classical Chinese tradition. Rather, its importance lies in its capacity to explore new areas of literature which were, by the older standards, unpoetic or low in style, while at the same time securely maintaining a concentrated lyric vision. In view of this fact, we have attempted in the foregoing chapters to trace some of the possible influences of popular songs on the *tz'u* development.

The traditional popular songs were commonly noted for their narrative elements, dramatic tendencies, colloquial diction, and hypotactic syntax. In spite of the conscious rejection of such elements on the part of the early "orthodox" *tz'u* poets, the "revolutionary" poets during the ninth and tenth centuries, notably

Wei Chuang and Li Yü, continued to borrow techniques from the popular song tradition. When Liu Yung emerged as a _man-tz'u_ specialist in the eleventh century, the intrusion of the popular song style into the elitist literary tradition became so obvious that the old separation of styles was immediately destroyed. The hypotactic syntax, formerly thought to characterize the "low" style of the popular song tradition, had now become an important ingredient in the newly engendered "elevated" style of _tz'u_ poetry, and could now feel at home in the poetic world of sublimity. When Su Shih broadened the horizons of the poetic world in _tz'u_ by borrowing important devices from the _shih_ tradition, the esteem of _tz'u_ poetry became unquestioned.

My main concern has been to see how the history of poetics in China, as in other traditions, exhibits continual changes in the manipulation of certain norms. I have mentioned that both _tz'u_ and _chüeh-chü_ poetry were originally song-forms, but later they freed themselves from the realm of music. It is worth noting that the _tz'u_ form replaced the _chüeh-chü_ form in terms of its musical function. During the High T'ang the _chüeh-chü_ poetry was a major song-form made popular by poets and singing girls. Gradually, as the _tz'u_ became the major song-form, the _chüeh-chü_ lost its original connection with the musical world. Later when the new _ch'ü_ form emerged in the Yuan dynasty, the _tz'u_ poetry suffered the same ultimate fate as _chüeh-chü_. All these changes in function, of course, resulted from changes in music.

But such systematic transformations point to something very important in our understanding of generic changes. In both the _chüeh-chü_ and the _tz'u_ traditions, this change seems to reinforce a definite

shift from a public function to an individualized expression of private feelings. When the main purpose of writing poetry is no longer to meet the demand of musical performers, the poet tends to concentrate on a world which is entirely personal.

The _tz'u_ poetry also shared a similar direction in stylistic developments with the tradition of _lü-shih_. In each case, right after the pioneer stage of generic development there were many influential poets who expressed thoughts in a straightforward fashion, or in my terminology, through the rhetoric of explicit meaning. On the other hand, most of the leading poets in the later period appeared to be more interested in the manipulation of poetic images for the purpose of constructing a private symbolic world. If we compare the stylistic tendencies of the _shih_ poets in the Early T'ang and those in the Late T'ang, or compare the _tz'u_ poets in the Northern Sung and those in the Southern Sung, we find that such was indeed the case.

This, however, does not mean that all genres are identical in their poetic functions. Each genre emerges in a special situation, as a response to a particular need for expression. When Wen T'ing-yün began to write in the _tz'u_ form with a particular emphasis on color and other sensual images, it seemed as though he was merely exaggerating the general style of the late T'ang _lü-shih_. But the fact that he needed a new genre to accomplish his poetic purpose suggests that he did attempt to express certain shades of feeling which were no longer possible to deal with in the old genre. What he did was to present a new dimension of aestheticism, which in all its implications reflected a fine emotional sensitivity, finer than any previous awareness of

human feelings in the poetic tradition. This level of aestheticism, first explored by Wen T'ing-yün, has remained for all these centuries one of the most important qualities of _tz'u_ poetry. However enlarged the poetic world in _tz'u_ might become as in the case of Su Shih, this essential quality has always been maintained, though it has by no means confined the scope of the generic development. In this fashion, _tz'u_ poetry has continued up to the present to project a unique world of aestheticism which is characteristic of the genre.

Appendix: Examples of *Man-tz'u* Poetry in the Tun-huang Collection

(1) *Feng kuei yün*

Alone, I sit by the green window
And finish a letter to you.
Your garment, I have just completed;
And I am sending it to you in the frontier faraway. 4
Imagining that for the emperor's sake you are fighting
valiantly,
Undaunted by the rugged path,
You are in the desert all day,
And only relying on your sword, 8
You fight our deadly foe.

How could you know that on my powdered face
Tears fall like pearls?
In vain I divined by the golden hairpins;-- 12
Each time I told my fortune it proved false.
I dream of you faraway--without a moment's reprieve,
And I lie in bed sighing endlessly.
When you return as a high-ranking official, 16
My features will be worn--
What, then, will we face each other?

(THC, #002)

鳳歸雲

綠窗獨坐
修得君書
征衣裁縫了
遠寄邊隅
想您為君貪苦戰
不憚崎嶇
終朝沙磧裏
只憑三尺
勇戰奸愚

豈知紅臉
淚滴如珠
枉把金釵卜
卦卦皆虛
魂夢天涯無暫歇
枕上長噓
待公卿回故里
容顏憔悴
彼此何如

(2) _Ch'ing-pei lo_

I remember when I turned fifteen,
I did not yet understand the feelings of separation
and union.
I grew up in the inner chamber--
I lay leisurely on the embroidered bed, 4
With needles I often
Created images, pairs of dancing, flying phoenixes.
At my dressing table I painted my face again and again,
Only to enjoy looking at myself, 8
Never thinking I would be seen by others.
And then the clever matchmaker
Came with a flattering tongue to beguile me.

Whenever people talked about mandarin ducks living 12
by the water,
I thought of only the paired swallows on the roof.
When my parents arranged a marriage for me,
I accepted it as a predestined union.
Then one day I was married to this crazy fool; 16
He immersed himself in studying, and deserted me to
seek official rank.
Even if he succeeds
And becomes a high-ranking official,
The honor and glory--can they ever be secure? 20

(THC, #20)

傾杯樂

憶昔笄年
未省離合
生長深閨院
閑凭着繡床
時拈金針
擬貌舞鳳飛鸞
對妝台重整嬉恣面
自身兒算料
豈教人見
又被良媒
苦出言詞誘炫

每道說水際鴛鴦
惟指梁間雙燕
被父母將兒匹配
便認多生宿姻眷
一旦娉得狂夫
攻書業抛妾求名宦
縱然選得
一時朝要
榮華爭穩便

Notes

I. Introduction

[1] Wang Cho, *Pi-chi man-chih*, in THTP, I, 20. See also James J. Y. Liu, *Major Lyricists of the Northern Sung* (Princeton: Princeton Univ. Press, 1974), pp. 3-4.

[2] For example, Shen I-fu's criticism on *tz'u* was entitled *Yüeh-fu chih-mi*, and Ho Chu's collection of *tz'u* was named *Tung-shan yüeh-fu*.

[3] Except for a few *tz'u* songs reconstructed by L. E. R. Picken. See Picken's "Secular Chinese Songs of the Twelfth Century," *Studia Musicologica Academiae Scientiarum Hungaricae*, 8 (1966), 125-172.

[4] Hans H. Frankel, *The Flowering Plum and the Palace Lady* (New Haven: Yale Univ. Press, 1976), p. 217.

[5] Edward H. Schafer has dealt with this subject with insight. In "The Capeline Cantos: Verses on the Divine Loves of Taoist Priestesses" (forthcoming in *Sinologische Studien*) he discusses in detail the recurrence of Taoist images and the various stereotypes representing the iconography of Taoist priestesses in the poems set to the tune *Nü-kuan tzu*. Elsewhere he describes how the poems to the tune *Nan-hsiang tzu* express the true tropical flavor typical of the "warm, amorous south." (See *The Vermilion Bird*, Berkeley: Univ. of California Press, 1967, p. 84).

[6] Wan Shu, [*So-yin pen*] *Tz'u-lü*, rpt. with supplements by Hsü Pen-li (Taipei: Kuang-wen shu-chü, 1971).

[7] However, in prosodic terms one can still distinguish a *tz'u* poem to the *Yü-lou ch'un* tune from a 7-character line *lü-shih*: first of all, a *Yü-lou ch'un tz'u* poem must use oblique tone rhymes, while a *lü-shih* poem usually employs level tone rhymes. Moreover, a *tz'u* poem lacks the linking device called *nien*, an absolute requirement in the structure of *lü-shih*. The use of *nien* in *lü-shih* reflects its general attempt to stress the sense of recurrence and regularity, for it is a technical device which prescribes that the second syllable in lines 3, 5, 7 should repeat the tone of the second syllable in the previous line.

[8] Wang Li, *Han-yü shih-lü hsüeh* (1958; rpt. Hong Kong: Chung-hua shu-chü, 1973), p. 304.

[9] It is generally believed that the Chinese were not conscious of tonal distinctions until the Han or immediate post-Han era. This in part explains the new role of tones in prosody during the Six Dynasties period.

[10] *Literature as System* (Princeton: Princeton Univ. Press, 1971), pp. 135-158.

[11] Wang Li, p. 50. It should be noted that, in contrast to this, the oblique tone rhymes were often used in Ancient Style poetry.

[12] The materials preserved in the Tun-huang Caves for nearly a thousand years were first discovered by the Taoist monk Wang Yüan-lu shortly before 1900. Yet the value of these findings was not recognized by scholars until Sir Aurel Stein and Paul Pelliot came to visit the Tun-huang caves around 1907.

[13] For the dating of the Tun-huang songs, see Jen Erh-pei, Tun-huang ch'ü ch'u-t'an (Shanghai: Wen-i lien-ho ch'u-pan-she, 1954), p. 222 et passim.

[14] 228 songs belong to the first category, and 318 songs belong to the second category.

[15] e.g., Shui-tiao tz'u, Lo-shih tz'u, and Huang-ti kan.

[16] See Hu Shih, "Tz'u ti ch'i-yüan," in "Appendix" to his Tz'u-hsüan (Shanghai: Commercial Press, 1927). See also Shih-ch'üan Ch'en, "The Rise of the Tz'u, Reconsidered," Journal of the American Oriental Society, 90, No. 2 (1970), 232-242.

[17] For details of this controversy, see Chang Wan, "P'u-sa man chi ch'i hsiang-kuan chih chu wen-t'i," Ta-lu tsa-chih, 20, No. 1 (1960), 19-24; 20, No. 2 (1960), 15-17; 20, No. 3 (1960), 27-32.

[18] The two collections of Wen's tz'u, Wo-lan chi (3 chüan) and Chin-ch'üan chi (10 chüan), are no longer extant. The extant tz'u by Wen can be found in the following anthologies: Chin-lien chi, Tsun-ch'ien chi, and Hua-chien chi. Among these Hua-chien chi has the most complete selection of Wen's work (66 songs).

[19] Ts'ui Ling-ch'in, Chiao-fang chi [chien-ting], annotated by Jen Pan-t'ang (Jen Erh-pei), Shanghai: Chung-hua shu-chü, 1962, p. 4.

[20] Chang Wan, 20, No. 2 (1960), 16-17.

[21] According to the "Yüeh chih" of Sung shih (Chüan 142), T'ai-tsung invented 390 new tunes and Jen-tsung 54 tunes.

[22] As to the exact locations of chiao-fang quarters, see Kishibe Shigeo, Tōdai ongaku no rekishiteki kenkyū--gakuseihen, I (Tokyo: Univ. of Tokyo Press, 1960), pp. 286-313.

[23] Ibid., I, 21. Su-yüeh became part of yen-yüeh in Sung times (Ibid., I, 86-87). This su-yüeh, taken to mean "vulgar" music in T'ang China, was later transmitted to Japan and regarded by the Japanese as elegant music (Ibid., I, 7).

[24] The "Yin-yüeh chih" of Chiu T'ang-shu (Chüan 30) describes this in the following words: "Since the years of K'ai-yüan singers mixed foreign music with songs of the streets."

[25] In Chu Tsu-mou, ed., Ch'iang-ts'un ts'ung-shu (Shanghai: n.p., 1922). Hsüan-tsung's other tz'u poems have all been lost: Yeh-pan yüeh, Ch'un-kuang hao, I-hu chu, etc. See Liu Tzu-keng, Tz'u shih (1931; rpt. Taipei: Hsüeh-sheng shu-chü, 1972), p. 25.

[26] The chiao-fang was restored during the second year of Su-tsung reign (757), but the scope of musical activities was never as extensive as before. See Kishibe Shigeo, I, 90.

[27] Ibid., I, 98.

[28] A famous story has it that Wang Ch'ang-ling, Kao Shih and Wang Chih-huan went to a banquet where courtesans were singing the chüeh-chü songs by all three of them without knowing the presence of these poets (See Wang Cho, Pi-chi man-chih, in THTP, I, 25).

[29] Frankel, The Flowering Plum and the Palace Lady, p. 94.

[30] Glen W. Baxter, "Metrical Origin of the Tz'u," in Studies in Chinese Literature, ed. John Bishop (Cambridge: Harvard Univ. Press, 1966), pp. 202-203. For examples of interpolations, see Huang-fu Sung's Chu-chih and Ts'ai-lien tzu songs (CTWT, I, 38-40).

[31] In Chung-kuo wen-hsüeh ts'an-k'ao tzu-liao hsiao ts'ung-shu, Ser. 1, No. 8 (Shanghai: Ku-tien wen-hsüeh ch'u-pan-she, 1957). Among

the 40 regular guests who visited pei-li 38 were scholar officials.

32 See Wang Jen-yü, K'ai-yüan T'ien-pao i-shih, rpt. in Shuo k'u (Taipei: Hsin-hsing shu-chü, 1963), 0245. See also Ou-yang Chiung's preface to Hua-chien chi in which he describes the tz'u milieu as something cultivated by the "bawdy air of the Northern Ward" (in Chao Ch'ung-tso, comp., Hua-chien chi [chiao], collated by Li I-mang, Hong Kong: Commercial Press, 1960).

33 Kishibe Shigeo, II, 20. See also Sun Ch'i, p. 22.

34 Sun Ch'i, pp. 27-28, 29-30, 31-32, 33-34.

35 Wang Shu-nu, Chung-kuo ch'ang-chi shih (Shanghai: Sheng-huo shu-tien, 1935), pp. 167-169.

36 The poet himself indicated that the songs were to "match Lo-t'ien's [Po Chü-i's] tz'u on spring, to the rhythm of the I chiang-nan tune" (CTWT, I, 22). This, according to Baxter, was the "first avowed instance of the practice of t'ien-tz'u" (p. 219).

37 Kishibe Shigeo, II, 101.

38 See, for example, Wei Chuang's tz'u in CTWT, I, 118 and Liu Yung's tz'u poems in CST, I, 34 for a contrast between Five Dynasties tz'u and Sung tz'u.

39 See Feng Meng-lung, "Chung ming-chi ch'un-feng tiao Liu Ch'i," in his Yü-shih ming yen, Chüan 12 (Hong Kong: Chung-hua shu-chü, 1965).

40 See Shih-lin shih-hua, as cited in Hsüeh Li-jo, Sung-tz'u t'ung-lun (1949; rpt. Taipei: K'ai-ming shu-tien, 1958), p. 88.

41 Chao Ch'ung-tso, p. 1.

42 For the dating of Yün-yao chi, see Jen Erh-pei, Tun-huang ch'ü ch'u-t'an, p. 204.

43 Earl Miner, "The Genres in Critical Systems and Literary Change" (paper, Princeton Conference on Genre and Its Problems, Apr. 30-May 1, 1976), p. 7.

44 e.g., two Keng-lou tzu songs by Wen T'ing-yün and Ou-yang Chiung, and one P'u-sa man poem by Ou-yang Chiung (THC, # 139, 140, 053).

45 See Miao Yüeh, Shih-tz'u san-lun (Taipei: K'ai-ming shu-tien, 1966), pp. 45-48. See also Jonathan Chaves, "The Tz'u Poetry of Wen T'ing-yün," M.A. thesis, Columbia University 1966, pp. 25-32.

46 This is based on the research done by Jen Erh-pei. Jen discovered that at least 74 songs out of the 500 and more Tun-huang songs belong to the yen ku-shih category. (See Tun-huang ch'ü ch'u-t'an, p. 303).

47 Ibid., pp. 16, 273, 297-309, 323. According to Jen Erh-pei the Feng kuei yün series (#003-004) was the earliest "dramatic" song-set in Chinese literature (p. 462).

48 Ibid., p. 348.

49 For the definition and types of "verbs of thought," see Yuen Ren Chao, A Grammar of Spoken Chinese (Berkeley: Univ. of California Press, 1968), p. 110.

50 Yu-kung Kao and Tsu-lin Mei, "Ending Lines in Wang Shih-chen's Ch'i-chüeh: Convention and Creativity in the Ch'ing," in Artists and Traditions, ed. Christian F. Murck (Princeton: Princeton Univ. Press, 1976), pp. 131-135.

51 The tune used by Po Chü-i is called I chiang-nan, which is also known as Wang chiang-nan, Wang chiang-mei, Meng chiang-nan, etc.

[52] Chou Fa-kao, _Chung-kuo ku-tai yü-fa: tsao-chü pien_ (rpt. Taipei: Chung-yang yen-chiu-yüan li-shih yü-yen yen-chiu so, 1972), pp. 22-54. See also Yuen Ren Chao, pp. 501-502.

[53] Statistically _Yang-liu chih_ (39 songs), _Chu-chih_ (27 songs) and _Lang t'ao sha_ (17 songs) were the three most popular tunes among the early literati _tz'u_ poets.

[54] Generally the most effective device for evoking overtones in _chüeh-chü_ poetry, according to traditional critics, is to bring a poem to its closure with an image of a scene which immediately follows an introspective expression. Contrary to this practice is another popular device which uses interrogatives, hypothetical statements, rhetorical questions, and negatives in the final couplets. These two devices seem to go in opposite directions, but they share the common purpose of creating overtones.

[55] Ch'en Chung-fan, _Chung-kuo yün-wen t'ung-lun_ (Taipei: Chung-hua shu-chü, 1959), p. 194.

[56] Chang Yen, _Tz'u yüan_, in _Tz'u-hsüeh yen-chiu_, ed. Lo Fang-chou, 2nd ed. (Shanghai: Chiao-yü shu-tien, 1947), p. 25.

[57] _Ibid._, p. 29.

[58] See Shen I-fu, _Yüeh-fu chih-mi_, in _Tz'u-hsüeh yen-chiu_, ed. Lo Fang-chou, p. 39. Shen holds that "the final couplet in _tz'u_ must be closed so as to suggest overtones" and that "to use a sensory image of the scene to conclude an expression of inner feelings is the best device of all." See also Li Yü (1611-1680), _K'uei tz'u kuan-chien_, in THTP, II, 545-561. Li claims that the merit of a _tz'u_ lies in the power of its ending lines which, like "the last bewitching look of a

beautiful woman," will "without fail make one lose all self-consciousness." Wang Kuo-wei's famous theory of the "poetic world" (ching-chieh) in tz'u apparently refers to the hsiao-ling poetry rather than to the longer man-tz'u, as the shorter hsiao-ling is more preoccupied with the purpose of evoking lingering associations beyond words.

59 Hsia Ch'eng-t'ao and Wu Hsiung-ho, Tu tz'u ch'ang-shih (Peking: Chung-hua shu-chü, 1962), p. 55.

60 See chüan 81 and 82 of Yüeh-fu shih-chi, in Ssu-pu ts'ung-k'an ch'u-pien so-pen (Taipei: Commercial Press, 1967), Vol. 104, pp. 555-567. These tz'u poems were set to such tunes as Yang-liu chih, Chu-chih, Ch'ing-p'ing tiao, Hui-p'o yüeh, Lang t'ao sha, P'ao-ch'iu lo, Ho-na ch'ü, Kung-chung t'iao-hsiao.

61 See Wang Li, p. 518. To be a little more flexible, Wang Li defines hsiao-ling as a tz'u poem which does not exceed 62 characters.

62 Critics such as the Ch'ing scholar Chin Sheng-t'an attempted to treat the lü-shih poem as having two structural units. Such a method of reading, however, does not correspond to the general structure of lü-shih poetry.

63 A statement made by Chang Ti-chung, as quoted in Hsieh Wu-liang, Tz'u-hsüeh chih-nan (Taipei: Chung-hua shu-chü, 1959), p. 29.

II. Wen T'ing-yün and Wei Chuang: Toward a Formation of Conventions

1 A legend has it that Liu An, the Lord of Southern Huai in the Han Dynasty, successfully achieved immortality and that when he

ascended to heaven his chickens and dogs followed him.

2 Emperor Yang of the Sui Dynasty (581-618) was strangled to death by rebels led by the Toba of the Yü-wen family when he established his government later in the south. This allusion, as well as the one about the Lord of Huai, is to suggest the illusoriness of the human world.

3 Wu-ling ("five tombs") refers to the tombs of Han emperors in Ch'ang-an. In poetry the term is often associated with rich and handsome young men from that area.

4 Wu Chi (literally "no restraint") alludes to a historical figure, the so-called "Hsin-ling Lord" in the Wei Dynasty (220- 264). Mo Ch'ou (literally "no sorrow") was a famous singer in the T'ang Dynasty. The two names here refer to those rich youths and beautiful maidens who visited the Wu-ling area.

5 For this interpretation, see Chan An-t'ai, "Wen *tz'u* kuan-k'uei," in *I-lin ts'ung-lu* (Hong Kong: Commercial Press, 1961-1966), IV, 95-103.

6 See Wayne C. Booth's distinction between the art of "showing" and that of "telling" in *The Rhetoric of Fiction* (Chicago: Univ. of Chicago Press, 1961), pp. 3-20.

7 For "deictic categories," see John Lyons, *Introduction to theoretical Linguistics* (Cambridge: Cambridge Univ. Press, 1968), pp. 275-281.

8 The "Hsieh family" is a euphemism for the brothel.

9 *Mimesis*, trans. Willard R. Trask (Princeton: Princeton Univ. Press, 1953).

10 See Lun tz'u tsa-chu, in Tz'u-hsüeh yen-chiu, ed. Lo Fang-chou, p. 96.

11 In his Tu tz'u ou-te (Taipei: K'ai-ming shu-tien, 1957), p. 14.

12 Chia-ling t'an tz'u (Taipei: Ch'un-wen-hsüeh ch'u-pan-she, 1970), p. 48.

13 The Jade Pass is a gate on the Great Wall in Kansu Province, but here it is taken to mean the frontier.

14 Feeling and Form (New York: Charles Scribner's Sons, 1953), p. 228, Note 22.

15 Poetic Closure (Chicago: Univ. of Chicago Press, 1968), p. 137.

16 The oriole here may be a metaphor for the lady.

17 The embankment, named after the Prince of Wei, Ts'ao Chih (192-232), was a famous scenic area in Lo-yang.

18 Aoyama Hiroshi, "Kakan shū no shi, 2--I Sō no shi ," Kangaku kenkyū, 9 (1972), 23, Note 23. See also Yeh Chia-ying, Chia-ling t'an tz'u, pp. 69-91.

19 Miao Yüeh, p. 67.

20 See, for instance, Poems # 098, #133, #202, #203 in Chang Ts'ui-pao, "Wen T'ing-yün shih-chi yen chu," M.A. thesis, National Taiwan Normal Univ. 1975.

21 The "mound at Tu" (Tu-ling) refers to the grave of the Han Emperor Hsüan-ti (1st century B.C.), situated in an area near Ch'ang-an.

22 See also Yu-kung Kao and Tsu-lin Mei, "Syntax, Diction and Imagery in T'ang Poetry," Harvard Journal of Asiatic Studies, 31 (1970), p. 57 et passim.

23 In Wei Tuan-chi shih chiao-chu, annotated by Chiang Ts'ung-p'ing (Taipei: Chung-hua shu-chü, 1969), p. 272.

24 Although it should be noted that the two narrative poems entitled Pei-fen shih by the Han poetess Ts'ai Yen do reveal an interest in historicity (CHSK, I, 51-52).

III. Li Yü and the Full Flowering of the Hsiao-ling Form

1 Except for Liang (907-923) and Chou (951-960) all the dynasties during this period (which lasted from 923 to 950) were ruled by non-Chinese.

2 Except for the two T'ang poets, Wen T'ing-yün and Huang-fu Sung, and the four Five-Dynasties poets Wei Chuang, Chang Mi, Ho Ning, and Sun Kuang-hsien, all the authors included in the anthology were born in the Shu area. Among those poets who were not born in Shu, Ho Ning was the only one who had no connection with the Shu culture.

3 Wang Kuo-wei, Jen-chien tz'u-hua, in THTP, XII, 4245.

4 Of course, according to M. H. Abrams, a lyric persona has to adapt himself to "the particular lyric situation and effect," so his lyric expression is "artistically ordered into a whole which is independent of outside biographical information" ("Lyric," A Glossary of Literary Terms, 3rd ed., New York: Holt, Rinehart and Winston, 1971). However, we are now comparing the two kinds of poetic voice--the one which seems objective, and the other which is more "personal" even to the extent of being autobiographical.

5 18 of his lü-shih poems are extant. See Nan-T'ang erh-chu shih-

tz'u, ed. Ho Yang-ling (Shanghai: Kuang-hua shu-chü, 1930), pp. 47-53.

6 See, for example, Liu Tzu-keng, p. 36, and Yeh Chia-ying, Chia-ling t'an tz'u, p. 119.

7 Wang Kuo-wei, Jen-chien tz'u-hua, in THTP, XII, 4246.

8 Miao Yüeh, p. 13.

9 These few lines from Li Yü's P'o-chen tzu were criticized by the Sung poet Su Shih for a lack of concern about public affairs (SHTK, II, 1124).

10 Yeh Chia-ying, Chia-ling t'an tz'u, p. 130.

11 The Prose Works of William Wordsworth, ed. W. J. B. Owen and Jane Worthington Smyser (Oxford: Clarendon, 1974), I, 126. I owe this particular point to Stuart Curran's paper, "The Reformation of Genres in the Romantic Period," Princeton Conference on Genre and Its Problems, April 30-May 1, 1976.

12 The Concept of Expression (Princeton: Princeton Univ. Press, 1971), p. 97.

13 Ibid., p. 11.

14 In ancient China women used to wash clothes by pounding them with a mallet.

15 Auerbach, pp. 75, 101.

16 Liu Ta-chieh, Chung-kuo wen-hsüeh fa-chan shih, II (Shanghai: Chung-hua shu-chü, 1962), 189.

17 Leo Spitzer, Linguistics and Literary History (Princeton: Princeton Univ. Press, 1948), p. 181.

18 These poets include Mao Wen-hsi, Li Hsün, Ku Hsiung, Lu Ch'ien-i, Yen Hsüan, and Sun Kuang-hsien.

[19] The "Hai-men" ("the door to the sea") County, located in Kiangsu Province, is actually a sandy islet. Since Yuan and Ming times this piece of land has been continually sinking into the sea.

[20] The Wu Garden (Wu-yüan) is located in the Wu County of Kiangsu Province. "Kuangling" is the name of an old county, situated near today's Kiangtu County of Kiangsu Province.

[21] The original line reads literally," We four brothers and the three hundred family members."

[22] Tormey, pp. 64-66.

[23] Ibid., p. 67.

[24] See Ou-yang Hsiu's lines: "The sorrow of separation becomes deeper as you go / Extending far and endlessly like spring waters" (T'a so hsing, CST, I, 123). See also Ch'in Kuan's lines: "I lean on the high tower, my sorrow like the spring grass / So dense, you cut it and yet it grows back" (Pa-liu tzu, CST, I, 456).

[25] A frontier outpost in Shensi Province.

[26] Chiang Shang-hsien, T'ang Sung ming-chia tz'u hsin hsüan, p. 87. For variant readings of this poem, see CTS, XII, 10158 and CTWT, I, 238.

[27] Li Ching, Li Yü tz'u, ed. Chan An-t'ai, p. 25. See also variant readings of this poem in CTWT, I, 225-226 and CTS, XII, 10044.

[28] See "Li Yü ho t'a ti tz'u," in T'ang Sung tz'u yen-chiu lun-wen chi, ed., Chung-kuo yü-wen hsüeh-she (Peking: n.p., 1969), p. 25.

[29] In the original Chinese text "painted screens" reads as "little hills." According to most tz'u scholars, "little hills" is an allusion to landscape screens, as it signifies either the hills painted on the

screen or the hill-like screens. There are other interpretations of this line which are equally plausible--for example, in his "The *Tz'u* Poetry of Wen T'ing-yün," Jonathan Chaves believes that this line refers to a particular hairstyle when the hair is "piled up and coifed with gold."

[30] See Li Yü (1611-1680), *K'uei tz'u kuan-chien*, in THTP, II, 548.

[31] The original line reads "locked in the P'eng-lai garden, a T'ien-t'ai woman." Both P'eng-lai and T'ien-t'ai are mountains where fairies reside.

[32] "Rain and Clouds" (line 5) is a famous allusion in Chinese literature which refers specifically to sexual intercourse. The phrase originated in Sung Yü's *Kao T'ang fu* where the King of Ch'u dreamt that he made love to a fairy who assumed the form of a cloud at sunrise and turned into rain at night. For line 6 I have followed a more popular reading than the one offered by CTWT where it reads, "As soon as we met, we expressed our innermost feelings."

IV. Liu Yung and the Formation of the *Man-tz'u* Form

[1] T'ang Kuei-chang and Chin Ch'i-hua, "Lun Liu Yung ti *tz'u*," in *T'ang Sung tz'u yen-chiu lun-wen chi*, pp. 70-79.

[2] For example, both Liu Ta-chieh and Lung Mu-hsün hold this view. See Liu's *Chung-kuo wen-hsüeh fa-chan shih*, II, 602, and Lung's "Liang-Sung *tz'u*-feng chuan-pien lun," in *Tz'u-hsüeh chi-k'an* (1933-1936; rpt. Taipei: Hsüeh-sheng shu-chü, 1967), II, 1-23.

[3] Feng Ch'i-yung, "Lun pei-Sung ch'ien-ch'i liang-chung pu-t'ung ti tz'u-feng," in _T'ang Sung tz'u yen-chiu lun-wen chi_, pp. 43-69.

[4] The great impact of Feng Yen-ssu on the Northern Sung _hsiao-ling_ poets was sufficiently observed by traditional critics. See, for instance, Liu Hsi-tsai's statement: "As for the _tz'u_ poetry of Feng Yen-ssu, Yen T'ung-shu [Yen Shu] has received its elegance, and Ou-yang Yung-shu [Ou-yang Hsiu] has inherited its profundity" (_Tz'u kai_, in THTP, XI, 3770).

[5] Jen Erh-pei, _Tun-huang ch'ü ch'u-t'an_, p. 222. For the examples of _man-tz'u_ poems in the _Yün-yao chi_, see Appendix.

[6] See also James J. Y. Liu, _Major Lyricists of the Northern Sung_, p. 98.

[7] As cited in Wang Li, p. 528.

[8] These major cities were K'ai-feng, Soochow, K'uai-chi, and Ch'ang-an.

[9] See Lo Ta-ching, _Ho-lin yü-lu_, as cited in Hu Yün-i, _Sung tz'u hsüan_ (Shanghai: Chung-hua shu-chü, 1965), p. 42.

[10] See Chapter I, Note 61.

[11] Mao Hsien-shu, _T'ien-tz'u ming-chieh_, rpt. in _Tz'u-hsüeh ch'üan-shu_, ed. Cha P'ei-chi (Taipei: Kuang-wen shu-chü, 1971). Traditional scholars seem to agree that there are two intermediate forms between _hsiao-ling_ and _man-tz'u_, the so-called _yin_ and _chin_. Yet both Wang Li and Hsia Ch'eng-t'ao believe that _yin_ does not necessarily designate a greater length than the _hsiao-ling_. (See Wang Li, p. 526; Hsia Ch'eng-t'ao and Wu Hsiung-ho, pp. 33-34). But most of the extant _tz'u_

poems written in the chin form are indeed longer than hsiao-ling and thus may be properly called the "medium-length tune" (chung-tiao). What is significant about the terms yin and chin is that they did not appear until the Sung. Such terms, as well as the word man-tz'u, might have been merely used to designate those new musical forms invented in early Sung times.

12 In "Fa-fan," [So-yin pen] tz'u-lü, p. 1. Also cited in Wang Li, p. 518.

13 Wang Li, pp. 518-534.

14 The Transformation of the Chinese Lyrical Tradition (Princeton: Princeton Univ. Press, 1978), pp. 106-107.

15 Although the rule is that the ending line of a strophe must coincide with the rhyme, other lines in the same strophe may also end in rhyme without suggesting a syntactic conclusion.

16 See Shuen-fu Lin, p.128.

17 These are Chu-ying yao hung (96 characters), An kung tzu (102 characters), Kuei-ch'ao huan (104 characters).

18 Hua man lu, as cited in T'ang Kuei-chang and Chin Ch'i-hua, p. 258.

19 See Tsui-weng ch'in-ch'ü wai-p'ien. These tz'u poems were considered by traditional critics to be forgeries made by the poet's political enemies to belittle his name, but many modern scholars have tried to prove the authenticity of the authorship. For the controversy of this issue, see James J. Y. Liu, Major Lyricists of the Northern Sung, pp. 48-49; and James T. C. Liu, Ou-yang Hsiu (Stanford: Stanford Univ. Press, 1967, p. 137.

[20] The "paper and pen" in the original line refers to the colorful paper produced in Szechwan Province and brush-holders made of ivory.

[21] In Yüan jen tsa-chü ch'üan-chi, ed. Lu Ch'ien (Lu Chi-yeh) (Shanghai: Shanghai tsa-chih kung-ssu, 1936), I, 29-58.

[22] See Lo Yeh, "Hua-ch'ü shih-lu," in Tsui-weng t'an-lu (rpt. Shanghai: Ku-tien wen-hsüeh ch'u-pan-she, 1957), pp. 31-35; Hung P'ien, "Liu Ch'i-ch'ing shih-chiu wan chiang-lou chi," in Ch'ing-p'ing shan-t'ang hua-pen (rpt. Shanghai: Ku-tien wen-hsüeh ch'u-pan-she, 1957), pp. 1-5; Feng Meng-lung, "Chung ming-chi ch'un-feng tiao Liu Ch'i," in Yü-shih ming-yen (rpt. Hong Kong: Chung-hua shu-chü, 1965), pp. 176-186.

[23] Major Lyricists of the Northern Sung, p. 53.

[24] Pi-shu lu-hua, rpt. in Ts'ung-shu chi-ch'eng chien-pien (Taipei: Commercial Press, 1966), Vol. 717, p. 49.

[25] Li Ch'ing-chao, "Tz'u lun," in Hu Tzu, T'iao-hsi yü-yin ts'ung-hua (rpt. Taipei: Shih-chieh shu-chü, 1966), II, 666.

[26] Pi-chi man-chih, in THTP, I, 34.

[27] Yüeh-fu chih-mi, in Tz'u-hsüeh yen-chiu, p. 38.

[28] T'ang Kuei-chang and Chin Ch'i-hua, p. 258.

[29] The later Liu Yung held official positions in Lo-yang, Yü-hang, Ting-hai, etc., and visited such cities as Ch'ang-an, Ch'eng-tu, Yang-chow, Chien-ning, Ku-su. He was finally buried in Jun-chou, Kiangsu.

[30] Hui-feng tz'u-hua, ed. Wang Yu-an, printed with Jen-chien tz'u-hua (Hong Kong: Commercial Press, 1961), p. 61.

[31] The Three Wu usually alludes to the three cities, Soochow, Ch'ang-chou, and Hu-chou.

[32] Jen Erh-pei, Tun-huang ch'ü ch'u-t'an, p. 396. Jen explains

that Tun-huang songs resemble the Chin and Yüan Northern _ch'ü_ in terms of overall poetic style, as distinguished from the later Southern _ch'ü_ (_nan-ch'ü_) which seemed to carry on the literati _tz'u_ tradition.

33 Liu Yung's family always belonged to the class of scholar-official, and not to that of the common people. For example, his father Liu I served in the government of the Southern T'ang and was respected by the monarch and poet Li Yü. See Winnie Lai-fong Leung,"Liu Yung and His _Tz'u_," M.A. thesis, University of British Columbia 1976, p. 6.

34 They are _Ting feng-po_, _P'o-lo men_, _Ch'ang hsiang-ssu_, _Wang yüan hsing_, _Shih-erh shih_.

35 Jen Erh-pei, _Tun-huang ch'ü ch'u-t'an_, p. 389.

36 These scholars include Wang Kuo-wei, Yü P'ing-po (see discussion in Jen Erh-pei, _Tun-huang ch'ü ch'u-t'an_, pp. 83-84), Hu Yün-i (_Chung-kuo tz'u-shih_, p. 117) and Wang Li (_Han-yü shih-lü hsüeh_, p. 578).

37 Lu Fu-chih, "_Tz'u_ chih," in THTP, I, 14. Lu lists 33 kinds of one-character _ling-tzu_.

38 These two-character and three-character _ling-tzu_ are taken from Chang Yen, _Tz'u yüan_, in _Tz'u-hsüeh yen-chiu_, ed. Lo Fang-chou, pp. 12-13.

39 See Wang Li, p. 659, and James J. Y. Liu, _Major Lyricists of the Northern Sung_, p. 97.

40 Wang Cho, _Pi-chi man-chih_, in THTP, I, 34.

41 See Chou Chi, comp., _Sung ssu-chia tz'u-hsüan_ [_chien-chu_], annotated by K'uang Shih-yüan (Taipei: Chung-hua shu-chü, 1971), p. 72.

42 Wang Ch'in-hsi, "Sung-*tz'u* shang ch'ü sheng tzu yü chü-ch'ü kuan-hsi chi ssu-sheng t'i k'ao-cheng," in *Wen shih*, ed. Hsin chien-she pien-chi-pu, II (Peking: Chung-hua shu-chü, 1963), 157-159.

43 See Shen I-fu, *Yüeh-fu chih-mi*, in *Tz'u-hsüeh yen-chiu*, ed. Lo Fang-chou, p. 42; Hsia Ch'eng-t'ao and Wu Hsiung-ho, *Tu tz'u ch'ang-shih*, pp. 59-60.

44 Hu Tzu, *T'iao-hsi yü-yin ts'ung-hua* (rpt. Taipei: Shih-chieh shu-chü, 1966), II, 733.

45 Liu T'i-jen, *Ch'i-sung-t'ang tz'u-i*, in THTP, II, 627.

46 Chang Yen, *Tz'u yüan*, in *Tz'u-hsüeh yen-chiu*, ed. Lo Fang-chou, p. 9.

47 Both "Ch'in tower" and "Ch'u house" are euphemisms for brothels. The "colorful phoenix" and the "morning cloud" refer to the courtesans living in the brothels.

48 There was a custom for fishermen to beat their boats with long sticks to produce sounds so that the fish would be startled and caught in the nets.

49 Ralph Freedman, *The Lyrical Novel* (Princeton: Princeton Univ. Press, 1963), p. 21.

50 *Ibid.*, pp. 26, 21.

51 The River Pass is situated between Ching-men Mountain (South of Yangtze) and Hu-ya Mountain (North of Yangtze) of Hupei Province. This section of Yangtze River is considered to be hazardous.

52 In *Ta-ho shan-jen tz'u-lun*, as cited in Chu Tsu-mou, comp., *Sung-tz'u san-pai-shou chien-chu*, annotated by T'ang Kuei-chang (Hong Kong: Chung-hua shu-chü, 1961), p. 29.

[53] Wang I-ch'ing, et al., [Yü-chih] tz'u-p'u (rpt. Taipei: privately printed, 1964), p. 311.

[54] Ibid., p. 631.

[55] Wan Shu, p. 230.

[56] Ibid., p. 252.

[57] Hsia Ching-kuan, "P'ing Chang Tzu-yeh tz'u," as cited in Lung Mu-hsün, ed., T'ang Sung ming-chia tz'u-hsüan (Shanghai: Ku-tien wen-hsüeh ch'u-pan-she, 1956), p. 57.

[58] Hu Yün-i, Chung-kuo tz'u-shih, p. 130.

V. Su Shih and the Elevation of the Tz'u Genre

[1] Tz'u kai, in THTP, XI, 3771.

[2] As quoted in "Preface," Tung-p'o tz'u, ed. Ts'ao Shu-ming (Hong Kong, 1968; rpt. Taipei: Hua-cheng shu-chü, 1975), p. 22.

[3] Hu Tzu, II, 66.

[4] Kong Yun Fun, Tz'u-hsüeh p'ing-lun shih-kao (Hong Kong: Lung Men Bookstore, 1966), p. 18.

[5] Of course, he did compose a few tz'u tunes with the help of musicians, as in the case of Shao p'ien and Tsui-weng ts'ao.

[6] Tung-p'o (meaning "eastern slope") was the style of Su Shih. The name was acquired sometime during his exile in Hangchow (1080 A.D.-1083 A.D.).

[7] See, for example, Chiang-ch'eng tzu (#7, CST, I, 299), Shao p'ien (CST, I, 307), Man-t'ing fang (#1, CST, I, 278).

[8] Tseng-ch'eng may refer to the so-called Black Stone Hill (Wu-

shih shan) upon which the Fallen Star Temple (Lo-hsing ssu) is built or to the temple itself. However, many critics believe that it is the name of a mountain near Hsieh Brook.

[9] This, along with the previous lines, alludes to a famous poem by T'ao Ch'ien entitled "An Outing on Hsieh Brook." In his preface to the poem, T'ao Ch'ien writes: "Facing the long river, I gazed upon the Tseng-ch'eng Hill." See also James Robert Hightower, The Poetry of T'ao Ch'ien (Oxford: Clarendon Press, 1970), pp. 56-58.

[10] See Nan-ko tzu (#2, CST, I, 292), Lin-chiang hsien (#11, CST, I, 287), Hao-shih chin (#2, CST, I, 294).

[11] Shuen-fu Lin, p. 87.

[12] See Yu-kung Kao and Tzu-lin Mei, "Meaning, Metaphor, and Allusion in T'ang Poetry," draft, to be published, p. 61.

[13] Ibid.

[14] Chou Yü (175-210), the famous general of the Wu Kingdom, defeated Ts'ao Ts'ao by fire at Red Cliff. Yet there are three places in today's Hupeh Province which are all called Red Cliff. It was suggested that the one visited by the poet was not where the Red Cliff Battle was fought.

[15] Ch'en Shih-tao, Hou-shan shih-hua, in SHTK, I, 91-92.

[16] Miao Yüeh, pp. 1-15. For a stylistic distinction between T'ang and Sung poetry, see Kōjirō Yoshikawa, An Introduction to Sung Poetry, trans. Burton Watson (Cambridge: Harvard Univ. Press, 1967), pp. 28-35.

[17] P'u-sa man (#1, CST, I, 303), Chien-tzu mu-lan hua (#2, #6, #7, CST, I, 322-323), T'i-jen chiao (#1, CST, I, 308), Che-ku t'ien (#2, CST, I, 288), Lin-chiang hsien (#12, CST, I, 287).

[18] For a more detailed discussion of this poem, see Section 3 of this chapter.

[19] The P'eng-tsu Tower, in today's Hsü-chou, was built as a homage to the legendary official of the Shang, P'eng-tsu, who was supposed to have lived for 800 years.

[20] The Racing-horse Platform (*hsi-ma t'ai*), said to be built by Hsiang Yü, is located in the south of P'eng City in Kiangsu Province.

[21] This refers to the founder of the Han Dynasty, Liu Pang.

[22] Like the ancient ruler Shun (ca. 2200 B.C.), Hsiang Yü was alleged to have eyes with double pupils.

[23] The White Gate alludes to Chien-k'ang (i.e., today's Nanking). Lü Pu, a general in the later Han, was defeated by Ts'ao Ts'ao and beheaded near this place.

[24] The "Great Star" refers to a T'ang general, Li Kuang-pi (708-764), who was installed as the Lord of Lin-huai in An-hui Province.

[25] i.e., Liu Yü, the Sung Wu-ti (Emperor Wu) during the Southern Dynasties period.

[26] One is an adaptation of Tu Mu's 7-character *lü-shih* (in *Tung-p'o tz'u*, ed. Ts'ao Shu-ming, #263), and the other an adaptation of his own *lü-shih* poem entitled "Red Plum" (STP, I, 180).

[27] The "old poet" refers to Shih Yen-nien (994-1041) who once wrote a poem on red plums.

[28] The former category includes poems to such tunes as *Lin-chiang hsien*, *P'u-sa man*, and *Nan-ko tzu*, and the latter category to such tunes as *Shui-lung yin*, *Shao p'ien*, *Nien-nu chiao*, *Man-chiang hung*, *Ch'i shih*, *Tsui P'eng-lai*.

[29] See Frankel, _The Flowering Plum and the Palace Lady_, p. 212.

[30] Hung Wei-fa, _Chüeh-chü lun_ (Shanghai: Commercial Press, 1934), p. 39.

[31] _Ibid._, p. 40.

[32] Hsü-chou is in Kiangsu Province, famous for its strategic position.

[33] In today's Kiangsu Province.

[34] For variant readings of lines 15-17, see James J. Y. Liu, _Major Lyricists of the Northern Sung_, pp. 143-144.

[35] Su Shih stayed overnight in the Swallow Tower in Hsü-chou where he dreamt of the ancient beauty P'an-p'an, the favorite concubine of a T'ang general Chang Chien. The tower belonged to Chang Chien, and P'an-p'an lived there alone even after Chang's death.

[36] e.g., _Shui-lung yin_ (#3, CST, I, 277), _Hsi-chiang yüeh_ (#10, CST, I, 284), _Ting feng-po_ (#7, CST, I, 289), _Nan-hsiang tzu_ (#11, CST, 291), _Ho-hua mei_ (CST, I, 319), _Tien chiang ch'un_ (#1, CST, I, 324), _Chiang-ch'eng tzu_ (#3, CST, I, 299), _Ho hsin-lang_ (CST, I, 297).

[37] See _Ho sheng-ch'ao_ by an earlier poet, Yeh Ch'ing-ch'en (1003-1049), in CST, I, 119.

[38] The Hu-tzu area may be in today's Hopeh Province.

[39] Chü-yeh Lake was an ancient lake in Shantung Province.

[40] The 4th century writer and calligrapher Wang Hsi-chih wrote his famous "Preface to Orchid Pavilion" at a drinking party in the Orchid Pavilion (in Chekiang Province) which he held on the third day of the third month in A.D. 353. Later it became a convention for

Chinese literati to hold similar drinking parties at some scenic spot on the same date each year, supposedly to exorcise evil influence.

[41] Yang Yü-huan (719-756) was a favorite concubine of the T'ang Emperor Hsüan-tsung, and Chao Fei-yen a favorite concubine of the Han Emperor Ch'eng (Ch'eng-ti). Both women were noted for their beauty.

[42] Hans H. Frankel, "Yüeh-fu Poetry," in Studies in Chinese Literary Genres, ed. Cyril Birch (Berkeley: Univ. of California Press, 1974), p. 82. For Su Shih's Ancient Style poems which use this device, see Su Shih shih-hsüan, ed. Ch'en Erh-tung (Peking: Jen-min wen-hsüeh ch'u-pan-she, 1957), pp. 98, 154, 169, 189, 212, 245.

[43] These poets include Hsin Ch'i-chi and Liu K'o-chuang. See also Wang Li, p. 663.

[44] An ancient name for the T'ai Lake which lies across Kiangsu and Chekiang Provinces.

[45] In Szechwan Province.

[46] See Kong Yun Fun, Tz'u-hsüeh p'ing-lun shih-kao, p. 20.

[47] The poem was written during the Hangchow years, possibly in 1074.

[48] Langer, pp. 208-235.

[49] Ibid., p. 212.

[50] Ibid., p. 219.

[51] Ibid.

[52] For the style of Wu's tz'u poetry, see Chia-ying Yeh Chao (Yeh Chia-ying), "Wu Wen-ying's Tz'u, " in Studies in Chinese Literary Genres, ed. Cyril Birch, pp. 154-191. For a detailed discussion of Chiang K'uei and Southern Sung tz'u poetry, see Shuen-fu Lin's book.

[53] James J. Y. Liu, *Major Lyricists of the Northern Sung*, p. 190.

A Selected Bibliography

Abbreviations

CHSK — *Ch'üan Han San-kuo Chin Nan-pei-ch'ao shih* 全漢三國晉南北朝詩. Ed. Ting Fu-pao 丁福保. 3 vols. Taipei: Shih-chieh shu-chü, 1969.

CST — *Ch'üan Sung-tz'u* 全宋詞. Ed. T'ang Kuei-chang 唐圭璋. 5 vols. Peking: Chung-hua shu-chü, 1965.

CTS — *Ch'üan T'ang-shih* 全唐詩. Ed. P'eng Ting-ch'iu 彭定求 (1645-1719), et al. 1907; rpt. in 12 vols. Peking: Chung-hua shu-chü, 1960.

CTWT — *Ch'üan T'ang Wu-tai tz'u hui-pien* 全唐五代詞彙編. Ed. Yang Chia-lo 楊家駱. 2 vols. Taipei: Shih-chieh shu-chü, 1967.

SHTK — *Shih-hua ts'ung-k'an* 詩話叢刊 (original title: *Keisetsuken sōsho* 螢雪軒叢書). Ed. Kondō Gensui 近藤元粋. 2 vols. 1892; rpt. Taipei: Hung-tao wen-hua shih-yeh yu-hsien kung-ssu 弘道文化事業有限公司, 1971.

STP — *Su Tung-p'o ch'üan-chi* 蘇東坡全集. 2 vols. Taipei: Shih-chieh shu-chü, 1974.

THC — *Tun-huang ch'ü chiao-lu* 敦煌曲校錄. Ed. Jen Erh-pei 任二北. Shanghai: Wen-i lien-ho ch'u-pan-she, 1955.

THTP Tz'u-hua ts'ung-pien 詞話叢編. Ed. T'ang Kuei-chang 唐圭璋. 1935; rpt. Taipei: Kuang-wen shu-chü, 1967.

Aoki Masaru 青木正兒. "Shikaku no chōtanku no hattatsu no gen'in ni tsuite" 詞格の長短句の發達の原因に就て. Shina bungei ronsō 支那文藝論藪. Tokyo, 1923, pp. 67-85.

Aoyama Hiroshi 青山宏. "Kakan shū no shi, 2 -- I Sō no shi" 花間集の詞(2) -- 韋莊の詞. Kangaku kenkyū 漢學研究, 9 (1972), 15-30.

__________. "Kakan shū no shi, 1 -- On Teiin no shi" 花間集の詞(1) -- 温庭筠の詞. Nihon Daigaku Jimbun Kagaku Kenkyūjo kenkyū kiyō 日本大學人文科學研究所研究紀要, 12. Rpt. in Chūgoku kankei ronsetsu shiryō 中国関係論說資料, 13, Pt. 2-2 (1971), 249-256.

__________. "Kakan shū no shi, 4 --Kakan shū shi no keishiki ni tsuite" 花間集の詞(4) -- 花間集詞の形式について. Nihon Daigaku Jimbun Kagaku Kenkyūjo kenkyū kiyō 日本大學人文科學研究所研究紀要, 16. Rpt. in Chūgoku kankei ronsetsu shiryō 中国関係論說資料, 16, Pt. 2-2 (1974), 292-301.

Auerbach, Erich. Mimesis: The Representation of Reality in Western Literature. Trans. Willard R. Trask. Princeton: Princeton Univ. Press, 1953.

Ayling, Alan and Duncan Mackintosh. A Collection of Chinese Lyrics. London: Routledge and Kegan Paul, 1965.

__________. A Further Collection of Chinese Lyrics. London: Routledge

and Kegan Paul, 1969.

Bate, Walter Jackson, ed. *Criticism: the Major Texts*. Enl. ed. New York: Harcourt Brace Jovanovich, 1970.

Baxter, Glen W. *Index to the Imperial Register of Tz'u Prosody* (*Ch'in-ting tz'u-p'u*). Harvard-Yenching Institute Studies, XV. Cambridge: Harvard Univ. Press, 1956.

__________. "Metrical Origin of the *Tz'u*." In *Studies in Chinese Literature*. Ed. John L. Bishop. Cambridge: Harvard Univ. Press, 1966, pp. 186-225.

Birch, Cyril, ed. *Studies in Chinese Literary Genres*. Berkeley: Univ. of California Press, 1974.

Booth, Wayne C. *The Rhetoric of Fiction*. Chicago: Univ. of Chicago Press, 1961.

Chafe, Wallace L. *Meaning and the Structure of Language*. Chicago: Univ. of Chicago Press, 1970.

Chan An-t'ai 詹安泰. "T'an Liu Yung ti *Yü lin ling*" 談柳永的雨霖鈴. *Yü-wen hsüeh-hsi* 語文學習, No. 67 (1957), 1-4.

__________. "Wen *tz'u* kuan-k'uei" 溫詞管窺. In *I-lin ts'ung-lu* 藝林叢錄. Hong Kong: Commercial Press, 1961-1966, IV, 95-103.

Chang Ching-wen 張敬文. *T'ang Sung shih-tz'u yen-chiu* 唐宋詩詞研究. Taipei: Commercial Press, 1968.

Chang Chung-chiang 張忠江. *Chi-nü yü wen-hsüeh* 妓女與文學. Taipei: K'ang-nai-hsin ch'u-pan-she, 1969.

Chang Hui-yen 張惠言 (1761-1802), comp., *Tz'u hsüan* [*chien-chu*] 詞選[箋注]. Annotated by Chiang Liang-fu 姜亮夫.

Shanghai: Pei-hsin shu-chü, 1933.

Chang Shih-lu 張世祿. *Chung-kuo wen-i pien-ch'ien lun* 中國文藝變遷論. Shanghai: Commercial Press, 1934.

Chang Ts'ui-pao 張翠寶. "Wen T'ing-yün shih-chi yen chu" 温庭筠詩集研註. M.A. thesis. National Taiwan Normal Univ. 1975.

Chang Wan 張琬 (pseud.). "*P'u-sa man* chi ch'i hsiang-kuan chih chu wen-t'i" 菩薩蠻及其相關之諸問題. *Ta-lu tsa-chih* 大陸雜誌, 20, No. 1 (1960), 19-24; 20, No. 2 (1960), 15-17; 20, No. 3 (1960), 27-32.

Chao Ch'ung-tso 趙崇祚 (fl. 934-965), comp. *Hua-chien chi* [*chiao*] 花間集[校]. Collated by Li I-mang 李一氓. Hong Kong: Commercial Press, 1960.

Chao, Yüan Ren. *A Grammar of Spoken Chinese*. Berkeley: Univ. of California Press, 1968.

Chaves, Jonathan. *Mei Yao-ch'en and the Development of Early Sung Poetry*. New York: Columbia Univ. Press, 1976.

__________. "The *Tz'u* Poetry of Wen T'ing-yün." M.A. thesis. Columbia Univ. 1966.

Ch'en Chung-fan 陳鐘凡. *Chung-kuo yün-wen t'ung-lun* 中國韻文通論. Taipei: Chung-hua shu-chü, 1959.

Ch'en, Shih-ch'üan. "The Rise of the *Tz'u*, Reconsidered." *Journal of American Oriental Society*, 90, No. 2 (1970), 232-242.

Cheng Chen-to 鄭振鐸. *Ch'a-t'u pen Chung-kuo wen-hsüeh shih* 插圖本中國文學史. 4 vols. 1932; rpt. Hong Kong: Commercial Press, 1961.

__________. *Chung-kuo su-wen-hsüeh shih* 中國俗文學史. 3 vols. Peking: Tso-chia ch'u-pan-she, 1954.

Cheng Ch'ien 鄭騫. *Ts'ung shih tao ch'ü* 從詩到曲. Taipei: K'o-hsüeh ch'u-pan-she, 1961.

__________, ed. *Tz'u hsüan* 詞選. 1954; rpt. Taipei: Hua-kang ch'u-pan-pu, 1973.

Chi Che 嵇哲. *Chung-kuo shih-tz'u yen-chin shih* 中國詩詞演進史. 1954; rpt. Taipei: Li-hsing shu-chü, 1958.

Chiang Shang-hsien 姜尚賢. *T'ang Sung ming-chia tz'u hsin-hsüan* 唐宋名家詞新選. Rev. ed. Tainan: Privately printed, 1971.

Ch'ien Chung-shu 錢鍾書, ed. *Sung-shih hsüan-chu* 宋詩選註. Peking: Jen-min wen-hsüeh ch'u-pan-she, 1958.

Chou Chen-fu 周振甫. *Shih-tz'u li-hua* 詩詞例話. Peking: Chung-kuo ch'ing-nien ch'u-pan-she, 1962.

Chou Chi 周濟 (1781-1839), comp. *Sung ssu-chia tz'u-hsüan [chien-chu]* 宋四家詞選〔箋注〕. Annotated by K'uang Shih-yüan 鄺士元. Taipei: Chung-hua shu-chü, 1971.

Chou Fa-kao 周法高. *Chung-kuo ku-tai yü-fa* 中國古代語法. 3 vols. 1959-1961; rpt. Taipei: Chung-yang yen-chiu-yüan li-shih yü-yen yen-chiu-so, 1972.

Ch'ü Hsüan-ying 瞿宣穎. *Chung-kuo she-hui shih-liao ts'ung-ch'ao (chia chi)* 中國社會史料叢鈔（甲集）. 1937; rpt. Taipei: Commercial Press, 1965.

Chu I-tsun 朱彝尊 (1629-1709), comp. *Tz'u tsung* 詞綜. Rpt. in *Wen-hsüeh ts'ung-shu* 文學叢書. Ed. Yang Chia-lo 楊家駱. Taipei: Commercial Press, 1965. Ser. 2, Vol. 6.

Chu Tsu-mou 朱祖謀 (1857-1931), ed. *Ch'iang-ts'un ts'ung-shu* 彊邨叢書. 40 vols. in 5 portfolios. Shanghai: n.p., 1922.

__________, comp. *Sung-tz'u san-pai-shou chien-chu* 宋詞三百首箋注. Annotated by T'ang Kuei-chang 唐圭璋. Hong Kong: Chung-hua shu-chü, 1961.

Chu Tung-jun 朱東潤. *Chung-kuo wen-hsüeh p'i-p'ing shih ta-kang* 中國文學批評史大綱. 1957; rpt. Taipei: K'ai-ming shu-chü, 1960.

__________. *Shih-yen-chih pien* 詩言志辨. 1956; rpt. Taipei: K'ai-ming shu-tien, 1972.

Culler, Jonathan. *Structuralist Poetics: Structuralism, Linguistics, and the Study of Literature.* Ithaca: Cornell Univ. Press, 1975.

Fang Yü 方瑜. "Liu Meng-te ti t'u-feng *yüeh-fu* yü *chu-chih tz'u*" 劉夢得的土風樂府與竹枝詞. *Wen-hsüeh p'ing-lun* 文學評論, 2 (1975), 81-105.

Feng Meng-lung 馮夢龍 (ca. 1574-1645). "Chung ming-chi ch'un-feng tiao Liu Ch'i" 眾名姬春風弔柳七. In his *Yü-shih ming-yen* 喻世明言. Rpt. Hong Kong: Chung-hua shu-chü, 1965. pp. 176-186.

Fong Nai Bun 方乃斌, ed. *Tz'u-shih ta-ch'üan* 詞史大全. Hong Kong: K'uei-lu ch'u-pan-she, 1963.

Frankel, Hans H. "The Chinese Ballad 'Southeast Fly the Peacocks.'" *Harvard Journal of Asiatic Studies*, 34 (1974), 248-271.

__________. *The Flowering Plum and the Palace Lady: Interpretation of Chinese Poetry.* New Haven: Yale Univ. Press, 1976.

__________. "The Formulaic Language of the Chinese Ballad 'Southeast Fly the Peacock.'" *Bulletin of the Institute of History and Philology, Academia Sinica*, 39, Pt. 2 (1969), 219-241.

Freedman, Ralph. *The Lyrical Novel: Studies in Hermann Hesse, Andre Gide, and Virginia Woolf*. Princeton: Princeton Univ. Press, 1963.

Frodsham, J. D., trans. *The Poems of Li Ho (791-817)*. Oxford: Clarendon Press, 1970.

Frye, Northrop. *Anatomy of Criticism: Four Essays*. Princeton: Princeton Univ. Press, 1957.

Fu Keng-sheng 傅庚生. *Chung-kuo wen-hsüeh hsin-shang chü-yü* 中國文學欣賞舉隅. Hong Kong: Nan-kuo ch'u-pan-she, 1969.

Gernet, Jacques. *Daily Life in China: On the Eve of the Mongol Invasion, 1250-1276*. Trans. H. M. Wright. Stanford: Stanford Univ. Press, 1962.

Guillén, Claudio. *Literature as System: Essays toward the Theory of Literary History*. Princeton: Princeton Univ. Press, 1971.

Han Sui-hsüan 韓穗軒. *Hsin-yüan-lou tz'u-hua* 心遠樓詞話. Hong Kong: n.p., 1972.

Hanan, Patrick. "Style as a Criterion of Date." In his *The Chinese Short Story: Studies in Dating, Authorship, and Composition*. Cambridge: Harvard Univ. Press, 1973, pp. 18-32.

Hightower, James Robert. *The Poetry of T'ao Ch'ien*. Oxford: Clarendon Press, 1970.

__________. *Topics in Chinese Literature: Outlines and Bibliographies*. Rev. ed. Cambridge: Harvard Univ. Press, 1971.

__________. "The *Wen Hsüan* and Genre Theory." In *Studies in Chinese Literature*. Ed. John L. Bishop. Cambridge: Harvard Univ. Press, 1966, pp. 142-163.

Hirsch, E. D. Jr. *Validity in Interpretation.* New Haven: Yale Univ. Press, 1967.

Hsia Ch'eng-t'ao 夏承燾. *T'ang Sung tz'u-jen nien-p'u* 唐宋詞人年譜. Shanghai: Ku-tien wen-hsüeh ch'u-pan-she, 1955.

________. *T'ang Sung tz'u lun-ts'ung* 唐宋詞論叢. Shanghai: Ku-tien wen-hsüeh ch'u-pan-she, 1956.

________ and Wu Hsiung-ho 吳熊和. *Tu tz'u ch'ang-shih* 讀詞常識. Peking: Chung-hua shu-chü, 1962.

Hsia Ching-kuan 夏敬觀. *Tz'u-tiao su-yüan* 詞調溯源. Taipei: Commercial Press, 1967.

Hsiao Kuo-chün 蕭國鈞. *T'ang wu-tai tz'u chih ti-yü fa-chan* 唐五代詞之地域發展. Hong Kong: Tz'u ch'ü hsüeh-hui, 1970.

Hsiao T'ung 蕭統 (501-531), comp. [*Chao-ming*] *Wen-hsüan* [昭明]文選. Annotated by Li Shan 李善 (d. 689). Rpt. Taipei: Ho-lo t'u-shu ch'u-pan-she, 1975.

Hsieh Wu-liang 謝无量. *Tz'u-hsüeh chih-nan* 詞學指南. Taipei: Chung-hua shu-chü, 1959.

Hsing Wen-fang 辛文房 (fl. 1304). *T'ang ts'ai-tzu chuan* 唐才子傳. Rpt. Shanghai: Ku-tien wen-hsüeh ch'u-pan-she, 1957.

Hsü Ch'iu 徐釚 (1636-1708). *Tz'u-yüan ts'ung-t'an* 詞苑叢談. Rpt. in *Kuo-hsüeh chi-pen ts'ung-shu* 國學基本叢書. Taipei: Commercial Press, 1968, 1968. Vol. 223.

Hsü Fu-kuan 徐復觀. *Chung-kuo wen-hsüeh lun-chi* 中國文學論集. 2nd ed. Taipei: Hsüeh-sheng shu-chü, 1974.

Hsü Ling 徐陵 (507-583), comp. *Yü-t'ai hsin-yung* 玉台新詠. Annotated by Wu Chao-i 吳兆宜 (Ch'ing). Rpt. in *Kuo-hsüeh chi-*

pen ts'ung-shu 國學基本叢書 . Taipei: Commercial Press, 1968. Vol. 205.

Hsüeh Li-jo 薛礪若 . *Sung-tz'u t'ung-lun* 宋詞通論 . 1949; rpt. Taipei: K'ai-ming shu-tien, 1958.

Hu Shih 胡適 . "*Tz'u* ti ch'i-yüan" 詞的起源 . In "Appendix" to his *Tz'u hsüan* 詞選 . Shanghai: Commercial Press, 1927.

Hu Ts'ai-fu 胡才甫 . *Shih-t'i shih-li* 詩体釋例 . 2nd ed. Taipei: Chung-hua shu-chü, 1969.

Hu Tzu 胡仔 (Sung). *T'iao-hsi yü-yin ts'ung-hua* 苕溪漁隱叢話 . Rpt. Taipei: Shih-chieh shu-chü, 1966.

Hu Yün-i 胡雲翼 . *Chung-kuo tz'u-shih* 中國詞史 . Hong Kong: I-wen ch'u-pan-she, 1966.

__________. *Chung-kuo wen-hsüeh shih* 中國文學史 . 1962, rpt. Taipei: San-min shu-chü, 1970.

__________, ed. *Sung-tz'u hsüan* 宋詞選 . Shanghai: Chung-hua shu-chü, 1965.

__________. *Sung-tz'u yen-chiu* 宋詞研究 . Shanghai: Chung-hua shu-chü, 1926.

__________, ed. *Tz'u-hsüeh hsiao ts'ung-shu* 詞學小叢書 . 2 vols. Shanghai: chiao-yü shu-tien, 1949.

Huang Hsü-wu 黄勗吾 . *Shih tz'u ch'ü ts'ung-t'an* 詩詞曲叢談 . 2nd ed. Hong Kong: Shanghai Book Co., 1969.

Huang Sheng 黄昇 (fl. 1240-1249). *Hua-an tz'u-hsüan* 花菴詞選 . Rpt. Hong Kong: Chung-hua shu-chü, 1962.

Hung P'ien 洪楩 (16th century), comp. "Liu Ch'i-ch'ing shih-chiu wan chiang-lou chi" 柳耆卿詩酒翫江樓記 . In *Ch'ing-*

p'ing shan-t'ang hua-pen 清平山堂話本 (compiled between 1541-1551). Rpt. Shanghai: Ku-tien wen-hsüeh ch'u-pan-she, 1957, pp. 1-5.

Hung Wei-fa 洪為法. *Chüeh-chü lun* 絶句論. Shanghai: Commercial Press, 1934.

Jao Tsung-i 饒宗頤. *Airs de Touen-houang*. Paris: éditions du Centre National de la Recherche Scientifique, 1971.

__________. *Tz'u-chi k'ao* 詞籍考. Hong Kong: Hong Kong Univ. Press, 1963.

Jen Erh-pei 任二北. *Tun-huang ch'ü ch'u-t'an* 敦煌曲初探. Shanghai: Wen-i lien-ho ch'u-pan-she, 1954.

Josephs, H. K. "The Chanda: A Sung Dynasty Entertainment." *T'oung Pao*, 62, No. 4-5 (1976), 167-198.

Kanaoka Shōkō 金岡照光, ed. *Tonkō shutsudo bungaku bunken bunrui mokuroku* 敦煌出土文學文献分類目錄. Tokyo: Tōyō Bundo Tonkō Bunken Kenkyū Iinkai, 1971.

Kao, Yu-kung and Tsu-lin Mei. "Ending Lines in Wang Shih-chen's *Ch'i-chüeh*: Convention and Creativity in the Ch'ing." In *Artists and Traditions*. Ed. Christian F. Murck. Princeton: Princeton Univ. Press, 1976, pp. 131-135.

__________. "Meaning, Metaphor and Allusion in T'ang Poetry." Draft, to be published, pp. 1-99.

__________. "Syntax, Diction and Imagery in T'ang Poetry." *Harvard Journal of Asiatic Studies*, 31 (1970), 49-136.

Kishibe Shigeo 岸邊成雄. *Tōdai ongaku no rekishiteki kenkyū--gakuseihen* 唐代音樂の歴史的研究 --樂制篇. 2 vols.

Tokyo: Univ. of Tokyo Press, 1960-1961.

Ko Tsai 戈載 (Ch'ing). Tz'u-lin cheng-yün 詞林正韻. Preface 1821. Rpt. with Tz'u-tiao tz'u-tien 詞調辭典. Taipei: Shih-chieh shu-chü, 1968.

Kong Yun Fun 江潤勳. Tz'u-hsüeh p'ing-lun shih-kao 詞學評論史稿. Hong Kong: Lung Men Bookstore, 1966.

Kuan Han-ch'ing 關漢卿 (1230-1280). "Ch'ien Ta-yin chih-ch'ung Hsieh T'ien-hsiang 錢大尹智寵謝天香. In Yüan jen tsa-chü ch'üan-chi 元人雜劇全集. Ed. Lu Ch'ien 盧前 (Lu Chi-yeh 盧冀野). Shanghai: Shanghai tsa-chih kung-ssu, 1936. I, 29-58.

K'uang Chou-i 況周頤 (1859-1926). Hui-feng tz'u-hua 蕙風詞話. Ed. Wang Yu-an 王幼安. Printed with Jen-chien tz'u-hua 人間詞話. Hong Kong: Commercial Press, 1961.

Kuo Mao-ch'ien 郭茂倩, ed. Yüeh-fu shih-chi 樂府詩集. Rpt. in Ssu-pu ts'ung-k'an ch'u-pien so-pen 四部叢刊初編縮本. Taipei: Commercial Press, 1967. Vol. 104.

Kuo Shao-yü 郭紹虞. Chung-kuo wen-hsüeh p'i-p'ing shih 中國文學批評史. 1955; rpt. Hong Kong: Hung-chih shu-chü, 1970.

Langer, Susanne K. Feeling and Form. New York: Charles Scribner's Sons, 1953.

Leung, Winnie Lai-fong. "Liu Yung and His Tz'u." M.A. thesis. Univ. of British Columbia 1976.

Levy, Dore Jesse. "Poetic Narrative in 'The Song of the Lady of Ch'in' and Its Tradition." B.A. thesis. Yale Univ. 1975.

Li Ching 李璟 and Li Yü 李煜. Li Ching, Li Yü tz'u 李璟

李煜詞 . Ed. Chan An-t'ai 詹安泰 . Peking: Jen-ming wen-hsüeh ch'u-pan-she, 1968.

__________. *Nan-T'ang erh-chu shih-tz'u* 南唐二主詩詞 . Ed. Ho Yang-ling 賀揚靈 . Shanghai: Kuang-hua shu-chü, 1930.

__________. *Nan-T'ang Erh-chu tz'u chiao-ting* 南唐二主詞校訂. Ed. Wang Chung-wen 王仲聞 . Peking: Jen-min wen-hsüeh ch'u-pan-she, 1957.

Li Fang 李昉 . *T'ai-p'ing kuang chi* 太平廣記 . 500 chüan. 978; rpt. Peking: Jen-min wen-hsüeh ch'u-pan-she, 1959.

Li O 厲鶚 (1692-1752) and Ma Yüeh-kuan 馬曰琯 (1688-1755), eds. *Sung-shih chi-shih* 宋詩紀事 . 100 *chüan*. Preface 1746; rpt. in 6 vols. Taipei: Ting-wen shu-chü, 1971.

Li Yü tz'u t'ao-lun chi 李煜詞討論集. Ed. Wen-hsüeh i-ch'an pien-chi-pu 文學遺產編輯部 . Peking: Tso-chia ch'u-pan-she, 1957.

Liang Ch'i-hsün 梁啓勳 . *Tz'u hsüeh* 詞學 . Preface 1932. Rpt. Taipei: Ho-lo t'u-shu ch'u-pan-she, n.d.

__________. *Tz'u-hsüeh ch'üan-heng* 詞學詮衡. Hong Kong: Shanghai Book Co., 1964.

Lin Mei-i 林玫儀. "Lun Tun-huang ch'ü ti she-hui hsing" 論敦煌曲的社會性 . *Wen-hsüeh p'ing-lun* 文學評論 , 2 (1975), 107-144.

Lin, Shuen-fu. *The Transformation of the Chinese Lyrical Tradition: Chiang K'uei and Southern Sung Tz'u Poetry*. Princeton: Princeton Univ. Press, 1978.

Lin, Yutang. *The Gay Genius: the Life and Times of Su Tungpo*. New York: John Day Co., 1947.

Liu Hsieh 劉勰. Wen-hsin tiao-lung 文心雕龍. Trans. Yu-chung Shih. The Literary Mind and the Carving of Dragons. New York: Columbia Univ. Press, 1959.

Liu, James J. Y. *The Art of Chinese Poetry*. Chicago: Univ. of Chicago Press, 1962.

__________. *Chinese Theories of Literature*. Chicago: Univ. of Chicago Press, 1975.

__________. *Major Lyricists of the Northern Sung: A.D. 960-1126*. Princeton: Princeton Univ. Press, 1974.

__________. *The Poetry of Li Shang-yin*. Chicago: Univ. of Chicago Press, 1969.

Liu, James T. C. *Ou-yang Hsiu: An Eleventh-century Neo-Confucianist*. Stanford: Stanford Univ. Press, 1967.

Liu Shao 劉劭 (3rd century). *Jen-wu chih* 人物志. Annotated by Liu Ping 劉昞. Rpt. Shanghai: Han-fen lou, n.d.

Liu Tzu-keng 劉子庚 (Liu Yü-p'an 劉毓盤). *Tz'u shih* 詞史. 1931; rpt. Taipei: Hsüeh-sheng shu-chü, 1972.

Liu Ta-chieh 劉大杰. *Chung-kuo wen-hsüeh fa-chan shih* 中國文學發展史. Rev. ed. 3 vols. Shanghai: Chung-hua shu-chü, 1962-1963.

Liu, Wu-chi and Irving Yucheng Lo, ed. *Sunflower Splendor: Three Thousand Years of Chinese Poetry*. New York: Anchor Books, 1975.

Liu Yün-hsiang 劉雲翔. "*Wu-ko* yü *tz'u*" 吳歌與詞. *T'ung-sheng yüeh-k'an* 同聲月刊, 2, No. 2 (1942), 119-134.

Liu Yung 柳永. Yüeh-chang chi 樂章集. Annotated by Cheng Wen-cho 鄭文焯 (1856-1918). Rpt. Taipei: Kuang-wen shu-chü, 1973.

Lo Fang-chou 羅芳洲, ed. Tz'u-hsüeh yen-chiu 詞學研究. Shanghai: Chiao-yü shu-tien, 1947.

Lo Ken-tse 羅根澤. "Chüeh-chü san-yüan" 絕句三源. In his Chung-kuo ku-tien wen-hsüeh lun-chi 中國古典文學論集. Peking: Wu-shih nien-tai ch'u-pan-she, 1955, pp. 28-53.

__________. Chung-kuo wen-hsüeh p'i-p'ing shih 中國文學批評史. Shanghai: Ku-tien wen-hsüeh ch'u-pan-she, 1957-1961.

__________. Yüeh-fu wen-hsüeh shih 樂府文學史. 1931; rpt. Taipei: Wen-shih-che ch'u-pan-she, 1964.

Lo Yeh 羅燁 (Sung). "Hua-ch'ü shih-lu" 花衢實錄. In Tsui-weng t'an-lu 醉翁談錄. 20 chüan. Rpt. Shanghai: Ku-tien wen-hsüeh ch'u-pan-she, 1957, pp. 31-35.

Lord, Albert B. The Singer of Tales. Harvard Univ. Press, 1960; rpt. New York: Atheneum, 1965.

Lou Tzu-k'uang 婁子匡 and Juan Ch'ang-jui 阮昌銳. "Chu-chih tz'u ti yen-chiu" 竹枝詞的研究. Chung-shan ta-hsüeh min-su ts'ung-shu 中山大學民俗叢書. Taipei: Chinese Association for Folklore, 1969. III, 19-33.

Lu Chi-yeh 盧冀野. Tz'u-ch'ü yen-chiu 詞曲研究. Taipei: Chung-hua shu-chü, 1960.

Lu K'an-ju 陸侃如 and Feng Yüan-chün 馮沅君. Chung-kuo shih-shih 中國詩史. 3 vols. Peking: Tso-chia ch'u-pan-she, 1957.

Lung Mu-hsün 龍沐勛 (Lung Yü-sheng 龍榆生). Chung-kuo yün-wen shih 中國韻文史. 1964; rpt. Taipei: Hung-shih ch'u-pan-she, 1974.

________, et al. Li Hou-chu ho t'a-ti tz'u 李後主和他的詞. Taipei: Hsüeh-sheng shu-chü, 1971.

________, ed. T'ang Sung ming-chia tz'u-hsüan 唐宋名家詞選. Shanghai: Ku-tien wen-hsüeh ch'u-pan-she, 1956.

________, ed. Tz'u-hsüeh chi-k'an 詞學季刊. 1933-1936; rpt. in 3 vols. Taipei: Hsüeh-sheng shu-chü, 1967.

________. Tung-p'o yüeh-fu chien 東坡樂府箋. Shanghai: Commercial Press, 1958.

Lyons, John. Introduction to Theoretical Linguistics. Cambridge: Cambridge Univ. Press, 1968.

Mao Chin 毛晉 (1598-1654), ed. Sung liu-shih ming-chia tz'u 宋六十名家詞. Rpt. in Chung-kuo wen-hsüeh chen-pen ts'ung-shu 中國文學珍本叢書. Shanghai: Shanghai tsa-chih kung-ssu, 1936.

Mao Hsien-shu 毛先舒 (1620-1688). T'ien-tz'u ming-chieh 填詞名解. Rpt. in Tz'u-hsüeh ch'üan-shu 詞學全書. Ed. Cha P'ei-chi 查培繼. Taipei: Kuang-wen shu-chü, 1971.

Meng Yüan-lao 孟元老 (Sung). Tung-ching meng-hua lu 東京夢華錄. 10 chüan. Preface 1147. Rpt. in Tung-ching meng-hua lu wai-ssu-chung 東京夢華錄外四種. Shanghai: Ku-tien wen-hsüeh ch'u-pan-she, 1957.

Miao Yüeh 繆鉞. Shih-tz'u san-lun 詩詞散論. Taipei: K'ai-ming shu-tien, 1966.

Miner, Earl. "The Genres in Critical Systems and Literary Change." Paper. Princeton Conference on Genre and Its Problems. April 30-May 1, 1976.

Mou Tsung-san 牟宗三. *Ts'ai-hsing yü hsüan-li* 才性與玄理. 1962; rpt. Taipei: Hsüeh-sheng shu-chü, 1975.

Murakami Tetsumi 村上哲見. "On Teiin no bungaku" 温庭筠の文学. *Chūgoku bungakuhō* 中国文学報, 5 (1956), 19-40.

_________, trans. *Ri Iku* 李煜. Chūgoku shijin senshū 中国詩人選集. No. 16. Tokyo: Iwanami, 1959.

_________. "Ryū ki kyō shi no keitai jō no tokushoku ni tsuite" 柳耆卿詞の形態上の特色について. *Tōhōgaku* 東方学, No. 43 (1972), 61-76.

_________. "Shi to shi to no aida--So Tōba no baai" 詩と詞とのあいだ -- 蘇東坡の場合. *Tōhōgaku* 東方学, No. 35 (1968), 68-82.

_________. *Sōshi* 宋詞. Chūgoku shibun sen 中国詩文選, No. 21. Tokyo: Chikuma, 1973.

_________. *Sōshi kenkyū--Tō Godai hokusō hen* 宋詞研究 -- 唐五代北宋篇. Tokyo: Sobunsha, 1976.

Nakada, Seiichi. "An Egocentric Conspiracy." Paper. Annual Meeting of the Association of Teachers of Japanese, San Francisco. Nov. 24-26, 1977.

Nakata Yūjirō 中田勇次郎. "Shiritsu ni mietaru chōjōin no rei ni tsuite" 詞律に見えたる重疊韻の例に就いて. *Shina-gaku* 支那学, 9, No. 2 (1938), 297-346.

Nishi Noriaki 西紀昭. "Tōba no shoki no sōbetsu-shi" 東坡の

初期の送別詞 . Chūgoku chūsei bungaku kenkyū 中国中世文學研究 , 7 (1968), 64-73.

Ogawa Tamaki 小川環樹, trans. So Shoku 蘇軾 . 2 vols. Chūgoku shijin senshū, ser. 2, nos. 5-6. Tokyo: Iwanami, 1962.

Okamura Shigeru 岡村繁 . "Tōmatsu ni okeru kyokushi-shi bungaku no seiritsu" 唐末における曲子詞文學の成立 . Bungaku kenkyū 文學研究, 65 (1968), 85-126.

Osada Natsuki 長田夏樹 . "Shi shi kyoku no setten 'Gakushō Shū'" 詩詞曲の接點'樂章集' . Kobe Gaidai ronsō 神户外大論叢 , 19, No. 3 (1968), 27-44.

Ōtsuka Shigeki 大塚繁樹. "Ko Teki no shiron ni okeru mondaiten" 胡適の詞論における問題点 . Ehime Daigaku kiyō 愛媛大學紀要 (Jimbun Kagaku 人文科學), 2, No 2 (1955), 271-281.

Owen, Stephen. The Poetry of the Early T'ang. New Haven: Yale Univ. Press, 1977.

Pian, Rulan Chao. Sonq Dynasty Musical Sources and Their Interpretation. Cambridge: Harvard Univ. Press, 1967.

Picken, L. E. R. "Secular Chinese Songs of the Twelfth Century." Studia Musicologica Academiae Scientiarum Hungaricae, 8 (1966), 125-172.

Po Hsing-chien 白行簡 (T'ang). "Li Wa chuan" 李娃傳 . Rpt. in Pai-pu ts'ung-shu chi-ch'eng 百部叢書集成 . Taipei: I-wen yin-shu-kuan, 1968. Vol. 22.

Robertson, Maureen. "To convey What Is Precious: Ssu-k'ung T'u's Poetics and the Erh-shih-ssu shih-p'in.'" In Transition and

Permanence: Chinese History and Culture, a Festschrift in Honor of Dr. Hsiao Kung-ch'üan. Ed. Frederick W. Mote and David C. Buxbaum. Hong Kong: Cathay Press, 1972.

Schafer, Edward H. *The Vermilion Bird: T'ang Images of the South*. Berkeley: Univ. of California Press, 1967.

__________. "The Capeline Cantos: Verses on the Divine Loves of Taoist Priestesses." Forthcoming in *Sinologische Studien*.

Sebeok, Thomas A., ed. *Style in Language*. Cambridge: The M.I.T. Press, 1960.

She Hsüeh-man 佘雪曼. *She Hsüeh-man tz'u-hsüeh yen-chiang lu* 佘雪曼詞學演講錄. Hong Kong: Hsüeh-man i-wen yüan, 1955.

Shu Meng-lan 舒夢蘭 (fl. 1796-1820). *Pai-hsiang tz'u-p'u* 白香詞譜. Rpt. Taipei: Wen-kuang t'u-shu kung-ssu, 1974.

Smith, Barbara Herrustein. *Poetic Closure: A Study of How Poems End*. Chicago: Univ. of Chicago Press, 1968.

Spitzer, Leo. *Linguistics and Literary History: Essays in Stylistics*. Princeton: Princeton Univ. Press, 1948.

Su Shih 蘇軾. *Su Shih shih-hsüan* 蘇軾詩選. Ed. Ch'en Erh-tung 陳邇冬. Peking: Jen-min wen-hsüeh ch'u-pan-she, 1957.

__________. *Tung-p'o tz'u* 東坡詞. Ed. Ts'ao Shu-ming 曹樹銘. Hong Kong: Universal Book Co., 1968; rpt. Taipei: Hua-cheng shu-chü, 1975.

Sun Ch'i 孫棨 (T'ang). *Pei-li chih* 北里志. Book completed in 884. Rpt. in *Chung-kuo wen-hsüeh ts'an-k'ao tzu-liao hsiao ts'ung-shu* 中國文學參考資料小叢書. Ser. 1, No. 8. Shanghai:

Ku-tien wen-hsüeh ch'u-pan-she, 1957.

Sun Kuang-hsien 孫光憲 (d. 968). *Pei-meng so-yen* 北夢瑣言. Rpt. in *Chung-kuo wen-hsüeh ts'an-k'ao tzu-liao ts'ung-shu* 中國文學參考資料叢書. Peking: Chung-hua shu-chü, 1960.

Suzuki Torao 鈴木虎雄. "Kōgo o shiyō seru tenshi" 口語を使用せる填詞. In his *Shina bungaku kenkyū* 支那文学研究. Kyoto: Kōbundō, 1925, pp. 491-499.

Tamori Noboru 田森襄. "Shikei yori mitaru chōtanku" 詩形より見たる長短句. *Saitama Daigaku kiyō* 埼玉大学紀要: Jimbun kagaku hen 人文科学篇, 3 (1954), 81-98.

Tanaka Kenji 田中謙二. "Ōyō Shū no shi ni tsuite" 歐陽修の詞について. *Tōhōgaku* 東方学, 7 (1953), 50-62.

T'ang Yüeh 唐鉞. *Kuo-ku hsin-t'an* 國故新探. 2 vols. Shanghai: Commercial Press, 1926.

T'ang Sung tz'u yen-chiu lun-wen chi 唐宋詞研究論文集. Ed. Chung-kuo yü-wen hsüeh-she 中國語文學社. Peking: n.p., 1969.

Tormey, Alan. *The Concept of Expression: A Study in Philosophical Psychology and Aesthetics*. Princeton: Princeton Univ. Press, 1971.

Ts'ui Ling-ch'in 崔令欽 (T'ang). *Chiao-fang chi* [*chien-ting*] 教坊記[箋訂]. Annotated by Jen Pan-t'ang 任半塘 (Jen Erh-pei 任二北). Shanghai: Chung-hua shu-chü, 1962.

Valery, Paul. *The Art of Poetry*. Trans. Denise Folleiot. Bollingen Series, XLV, 7. New York: Pantheon Books, 1958.

Wan Min-hao 宛敏灝. *Erh Yen chi ch'i tz'u* 二晏及其詞.

Shanghai: Commercial Press, 1934.

Wan Shu 萬樹 (fl. 1680-1692). [So-yin pen] Tz'u-lü [索引本] 詞律. Preface 1687; rpt. with supplements by Hsü Pen-li 徐本立. Index by Wang Ch'iung-shan 王瓊珊. Taipei: Kuang-wen shu-chü, 1971.

Wang Ch'in-hsi 王琴希. "Sung tz'u shang ch'ü sheng tzu yü chü-ch'ü kuan-hsi chi ssu-sheng t'i k'ao-cheng" 宋詞上去聲字與劇曲關係及四聲体攷證. In Wen shih 文史. Ed. Hsin-chien-she pien-chi-pu 新建設編輯部. Vol. II. Peking: Chung-hua shu-chü, 1963, pp. 139-162.

Wang Ch'ung-min 王重民, ed. Tun-huang ch'ü-tzu-tz'u chi 敦煌曲子詞集. 2nd ed. Shanghai: Commercial Press, 1954.

Wang Hsi-yüan 王熙元. Li-tai tz'u-hua hsü-lu 歷代詞話敘錄. Taipei: Chung-hua shu-chü, 1973.

Wang I 王易. Tz'u-ch'ü shih 詞曲史. 2 vols. 1971; rpt. in 1 vol. Taipei: Kuang-wen shu-chü, 1971.

Wang I-ch'ing 王奕清 (ca. 1644-ca. 1736), et al. [Yü-chih] Tz'u-p'u [御製] 詞譜. 1715; rpt. Taipei: privately printed, 1964.

Wang Jen-yü 王仁裕 (T'ang). K'ai-yüan T'ien-pao i-shih 開元天寶遺事. Rpt. in Shuo k'u 說庫. Taipei: Hsin-hsing shu-chü, 1963.

Wang Kuo-wei 王國維. Jen-chien tz'u-hua 人間詞話. Trans. Ching-i Tu. Poetic Remarks in the Human World. Taipei: Chung-hua shu-chü, 1970.

Wang Li 王力. Han-yü shih-lü hsüeh 漢語詩律學. 1958; rpt. Hong Kong: Chung-hua shu-chü, 1973.

Wang Shu-nu 王書奴. Chung-kuo ch'ang-chi shih 中國娼妓史.

Shanghai: Sheng-huo shu-tien, 1935.

Wang Yao 王瑤 . *Chung-ku wen-hsüeh ssu-hsiang* 中古文學思想 . 1953; rpt. Hong Kong: Chung-liu ch'u-pan-she, 1973.

Watson, Burton. *Chinese Lyricism: Shih Poetry from the Second to the Twelfth Century*. New York: Columbia Univ. Press, 1971

__________, trans. *Su Tung-p'o: Selections from a Sung Dynasty Poet*. New York: Columbia Univ. Press, 1965.

Wei Ch'ing-chih 魏慶之 (fl. 1240-1244). *Shih-jen yü-hsieh* 詩人玉屑 . Rpt. Taipei: Commercial Press, 1972.

Wei Chuang 韋莊 . *Wei Tuan-chi shih chiao-chu* 韋端己詩校注 . Annotated by Chiang Ts'ung-p'ing 江聰平 . Taipei: Chung-hua shu-chü, 1969.

Wellek, René. *Theory of Literature*. 3rd ed. New York: Harcourt, Brace & World, 1956.

Wen Ju-hsien 聞汝賢 . *Tz'u-p'ai hui-shih* 詞牌彙釋 . Taipei: privately printed, 1963.

Wen T'ing-yün 溫庭筠 . *Wen Fei-ch'ing shih-chi* 溫飛卿詩集 . Annotated by Tseng I-yüan 曾益原 (Ming). With supplementary notes by Ku Yü-hsien 顧予咸 (Ch'ing). Rpt. in *Kuo-hsüeh chi-pen ts'ung-shu* 國學基本叢書 . Taipei: Commercial Press, 1968. Vol. 276.

Wright, Arthur F. and Denis Twitchett, ed. *Perspectives on the T'ang*. New Haven: Yale Univ. Press, 1973.

Wu Mei 吳梅 . *Tz'u-hsüeh t'ung-lun* 詞學通論 . Shanghai: Commercial Press, 1932.

Yeh Chia-ying 葉嘉瑩 . "Ch'ang-chou *tz'u*-p'ai pi-hsing chi-t'o

chih shuo ti hsin chien-t'ao" 常州詞派比興寄託之說的新檢討. Hsien-tai wen-hsüeh 現代文學, No. 51 (1973), 62-90.

________. Chia-ling t'an tz'u 迦陵談詞. Taipei: Ch'un-wen-hsüeh ch'u-pan-she, 1970.

Yeh Meng-te 葉夢得 (1077-1148). Pi-shu lu-hua 避暑錄話. Rpt. in Ts'ung-shu chi-ch'eng chien-pien 叢書集成簡編. Taipei: Commercial Press, 1966. Vol. 717.

Yoshikawa, Kōjirō. An Introduction to Sung Poetry. Trans. Burton Watson. Cambridge: Harvard Univ. Press, 1967.

Yü P'ing-po 俞平伯. Ch'ing-chen tz'u shih 清真詞釋. Shanghai: K'ai-ming shu-tien, 1949.

________. "Chin ch'uan Li T'ai-po tz'u ti chen-wei wen-t'i" 今傳李太白詞的真偽問題. Wen-hsüeh yen-chiu chi-k'an 文學研究季刊, 1 (1951), 101-107.

________. Tu tz'u ou-te 讀詞偶得. Taipei: K'ai-ming shu-tien, 1957.

Yuh, Liou-yi. "Liu Yung, Su Shih and Some Aspects of the Development of Early Tz'u Poetry." Diss. Univ. of Washington 1972.

A Glossary of Chinese Characters

An kung tzu 安公子

An Lu-shan 安祿山

Ch'ang-chou 常州

Ch'ang hsiang-ssu 長相思

Chang Hsien 張先

Chang Mi 張泌

Chang San-ying 張三影

Ch'ang-shan 常山

Chang Ti-chung 張砥中

ch'ang-tiao 長調

ch'ang-tuan-chü 長短句

Chang Yen 張炎

Chao-tsung (T'ang) 昭宗

Che-ku t'ien 鷓鴣天

chen 真

ch'en-chü 襯句

Ch'en Shih-tao 陳師道

ch'en-tzu 襯字

cheng k'o 爭克

Ch'eng-ti (Han) 成帝

cheng-t'i 正体

Ch'eng-tu 成都

Cheng Wen-cho 鄭文焯

chi-kuan 妓館

Ch'i shih 戚氏

Ch'i-sung-t'ang tz'u-i 七頌堂詞繹

chia-men 家門

Chiang-ch'eng tzu 江城子

Chiang K'uei 姜夔

Ch'iang-t'ou ma-shang 牆頭馬上

chiao-fang 教坊

Chiao-fang chi 教坊記

Chiao-hung chuan 嬌紅傳

chiao wu-na 嬌無那

Chien-k'ang 建康

Chien-ning 建寧

Chien-tzu mu-lan hua 減字木蘭花

Chien-wen 簡文

chin 近

Chin Ch'i-hua 金啓華

Chin-ch'üan chi 金荃集

Ch'in-fu yin 秦婦吟

Ch'in Kuan (Shao-yu) 秦觀(少游)

chin-lien chi 金奩集

Chin Sheng-t'an 金聖嘆

chin-t'i shih 近體詩

Ch'in-yüan ch'un 沁園春

ching-chieh 境界

ch'ing-ching chiao-jung 情景交融

Ching-men 荊門

Ch'ing-pei lo 傾杯樂

Ch'ing-p'ing tiao 清平調

Ch'iu-yeh yüeh 秋夜月

Chou Pang-yen 周邦彥

ch'ü 曲

chu-chiao 助教

Chu-chih 竹枝

Ch'u-erh 楚兒

ch'ü-sheng 去聲

Ch'u-tz'u 楚辭

ch'ü-tzu-tz'u 曲子詞

Chu Ying-t'ai chin 祝英台近

Chu-ying yao-hung 燭影搖紅

Chu-yü tz'u 珠玉詞

ch'uan-ch'i 傳奇

Chuang-tzu 莊子

chüeh-chü 絕句

Ch'üeh t'a chih 鵲踏枝

Ch'un-kuang hao 春光好

chün pu-chien 君不見

Chung Fu 鍾輻

Chung-hsing yüeh 中興樂

Chung Hung 鍾嶸

chung-tiao 中調

Fa-ch'ü hsien-hsien-yin 法曲獻仙音

fa-fan 發凡

Feng Ch'i-yung 馮其庸

Feng kuei yün 鳳歸雲

Feng Yen-ssu 馮延巳

Fu-niang 福娘

Han-lin 翰林

hao-fang 豪放

Hao-shih chin 好事近

Hao shih-kuang 好時光

Ho Chu 賀鑄

Ho ch'uan 河傳

Ho hsin-lang 賀新郎

Ho-hua mei 荷華媚

Ho-lin yü-lu 鶴林玉露

Ho-na ch'ü 紇那曲

Ho Ning 和凝

ho-sheng 和聲

Ho sheng-ch'ao 賀聖朝

Ho-yeh pei 荷葉杯

Hou-shan shih-hua 後山詩話

Hsi-chiang yüeh 西江月

hsi-ch'ü 西曲

Hsi-hsiang chi 西廂記

Hsia Ching-kuan 夏敬觀

Hsiang-ho ko-tz'u 相和歌辭

Hsiang Yü 項羽

Hsiao-hsiang shen 瀟湘神

hsiao-ling 小令

Hsiao-niang 蕭娘

Hsiao-shan tz'u 小山詞

hsiao te 消得

hsiao-yao yu 逍遙遊

hsieh-erh ko 些兒箇

Hsieh-niang 謝娘

Hsin Ch'i-chi 辛棄疾

Hsin-ling 信陵

Hsing hsiang tzu 行香子

Hsing-lu nan 行路難

Hsü-chou 徐州

hsü-tzu 虛字

Hsüan-ti (Han) 宣帝（漢）

Hsüan-tsung (T'ang) 玄宗（唐）

Hsüeh Chao-yün 薛昭蘊

Hsüeh T'ao 薛濤

Hu-chou 湖州

Hu-ya 虎牙

Hu Ying-lin 胡應麟

hu-yüeh 胡樂

Hua-chien chi 花間集

Hua-chou 華州

Hua fan 花犯

Hua man lu 畫墁錄

huai le 壞了

Huan hsi sha 浣溪沙

huan-t'ou 換頭

huan-yu 還又

Huang Ch'ao 黃巢

Huang-fu Sung 皇甫松

Huang-ti kan 皇帝感

Huang T'ing-chien (Shan-ku) 黃庭堅（山谷）

Hui-p'o yüeh 回波樂

i 伊

I chiang-nan 憶江南

I-hu chu 一斛珠

i shih wei tz'u 以詩為詞

I-ts'un chin 一寸金

I-ts'ung hua 一叢花

i-tzu tou 一字豆

Jen-tsung (Sung) 仁宗（宋）

Ju-meng ling 如夢令

Ju yü shui 如魚水

Jun-chou 潤州

k'an 看

Kao Shih 高適

Kao T'ang fu 高唐賦

Keng-lou tzu 更漏子

keng neng hsiao 更能消

Ku Hsiung 顧夐

ku-shih 古詩

Ku-su 姑蘇

Kuei-ch'ao huan 歸朝歡

K'uei tz'u kuan-chien 窺詞管見

kuei-yüan 閨怨

Kung-chung t'iao-hsiao 宮中調笑

kung-t'i shih 宮體詩

kuo-feng 國風

Lai-erh 萊兒

Lan-ling wang 蘭陵王

lang 郎

Lang t'ao sha 浪淘沙

Li Chieh 李傑

Li Ching 李璟

Li Ch'ing-chao 李清照

Li Hsün 李珣

Li Kuang-pi 李光弼

Li Mao-chen 李茂貞

Li Po 李白

Li Ts'un-hsü 李存勗

Li Wa chuan 李娃傳

Li Yü (Hou-chu) 李煜(後主)

Li Yü (1611-1680) 李漁

liao 料

lien-chang 聯章

Lin-chiang hsien 臨江仙

Lin-huai 臨淮

ling-tzu 領字

Liu An 劉安

Liu Ch'i 柳七

Liu ch'ou 六醜

Liu Hsi-tsai 劉熙載

Liu Hsieh 劉勰

Liu I 柳宜

Liu-i tz'u 六一詞

Liu K'o-chuang 劉克莊

Liu Pang 劉邦

Liu T'i-jen 劉體仁

Liu Yü 劉裕

Liu Yü-hsi 劉禹錫

Liu Yung (Ch'i-ch'ing, San-pien, T'un-t'ien) 柳永(耆卿, 三變, 屯田)

Lo-hsing ssu 落星寺

Lo-shih tz'u 樂世詞

Lo Ta-ching 羅大經

Lu Ch'ien-i 鹿虔扆

Lu Fu-chih 陸輔之

Lü Pu 呂布

lü-shih 律詩

Lun-t'ai tzu 輪臺子

Lun tz'u tsa-chu 論詞雜著

Lung-hsing 龍興

Man-chiang hung 滿江紅

Man-t'ing fang 滿庭芳

man-tz'u 慢詞

Mao Wen-hsi 毛文錫

Meng chiang-nan 夢江南

Meng-chiang-nü 孟姜女

mo-shih 莫是

Mu-lan hua 木蘭花

na-k'an 那堪

nan-ch'ü 南曲

Nan-hsiang tzu 南鄉子

Nan-ko tzu 南歌子

nan-kuo ch'an-chüan 南國嬋娟

Nan T'ang 南唐

Nei chia chiao 内家嬌

Neng-kai-chai man-lu 能改齋漫錄

nien 黏

Nien-nu chiao 念奴嬌

Nü-kuan tzu 女冠子

nung 儂

Ou-yang Chiung 歐陽炯

Ou-yang Hsiu (Yung-shu) 歐陽修(永叔)

p'a 怕

Pa-liu tzu 八六子

Pa-sheng kan-chou 八聲甘州

P'an-p'an 盼盼

P'ao-ch'iu lo 拋球樂

pei-ch'ü 北曲

Pei-fen shih 悲憤詩

Pi-chi man-chih 碧雞漫志

p'ien 片

pien-t'i 變體

p'ien-wen 駢文

P'ing-k'ang *fang* 平康坊

P'o-chen tzu 破陣子

P'o-chen yüeh 破陣樂

Po Chü-i (Lo-t'ien) 白居易（樂天）

Po Hsing-chien 白行簡

P'o-lo men 婆羅門

P'u-sa man 菩薩蠻

Pu-suan-tzu man 卜算子慢

San-t'ai 三台

Shao-nien yu 少年遊

Shao p'ien 哨遍

shei 誰

shen 甚

Shen I-fu 沈義父

shih 詩

Shih-erh shih 十二時

shih-k'o ch'ü-tzu-tz'u 詩客曲子詞

shih le 是了

Shih-lin shih-hua 石林詩話

shih-tzu 實字

Shih Yen-nien 石延年

Shu 蜀

shuang-tiao 雙調

Shui-lung yin 水龍吟

Shui-tiao ko-t'ou 水調歌頭

Shui-tiao tz'u 水調詞

Shun 舜

Ssu-k'ung T'u 司空圖

Su Shih (Tung-p'o) 蘇軾（東坡）

Su-tsung (T'ang) 肅宗(唐)

su-yüeh 俗樂

Sun Kuang-hsien 孫光憲

Sung Yü 宋玉

Ta-ho shan-jen tz'u-lun 大鶴山人詞論

T'a so hsing 踏莎行

T'ai-tsung (T'ang) 太宗(唐)

tan 但

tan-tiao 單調

T'ang Kuei-chang 唐圭璋

T'ao Ch'ien (Yüan-ming) 陶潛(淵明)

Tao-lien tzu 搗練子

t'ao-shu 套數

t'i 體

T'i-jen chiao 殢人嬌

Tieh lien hua 蝶戀花

Tien chiang ch'un 點絳脣

T'ien-hsien tzu 天仙子

t'ien-tz'u 填詞

Ting feng-po 定風波

Ting-hai 定海

ting-ko lien-chang 定格聯章

tsa-ch'ü-tzu 雜曲子

Ts'ai-lien ch'ü 采蓮曲

Ts'ai-lien tzu 采蓮子

Ts'ai-sang tzu 採桑子

Ts'ai Yen 蔡琰

Ts'ang-lang shih-hua 滄浪詩話

Ts'ao Chih 曹植

Ts'ao Ts'ao 曹操

tsen jen te 怎忍得

Ts'en Shen 岑參

tsen sheng 怎生

Tsui P'eng-lai 醉蓬萊

Tsui-weng ch'in-ch'ü wai-p'ien 醉翁琴趣外篇

Tsui-weng ts'ao 醉翁操

tsui wu tuan 最無端

Tsun-ch'ien chi 尊前集

tsung 縱

Tu Mu 杜牧

Tung Chieh-yüan 董解元

Tung-hsien ko 洞仙歌

Tung-shan yüeh-fu 東山樂府

tz'u 詞

"*Tz'u* chih" 詞旨

tz'u-hua 詞話

Tz'u kai 詞概

tz'u-lü 詞律

"*Tz'u* lun" 詞論

tz'u-p'ai 詞牌

tz'u-p'u 詞譜

Tzu-yeh ko 子夜歌

Tz'u yüan 詞源

wan-yüeh 婉約

Wang An-shih (Ching-kung) 王安石（荊公）

Wang Ch'ang-ling 王昌齡

Wang chiang-mei 望江梅

Wang chiang-nan 望江南

Wang Chien 王建

Wang Chih-huan 王之渙

Wang Cho 王灼

Wang hai-ch'ao 望海潮

Wang Hsi-chih 王羲之

Wang Kuo-wei 王國維

Wang Wei 王維

Wang yüan hsing 望遠行

Wang Yüan-lu 王元籙

Wei-ch'eng ch'ü 渭城曲

Wei Chuang 韋莊

Wen T'ing-yün 溫庭筠

Wo-lan chi 握蘭集

wu-ko 吳歌

Wu-shan i-tuan yün 巫山一段雲

Wu-shih shan 烏石山

Wu-ti (Liu Sung) 武帝（劉宋）

Wu Ts'eng 吳曾

Wu Wen-ying 吳文英

Wu yeh t'i 烏夜啼

wu-yen shih 五言詩

ya-yüeh 雅樂

Yang-kuan ch'ü 陽關曲

Yang-liu chih 楊柳枝

Yeh Ch'ing-ch'en 葉清臣

Yeh Meng-te 葉夢得

Yeh-pan yüeh 夜半樂

Yen Chi-tao 晏幾道

Yen Hsüan 閻選

yen ku-shih 演故事

Yen Ling-pin 顏令賓

Yen Shu (T'ung-shu) 晏殊 (同叔)

Yen Yü 嚴羽

yen-yüeh 燕樂

yin 引

Yin O 尹鶚

"Yin-yüeh chih" 音樂志

Ying hsin-ch'un 迎新春

Yü-chieh hsing 御街行

yu ch'üeh shih 又卻是

Yü-chung-hua man 雨中花慢

Yü-fu 漁父

Yü-hang 餘杭

Yü hu-tieh 玉蝴蝶

Yü lin ling 雨霖鈴

Yü-lou ch'un 玉樓春

Yü mei-jen 虞美人

Yü-t'ai hsin-yung 玉台新詠

Yüeh-chang chi 樂章集

"Yüeh chih" 樂志

yüeh-fu 樂府

Yüeh-fu chih-mi 樂府指迷

"Yüeh Hsiao-she p'an-sheng mi-ou" 樂小舍拚生覓偶

Yün-yao chi 雲謠集

yung-wu tz'u 詠物詞

Yung yü lo 永遇樂

Abstract

This dissertation attempts to trace the early development of the Chinese poetic genre called *tz'u* in terms of its distinct linguistic characteristics, conventional requirements, aesthetic values and structural principles. The study grows out of the conviction that an examination of the evolution of a new genre is of intrinsic significance to the study of literary history, as it helps us define relations between literary forms, locate recurrent stylistic traits, and consider how individual writers make their important breakthroughs. Focusing on the five seminal poets, Wen T'ing-yün (ca. 812-ca. 870), Wei Chuang (ca. 836-910), Li Yü (937-978), Liu Yung (987-1053), and Su Shih (1036-1101), the present work undertakes a diachronic study which examines how a poet's personal style and his choice of material can often set guidelines for later generic requirements, insofar as convention can normally determine form and meaning for a specific genre.

The development of *tz'u* poetry was closely related to the impact of "popular" songs. In Chapter I the conventional criteria of separating literati poetry from popular literature are called into question. After examining the close affinity and mutual influences between the two traditions, it is further observed that whereas the T'ang popular *tz'u* employed many widely different forms simultaneously and without

discrimination, the contemporary literati *tz'u* was at first conditioned by the poetics of a previously entrenched literary genre, *chüeh-chü*, until a new set of structural principles slowly evolved for the *tz'u* genre around 850. This proves that the notion of a tradition is paramount in literati poetry, as distinguished from popular songs.

Chapter II discusses the two distinct stylistic modes (the rhetoric of implicit meaning and the rhetoric of explicit meaning) established by the pioneer poets Wen T'ing-yün and Wei Chuang, which were to develop into the two major schools of *tz'u* writing. It is argued that Wen's style was distinguished mainly by his use of paratactic syntax, and Wei's by hypotactic syntax, the former being under the influence of *lü-shih* and the latter under the influence of popular songs and *ku-shih*. Chapter III explains how Li Yü invented new devices by synthesizing these two modes. As the genre evolved from a simpler form (*hsiao-ling*) to a more complex form (*man-tz'u*), the *tz'u* poetics also underwent great changes. In Chapters IV and V we observe how Liu Yung and Su Shih continuously introduced new blood into the *tz'u* tradition by using (though in different ways) the rhetoric of explicit meaning and hypotactic syntax as a point of departure for their innovations. Liu's achievement lies mainly in the formal aspects of the *man-tz'u* form, and Su's in the extension of poetic scope in *tz'u* as a whole.